9

A Practical Approach to

COUNSELLING

A Practical Approach to
COUNSELLING

Margaret Hough

Lecturer in Social Care and Counselling Studies

 **LONGMAN**

PEARSON EDUCATION LIMITED
Edinburgh Gate, Harlow,
Essex CM20 2JE, England and
Associated Companies throughout
the world.

Visit us on the World Wide Web at:
http://www.pearsoneduc.com

First published in Great Britain 1994
Second impression 1995
Eighth impression 1999
Ninth impression 2000

© Longman Group Limited 1994

British Library Cataloguing in Publication Data
A CIP catalogue record for this book can be obtained from the British Library.

ISBN 0 273 60090 7

Typeset by ⚐ Tek-Art, Croydon, Surrey
Produced by Pearson Education Asia Pte Ltd
Printed in Singapore (CNC)

The publisher's policy is to use paper manufactured from sustainable forests.

Contents

Acknowledgements

Souvenir Press Ltd, London, for selected quotations and diagrams from the text of *Transactional Analysis in Psychotherapy* by Eric Berne.

Dr Albert Ellis and the Institute for Rational Emotive Therapy, New York, for the Personality Data Form.

Carol Publishing Group, New York, for selected quotations from *Reason and Emotion in Psychotherapy* by Albert Ellis.

Moira Jessup, John Redmond and Sue Redding for their help and advice.

David Hough for his support and collaboration in the writing of the book.

Introduction

Most trainee counsellors are introduced to the concept of eclecticism towards the end of their initial skills training and, as a consequence, develop an interest in the different models of counselling and their use. This interest represents a logical progression for students who wish to undertake further education and study, but the number of counselling models now in use is quite diverse and ever increasing, so that the prospect of fully understanding all of them is a daunting one. This book is intended merely as a starting point or introduction to the seven models which it outlines, because *real eclecticism* – which refers to the practice of using elements of different models of counselling when and if they are needed – can only be truly successful when practitioners have an in-depth knowledge of the models available to them.

When I first heard the word 'eclecticism' in relation to counselling theory, I was fascinated, amused and repelled by it. It seemed to me to be a grandiose term designed to mystify students and to deter everyone except the most intellectual or brave from venturing further into the realm of counselling education. In fact, I quickly learned that it is simply a word which describes the process of selecting methods and concepts from a variety of therapeutic systems, while taking into consideration the fact that each client is a unique individual whose problems and resources are quite different from anyone else's. In writing this book, I hope to illustrate some of the ways in which the various models of counselling – including Person-Centered, Psychodynamic, Gestalt, Behavioural, Rational-Emotive, Transactional Analysis and Groupwork – can accommodate these differences and promote therapeutic change and growth for clients. In order to do this I shall discuss the theoretical principles of each model, and then show how they can be applied to the actual counselling situation, using case material to highlight their relevance and usefulness. Since confidentiality is essential in every counselling situation, all the descriptions which I have included are altered in name and other important details so as to ensure that client anonymity is respected throughout.

When a counsellor is eclectic in her approach, it implies that she has knowledge of the theoretical basis of many models of counselling, and that she is able, in the practical situation, to adapt her approach to suit the needs of each client. This ability to adapt to clients' needs implies respect for them at the very deepest level. It also involves a dedication to training and a willingness to become acquainted with a fairly wide-ranging body of information. It is often the case that students of counselling become disheartened in the face of this rather intimidating kind of commitment, and decide to stick with the first model of counselling which they learned. But relying on one model of counselling can be limiting for both client and counsellor, because such reliance does not afford either the kind of broad vision or the range of possibilities which are accessible when an eclectic approach is used.

The problem arises when the trainee counsellor embarks on an initial search for information about other models of counselling, and is faced with a bewildering array of specialized books on every one of them. The purpose of this book is to offer an outline of the seven models examined in the hope that the student will be stimulated to do further research on each. In order to encourage this research, I have included a Further Reading section at the end of each chapter.

The use of the personal pronoun 'she', which is consistently followed throughout the book to describe the counsellor, is for convenience only. It is certainly not based on any conviction that all counsellors are, or should be, female, since this is clearly not the case in reality. Similarly, the use of the pronoun 'he' which is employed to describe many of the clients, is also a convenient way of maintaining coherence and continuity, and does not in any way reflect the gender ratio of clients who come for counselling.

CHAPTER 1

Psychodynamic counselling

The historical background

SIGMUND FREUD (1856–1939)

Sigmund Freud was born in 1856 in Moravia, Czechoslovakia, where he lived with his family until they moved to Vienna four years later. He remained in Vienna until 1938 and studied philosophy, zoology and medicine at the university there. As a student, Freud had a deep and abiding curiosity, and was probably more interested in science and scientific research than anything else. In 1881 he completed his medical training and started to work as a doctor at the General Hospital in Vienna. Later he spent some time in Paris working with Charcot who was Professor of Neuropathology there; it was as a direct result of this work with Charcot that Freud developed an interest in hypnosis, which he subsequently began to use in the treatment of his own patients.

Although his work with hypnosis was never entirely successful, Freud's initial involvement with it laid the foundation for his future work in psychoanalysis. He had encountered patients in his practice who suffered physical symptoms for which there seemed to be no organic cause and he concluded that these symptoms were related to the phenomenon of hysteria. Since his patients had no conscious knowledge of their origin, he became convinced that the cause lay in their unconscious minds. But Freud was not just interested in the cause of the hysterical symptoms which his patients displayed; he was also concerned to find ways of investigating the unconscious in order to understand it more fully. Because of this need to find out more, he developed the techniques of *free association*, *analysis of slips of the tongue* and *dream interpretation*, as well as clinical interviews to build up case studies of his patients. He also spent a great deal of time and energy in self-analysis, which he regarded as an essential component of his research and learning experience.

This method of psychoanalysis, pioneered by Freud, was the starting point for all future work carried out in the field of psychotherapy. His work has been adapted or developed by theorists of many different persuasions, some of whom have either used, changed or discarded the techniques which he began. Essentially they all subscribe to the basic view that a true knowledge of people and their problems is possible only through an understanding of all areas of the human psyche.

ID, EGO AND SUPER-EGO

Freud's analysis of his patients led him to structure the personality into three related elements: the id, the ego and the super-ego (see Fig. 1.1). He believed that these three systems or elements had to be balanced and in harmony in order to ensure the individual's psychological health. The id is that area of the personality which is primitive and represents the true unconscious; it is illogical and filled with instinctual energy which is constantly demanding recognition and release.

Present from birth and necessary for survival, the id is mainly concerned with securing food, comfort and pleasure. The ego, on the other hand, is more logical since it has been refined and modified through contact with the external world. Whereas the infant is dominated by the demands of the id, the developing child becomes more influenced by the ego when it real-

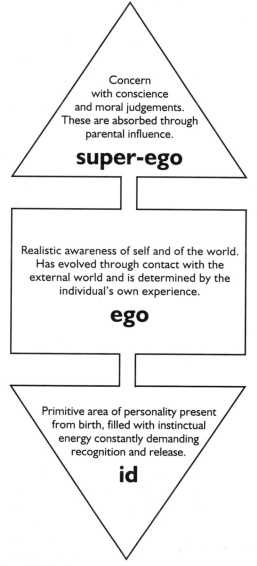

Concern
with conscience
and moral judgements.
These are absorbed through
parental influence.

super-ego

Realistic awareness of self and of the world.
Has evolved through contact with the
external world and is determined by the
individual's own experience.

ego

Primitive area of personality present
from birth, filled with instinctual
energy constantly demanding
recognition and release.

id

Fig. 1.1 *Freud's structure of personality*

izes that all its urges will not be instantly gratified. Thus the 'reality principle' of the ego, as opposed to the 'pleasure principle' of the id, becomes apparent when the child has developed a realistic awareness of self, and of the world. The super-ego, which is the third part of the personality, is beginning to develop by about three years of age. It is evolved from that part of the ego which has absorbed parental, cultural and familial influences. The 'morality principle' is the basis of the super-ego and its main function is to curb the demands of the id; for this reason it is primarily concerned with conscience and moral judgements.

For each individual there will always be conflict and compromises between the three parts of the personality. It may be that a person's ego is so dominated by a harsh and punitive conscience or super-ego, that an unhealthy imbalance is created. It may be also that the influence of the ego, which is essentially that of arbiter between the id and the super-ego, is so weakened by conflicting demands that it ceases to cope adequately as more and more anxiety is generated.

It is important for any student who is interested in studying psychodynamic counselling to understand the structure of personality as outlined by Freud, and to further understand the kind of conflicts which can arise within it. Even those people who do not wholly subscribe to Freud's views need to remember just how influential they have been in the twentieth century, not only in psychotherapy, but also in sociology, philosophy, literature and the arts.

TENSION AND CONFLICT

According to Freudian theory, we all experience tension and conflict between these three related elements – the id, the ego and the super-ego. Clashes occur and compromises are always being made. When the id demands instinctual expression or release, the ego has to balance these demands against the inhibiting or restraining forces of the super-ego. If moral standards are not sufficiently upheld, *guilt* is produced by the super-ego. It sometimes happens that an individual's ego will be guided consistently by the super-ego, so that impulses which are felt to be wrong are successfully kept in abeyance.

Occasionally, however, sexual and aggressive demands are so severely denied that an imbalance is created and the individual suffers as a consequence. Excessive restraints are often imposed by parents, religion or society, so that conflict between the two parts of the personality (id and super-ego) is increased. On the other hand, some restraining influence is necessary in order to contain the powerful forces of the id and this is achieved through the development of *defence mechanisms* which protect the individual against painful anxiety and ensure that the ego is not overwhelmed. Integrated behaviour evolves through a process of successfully balancing all three components of the personality, as well as through the use of *defence mechanisms* to reduce tension. The main goal of psychodynamic therapy is to help the individual to acquire a reasonable balance between the id, the ego and the super-ego.

Since the ego, or conscious self, is frequently put in the position of having to arbitrate between the id and the super-ego, anxiety is generated and this in turn motivates the individual to do something about the situation.

ANXIETY AND EGO DEFENCE MECHANISMS

Ego defence mechanisms are strategies which people use in order to cope with intrapsychic conflict and to reduce anxiety. Essentially, they are ways of expressing forbidden impulses in disguised form, so that punishment by society and condemnation by the super-ego are avoided. Ego defence mechanisms are therefore normal and not indicative of illness, although they can become restrictive and maladaptive. Each individual will use the defence mechanism which matches his or her own particular conflict, and the object of using the defence is to deny or distort reality. Since defence mechanisms function at an unconscious level, people are unaware that they are using them.

SUBLIMATION

Sublimation occurs when instinctual drives are redirected into creative or other acceptable expressions. Sport is an example of acceptable expression of *aggressive* feelings, and in this respect sublimation serves some useful purposes. For example, admiration and respect are frequently given to players, which in turn increases their self-esteem. The energy which is generated by hostility and anger can be adapted by sublimation and used in other positive ways as well, including business and work generally. Sexual energy can be channelled into creative enterprise, including painting, writing and music.

Sublimation is regarded as a very constructive defence mechanism, since it produces such beneficial and socially acceptable results, and because it is directed towards a reduction of guilt feelings (in common with other defence mechanisms) and helps to maintain the individual's equilibrium and sense of worth. Very often aggressive desires are redirected in areas of work which are not just socially acceptable, but socially necessary as well, including the armed services and the police force. Sexual drives are sometimes channelled into theatre and ballet, for these are areas in which physical display of the body is both acceptable and artistic. Socially unacceptable expressions of curiosity, such as voyeurism and gossip, which often lead to feelings of anxiety and guilt, can be transformed through sublimation into other acceptable areas where anxiety and guilt will not be generated. These include medicine, social work, psychology and, of course, psychotherapy and counselling.

REPRESSION

The word repression describes the mechanism whereby we push unacceptable feelings or emotions into the unconscious. If these feelings and emotions were permitted to surface to the conscious level, they would create deep anxiety. According to Freud, almost all of the traumatic events of early life are repressed and the process itself is unconscious. However, repression is often not complete, and feelings of insecurity, guilt and lack of self-worth often indicate that the process has not been wholly accomplished.

Repression is the most fundamental of all the defence mechanisms and it is also the bedrock on which the others are built.

Painful thoughts and feelings which have been excluded from conscious awareness can sometimes be converted into neurotic or physical symptoms. If this happens people can be helped to overcome the problem by reliving traumatic memories in a supportive therapeutic environment. The most important point about repression as a defence mechanism is that thoughts and feelings which have been repressed are *not* deactivated, but are always alive and present at an unconscious level, and can manifest themselves in various ways – for example, through slips of the tongue, errors in writing, memory lapses and dreams.

DENIAL

People frequently avoid disagreeable reality by simply denying it. Wishes, thoughts, needs and feelings which people cannot deal with without causing themselves a great deal of anxiety, are often disowned or disavowed. Like the other defence mechanisms, denial is unconsciously motivated and unconsciously acquired, and is developed as a means of protecting the ego from distress and unpleasantness.

Denial involves distortion of thoughts, feelings and perceptions, so that their true meanings are not acknowledged. It is used when people refuse to face the reality of their problems. It is often adopted as a defence mechanism by people who have been involved in distressing situations like war and natural disasters, and in this context it helps to shield them from overwhelming anxiety. Other examples include the denial of the reality of illness or death.

On a less dramatic level, denial can be used by people who are insecure about their age or looks, and who then dress, act and identify with others who are much younger. Denial, by its very nature, prevents people from looking at things which, if acknowledged, might very well lead to greater development and growth.

REGRESSION

The word 'regression', used in the context of defence mechanisms, refers to a process of reverting to an earlier and more childlike pattern of behaviour. It is prompted by the individual's unconscious wish to return to a much earlier time when life was less difficult and threatening. Stress, frustration and anxiety are all responsible for regression.

Adult life involves both independence and responsibility for self, and at times of threat or crisis these qualities may be rejected by some people who adopt instead a passive or childish position so as to provoke a caring reaction and attention from others. Children also use regression when under threat: a child may, for example, revert to an earlier stage of development when a new baby is born into the family. Regression in this instance could take the form of bed-wetting, thumb-sucking, temper tantrums, baby talk or other attention-seeking behaviour. Adult regression takes various forms too, including temper tantrums and sulking, when frustration levels are high, and crying and overdependence when emotional upset is experienced. Regression in adults is also common during illness, sometimes showing itself in passive behaviour, incontinence, and transference of childish feelings to those who are caring for them.

PROJECTION

Projection consists of ascribing one's own desires and unacceptable impulses to other people. As a defence mechanism, this ensures that a person is relieved of uncomfortable feelings, including guilt, and there is usually some element of denial as well, since the traits and emotions which are projected are also, as a consequence, disowned. A person may deny strong sexual feelings yet attribute them to others, and this is often accompanied by condemnation and blame. A man may deny homosexual feelings, for example, while at the same time persecuting others for their supposed or actual homosexual tendencies.

Projection is also evident when an individual blames others for his own shortcomings and inadequacy. This sometimes happens in the work situation when someone asserts that his colleagues are incompetent or uncooperative, thus projecting his own lack of communication and other skills on to them. Feelings of hostility and anger can also be projected on to other people, so that the person who actually experiences these feelings evades the hard work of dealing with them.

DISPLACEMENT

This is sometimes referred to as the 'kick the cat' syndrome. When a man has been harassed at work by a bullying colleague, he may react by displacing his own hostility on to his wife, his children, or even the cat. One way of coping with anxiety, especially when the legitimate target is too threatening or remote, is to release it on to the nearest safe, non-threatening target. Energy is therefore directed against someone or something else which is unlikely to retaliate. Quite often a small incident may trigger an outburst of anger against the innocent, non-offending object or person.

Children sometimes use displacement as a defence mechanism and some of the aggression and hostility which they may feel towards parents may be displaced on to toys. Displacement can also take the form of psychosomatic illness, and when this happens emotional distress is translated into a range of symptoms including headache, chest pain, gastric upset, skin conditions and asthma. Finally, people who experience disruption and tension in their domestic lives, may displace their feelings to others in the workplace. This is particularly serious when the victims of displacement are in lower status positions, or when they are dependent and vulnerable, as patients are in hospital.

RATIONALIZATION

Rationalization is the process of inventing good, but false, reasons to explain our actions or behaviour. For example, a person who steals may rationalize that the people he steals from are rich and therefore will not miss the money anyway. We have a number of ways of justifying our behaviour, and of excusing weakness or failure. People who are obese may explain their failure to lose weight by saying that their problem is a glandular one for which there is no remedy. When an applicant does not get the job she applied for, she may rationalize this on the grounds that she never seriously wanted the job in the first place.

Rationalization is essentially self-deception, and when people continually use it as a defence mechanism, they never successfully deal with their problems. The person with the weight problem is unlikely to diet or exercise so long as he believes that his hormones are to blame. In a similar way, the job applicant will never improve her interview skills if she closes her mind to the problem by denying that she wants to get ahead. In the short term, however, rationalization serves a useful purpose in that it cushions us against extreme disappointment and anxiety.

REACTION
FORMATION

Reaction formation is a way of concealing real feelings which people consider to be unacceptable. Impulses which are frightening or threatening can be held in abeyance by the simple expedient of developing and expressing views which are opposite to them. People who are attracted to pornography, for example, may cultivate conscious attitudes of censorship towards it. Similar attitudes are sometimes evident in people with a propensity to drink too much alcohol; in other words, their attraction to alcohol is marked by extreme views against it.

As a defence mechanism, reaction formation helps people to feel good about themselves, but it is not constructive in the long term since the original impulse or attraction is still there, and failing to acknowledge it leads to the development of more extreme and intolerant attitudes.

Sometimes people who are lonely or scared use reaction formation as a defence against intimacy. Their loneliness and vulnerability are hidden behind a 'couldn't care less' attitude which is cultivated to ward off the possibility of rejection or abandonment by others. To some extent, reaction formation serves a useful social function because it helps to preserve acceptable standards of behaviour. A problem arises, though, when its use leads to isolation and the intolerant and extreme attitudes mentioned earlier.

COMPENSATION

Compensation is a defence mechanism whereby people develop characteristics or personality traits to make up for their deficiencies in other areas. Sometimes people who lack social skills and who do not mix easily with others, compensate by developing intellectual or academic ability from which they derive great satisfaction. Children who have difficulty with schoolwork may compensate by becoming good at sports or outdoor pursuits. Responding in this way to an apparent or imagined deficiency has obvious value, but compensation as a defence mechanism is not always so constructive. Parents may compensate for their feelings of inferiority or low self-esteem, by imposing impossibly high standards of achievement and behaviour on their children. Children may be expected to do what their parents failed to do, academically, socially or in many other ways. The problem is compounded when children have real talent in areas that parents do not value. Very often these real talents have to be relinquished or neglected in order to satisfy parental demands. In the long term, this causes resentment, unhappiness and a sense of unfulfilled potential.

INTROJECTION

Introjection is used as a means of dealing with aspects of reality and the

Children who have difficulty with school work may compensate by becoming good at sports or outdoor pursuits.
Courtesy: Andrew Stewart

external world by incorporating them into, and then owning them as part of the self. Victims of kidnap may, for example, begin to accept the values and philosophy of the kidnappers, especially when these values are political or allied to a particular belief system. In this sense introjection enables the victim to survive (mentally) by warding off the extreme anxiety which would normally be generated in such a situation. Children, too, often use introjection to copy others (usually adults) and in this way frequently perpetuate destructive behaviour. For example, children who have been beaten or abused may continue the cycle by introjecting their parents' abusive behaviour and passing it on to the next generation.

Introjection can be, and frequently is, used in a positive way. Children introject values from parents which lead to the formation of the super-ego. In this last sense, parents or parental figures are referred to as *external objects*, while the values are referred to as the *introjects*.

The psychosexual stages of development

During the 1880s, while working in his medical practice, Freud became interested in the number of patients whose symptoms seemed to be traceable to childhood traumas involving sexual abuse. From the experience of working with these patients, he described what he regarded as the psychosexual stages of development from infancy to adolescence. Freud's theory of infantile sexuality was a radical departure from accepted Victorian views of childhood, and certainly encouraged people to look at children and their needs in a totally different light. Even so, the idea – implicit in Freud's theory – that a great deal of remembered sexual experience can be explained in terms of unconscious incestuous desires, is now being seriously questioned by many people. There is increasing awareness that the incidence of sexual abuse in childhood is high, and that it might, in fact, have always been so.

However, these discoveries do not entirely discredit Freud's views, since the stages which he described are concerned with sexuality in general, and not just with supposed incestuous desires. It is important for students of psychodynamic counselling to be familiar with Freud's psychosexual theories in order to understand the characteristics of the different stages, the needs related to these and the problems which can arise as a result of impaired development. Along with this, the psychodynamic counsellor needs to be aware of the connections between the developmental stages which Freud believed occurred during the first six years of life, and any later difficulties which clients experience, especially those related to sexuality and sexual feelings.

THE ORAL STAGE

The oral stage of development begins at birth and continues for the first year of life. During this time, the child's mouth is the centre of pleasure. An infant uses its mouth not just for eating, but for other purposes as well, including exploration of the world. A sense of power is achieved through sucking and biting. According to Freud, all psychical activity is centred on the mouth at this stage, and the pleasure that is derived from this activity is described as sexual. The word 'sexual' used in this context refers to any gratification arising from parts of the body, and not just to obvious sexual behaviour occurring in childhood. Student counsellors often find this point confusing, and frequently resist any suggestion that the term sexual can be applied to any childhood experience at all. Confusion can be dispelled, however, by encouraging students to discuss the issue, and by directing their attention to their own observations of babies in the first year of life.

Personality problems can occur later in life if the infant's oral needs have not been met, or when they have been overindulged. Thus an infant who has been weaned too early may long for the bottle later in childhood, and the infant whose weaning has been delayed may retain an intense attachment to the bottle, the breast and other forms of oral gratification. Later, in adult life, oral fixation may take the form of alcoholism, eating disorders and smoking. People who have become fixated at the *oral–aggressive* stage, when the infant is teething, may display hostile characteristics in adult life, including oral aggression and sarcasm. Other oral-fixated problems are thought to include low self-esteem, fear of rejection, depression and an inability to sustain relationships. Under stress, people may exaggerate the characteristics related to oral fixation, as part of regression to early behaviour.

THE ANAL STAGE

During the anal stage of development the focus of pleasure switches to the sphincter muscles of the lower bowel and the urinary system. This stage occurs in the second year of life and continues into the third year, which is a period when toilet training is an important aspect of the child's socialization process. During the previous oral stage of development, the infant's main preoccupation had been instant gratification of urges, so the id was in a dominant position. A shift in the balance of id and ego takes place once the anal stage has been reached, and the ego starts to exert some authority over the id. It is not the case, however, that one stage ends and another begins in a neat sequential fashion; the oral and anal stages can overlap and may be present at the same time.

The anal stage of development represents a significant milestone in the child's life, since approval and praise now have to be earned from parents. Unconditional love is no longer given, but depends to some extent on the child's behaviour. While the id is still demanding satisfaction through instant relief of bowel and bladder, the parents are concerned to teach control. This can result in conflict and have a lasting effect on the child' developing attitudes to authority. The way that the situation is dealt with by parents is important, and the methods of toilet training can have lasting effects on the child's future development. Parental attitudes to bodily functions are also crucial at this stage and will influence the child's feelings about his or her body later on.

A child can also learn to retain faeces and urine during this stage of development, and in doing so will gain pleasure as well as defying parental wishes. According to psychodynamic theory, unresolved conflicts from the anal stage can result in later problems and can even create personality types. An adult who was fixated at the anal stage might, for example, symbolically retain faeces by being overly possessive, tidy, obstinate and mean, while another adult fixated at this stage might symbolically expel faeces by being untidy, impulsive and generous. The first personality type is referred to as *anal retentive*, and the second as *anal expulsive*.

THE PHALLIC STAGE

The phallic stage, which occurs between three and six years of age, is a period during which the child is developing socially and is increasingly capable of making moral judgements about right and wrong. The third component of personality (i.e. the super-ego), which represents the inter-pretation of parental and societal standards, is exerting an influence on the way the child deals with problems and conflict. The focus of sensitivity now shifts to the genital area, which becomes a source of pleasure. Children become aware of sex differences at this stage, and they also learn how they are expected to behave in male and female roles.

According to Freud, children from around three years of age experience sexual feelings for their opposite-sex parent. He referred to this phase as *phallic* for boys, and described it as a situation in which the child uncon-sciously desires his mother, and wishes to get rid of his father who is his rival. These hostile fantasies cause great anxiety to the child, and fear of retaliation by the father is a result. The child's greatest fear is that of castra-tion, and this in turn leads him to repress his desire for his mother. This group of impulses is known as the *Oedipus complex* because Freud believed that it mirrored the plot of the Greek tragedy *Oedipus Rex*, in which Oedi-pus kills his father and marries his mother.

Repression of sexual desire for the mother is followed by a period in which the child seeks to identify with his father. In this way he is able to resolve the situation, and also achieve some vicarious satisfaction. As time goes on, the child becomes more like his father and in the process begins to develop male sex-role behaviour as well as the attitudes and standards which his father expresses. This strengthens the child's super-ego develop-ment, and also ensures his safety since his father is unlikely to attack some-one who is so much a part of himself.

Freud paid less attention to psychosexual development in girls, although he did outline a constellation of impulses which he believed applied to them, and is in some respects similar to the Oedipus complex. According to him, girls start with a strong attachment to the mother (as do boys) and later on turn to the father for love and affection. The reason for turning to her father is linked to the girl's realization that neither she nor her mother has a penis, whereas the father does. It should be remembered that the penis, in this context, represents more than just a physical attribute; it is also a symbol of potency, authority and power. The abandonment of her mother in favour of her father causes the young girl intense anxiety. This situation continues until it is eventually resolved through the young girl's identification with her mother and the adoption of female sex-role behaviour.

Needless to say, the *Electra complex*, which is how Freud described this situation, has caused some controversy in recent times, and has never been a popular theory as far as women are concerned. However, the phallic stage of development is important in general terms, especially from the point of view of counselling because some clients have ambivalent feelings about their own sexuality, and many may have difficulty in acknowledging and expressing sexual arousal. As well as this, a great many people experience extreme emotions of aggression, fear or passivity when dealing with au-thority figures like teachers and bosses. This may indicate some unresolved conflict with a parent of the same sex as the authority figure. Difficulty in maintaining intimate relationships may also be linked to faulty or unre-solved conflicts at the phallic stage. Moreover, although there has been opposition - justifiable in my view - to the theory of the Electra complex, there is a case for saying that women are symbolically castrated in our society since they are unable to attain positions of authority, power or prestige equivalent to those enjoyed by men.

THE LATENCY STAGE

During the latency period, between six and twelve years, sexual feelings tend to lie dormant. The child's attention is focused on education, hobbies, friendship and sport. The structure of personality - the id, the ego and the super-ego - has been formed and the socialization process continues. In psychoanalysis, this fourth stage of development is referred to as the *latency* stage, in order to indicate that the child's sexual preoccupations have been repressed only. During the next stage, (see below) sexual desires are reawakened and begin to make very powerful demands to satisfy the libido. During latency, the child's energies are directed towards the development of social and intellectual skills, and to the enjoyment of recreational activities. Before the latency period, children are inward-looking and self-centred, but now they become interested in other people and in relationships, especially in relationships with children of the same sex.

THE GENITAL STAGE

At the genital stage of development (12–18 years), sexual interest begins to re-emerge. Hormone levels alter, and body changes take place. Adolescents, at this stage, break free of adult influence as they work towards their own adult roles and responsibilities. The harmony between the id, the ego and the super-ego is disrupted as the sexual impulses of the id start to dominate and make demands. A balance is provided by an emergency sense of altruism, and a deepening interest in other people. The genital stage continues into adult life, and the happiness and fulfilment which the individual can ultimately achieve is, according to Freud, directly related to the successful resolution of conflict at earlier stages of development.

KEY WORDS

PSYCHODYNAMIC

The word 'psychodynamic' is an amalgam of two words, both of them Greek of origin. The first part, *psyche*, can be translated as spirit, mind or soul, while the second part, *dynamic*, can be translated as active, forceful, energetic or alive. The term thus coined aptly describes the active mental, emotional and spiritual processes which people constantly experience. In the context of counselling and therapy, the word 'psychodynamic' refers to a Freudian approach, or an approach whose origins are firmly rooted in Freudian theory. Such an approach would, for example, emphasize the constant interplay of unconscious mental processes in determining human feelings, thoughts and behaviour. It would also be concerned with the concepts of *resistance*, *defences*, *transference* and the history of a client's early childhood experiences.

PSYCHOANALYSIS

This is the theory of human behaviour and related therapy developed by Freud in the 1890s. Its main purpose is to help clients gain insight by recognizing and understanding the unconscious emotions and thoughts which are believed to cause their problems. Two of the techniques commonly used in psychoanalysis are *free association* and *dream analysis*, both of which are intended to help clients gain access to repressed mental conflicts. The analysis of resistance and transference, along with assessment and interpretation, also enables clients to uncover unconscious mental processes, and is central to the use of psychoanalysis. These techniques can be applied to both individual and group therapy.

PSYCHOTHERAPY

This term refers to the treatment of psychological disorders through the use of psychological, rather than physical, means. Verbal communication between therapist and client is the most significant element of psychotherapy, although the term includes a variety of other techniques. It can be carried out individually or in groups, and is concerned with the evaluation of problems and possible solutions, as well as with the encouragement of more adaptive ways of thinking and behaving. Although there are theoretical and practical differences between the various schools of psychotherapy, all of them subscribe to certain basic ideas, such as the need to establish a helping relationship which encourages the client to express deeply-felt issues and concerns, in an atmosphere that is non-judgemental and confidential

The Model

The psychodynamic model of counselling is one which places emphasis on past as well as present experiences. It is concerned to look at the way a person's early life, in particular a person's childhood and relationships with parents and family, has shaped their present personality, their way of thinking and behaving, and their current relationships with other people. According to the model, much of what happened to us in infancy and childhood is still present in the unconscious mind, and is thus capable of exercising an influence over our adult experiences.

Unconscious thoughts and feelings are, by definition, outside our awareness, and it is this lack of conscious awareness which is seen as a potential cause of problems in everyday life. Since few people are capable of recalling spontaneously the details of early childhood, a focus of psychodynamic counselling is to encourage and facilitate clients' endeavours to look more closely at the past in the hope that this will uncover significant memories. This recollection of significant events and feelings is regarded as being therapeutic for clients because it enables them to understand more fully the connections between past and present; the origins of a problem can be highlighted so that a new perspective is achieved, and it is this new perspective which forms the basis for healing and change.

To use the psychodynamic model effectively the counsellor needs to have a thorough understanding of its theoretical principles, along with a commitment to the time and work required for its effective practice. Although the techniques of Freud's original model have been modified in contemporary psychodynamic therapy, there is still an emphasis on working through unconscious motives in order to uncover emotional problems and achieve insight. The process can be time-consuming and lengthy, which means that clients also need to be prepared to spend some time and effort if the work is to be successful.

Training in psychodynamic counselling is not the same as training in psychoanalysis. The latter takes much longer, and is concerned with an in-depth study of Freudian theory and practice. However, counsellors of any theoretical orientation should benefit from psychodynamic training, if only to help them understand the basic concepts such as transference, resistance and ego-defence mechanisms.

THE UNCONSCIOUS

The word 'unconscious' has been used so far with the underlying assumption that most people will be familiar with the terminology, and its meaning in relation to the human mind. We have become so used to hearing the word in everyday language that it is easy to forget just how precise and specific Freud originally intended it to be. The distinction which he made between the conscious and the unconscious mind was quite clear: the former is accessible and encompasses all those thoughts and feelings of which we are aware; while the latter describes a realm of the mind whose content and material is normally inaccessible except through the experience of dreams, fantasies, or slips of the tongue. Nevertheless, unconscious impulses, Freud believed, are active in governing much of our everyday feelings and behaviour. He made a further distinction when he described what he called the *preconscious*, that area of psychic experience which, while not entirely conscious, is capable of becoming so through the ordinary use of memory.

REPRESSION AND RESISTANCE

If then the unconscious is an area of human experience which is normally hidden from us, it follows that there must be some reason for the mind to exercise censorship and secrecy. According to Freud, the action of hiding or burying memories and feelings follows from the individual perceiving them as threats. Memories that are painful, traumatic or shameful are often unacceptable to us, so we respond by repressing them from conscious awareness. It is this phenomenon of repression which Freud regarded as being of paramount importance in his formulation of psychoanalytic theory.

Allied to repression is the corresponding phenomenon of resistance: that which is repressed in the unconscious is firmly relegated there by the ways in which we obstinately resist any attempts to uncover it.

Repression and resistance are twin concepts central to an understanding of the psychodynamic model. Clients who are firmly committed to the idea of therapeutic change will, nevertheless, vigorously resist any endeavour to look closely at past experiences or events which are painful for them. The task of the counsellor is to encourage clients to acknowledge and, if possible, to talk freely about these events and experiences. This task can only be accomplished if the counsellor fully understands the reasons for the client's resistance, is aware that it is a propensity in all of us, and is sensitive towards the client who is engaged in the difficult process of change.

INTERPRETATION

In an attempt to uncover unconscious material, the client who has come for psychodynamic counselling is encouraged to talk freely, just as clients are encouraged to talk freely and at their own pace in most other counselling situations. What is different about the psychodynamic model is the degree to which the counsellor is prepared to act as an interpreter for the client, so that a meaningful reconstruction of past events is achieved. This interpretation necessitates careful attention and listening on the part of the counsellor, not just to the words which the client speaks, but also to underlying nuances, to the accompanying body language, as well as any signs of difficulty, hesitation or distress. Interpretations are not offered lightly, nor are they meant to be indications of the counsellor's superior knowledge or intelligence. They are thoughtfully considered and tentative, and acknowledge that only the client can judge how accurate they are. For this reason, interpretation is seen primarily as a means of enabling clients to gain insight into their own problems.

In order to help clients to understand themselves better, the psychodynamic counsellor is encouraged, therefore, to interpret some of the material which is revealed during the session, so that the client can consider it and ultimately decide whether or not it is correct. For an interpretation to be effective it should feel right for the client, and just as important , it should shed some light on the client's current preoccupations and problems. Very often an accurate interpretation will reveal to a client that which is already known, but has not been identified. If the truth of this revelation is uncomfortable or painful it will again be rejected. It is this tendency by clients to resist or reject which makes psychodynamic counselling a process requiring time, sensitivity and patience on the counsellor's part. It could be quite tempting to 'lead' the client, by way of interpretation and subtle pressure, to accept what the counsellor believes to be true. If this happens, a situation occurs in which the counsellor's own need for success becomes more important than the issues which rightly belong to the client. This would ultimately negate the whole purpose of the counselling process since it switches the focus away from the client's needs to those of the counsellor.

An example of how interpretation might work successfully in the counselling situation is outlined in the following case note. A client who has talked for some time in idealizing terms about his father, suddenly says that he wishes his father had spent more time with him when he was a child. His father was a wonderful man, but he hardly ever spent any time alone with him. The counsellor might respond to this by asking him to look more closely at his feelings, and to consider the possibility that he may have experienced sadness, or even anger because of his father's lack of attention and time. The client may reject this interpretation outright because the truth and the reality are too painful to accept. In any case, it is his decision to accept or reject it. What is important in this instance, is that the interpretation offered by the counsellor will have prompted the client to reconsider his relationship with his father, and in looking afresh at it the client may come to understand more clearly what it was really like for him and how it has influenced his present difficulties and problems. Very often this kind of reflection takes place outside the counselling situation when clients are reviewing their own progress before the next session takes place. It is important to remember this fact because it serves to place the counsellor's role as helper firmly in perspective, and to emphasize the central and active role of the client, not just in psychodynamic counselling, but in all other models as well.

FREE ASSOCIATION

The use of interpretation is effective, therefore, in the way it encourages clients to think again about their past experiences, and to connect these in a coherent and meaningful way to their present situation. But in order to make this process work, clients need to be allowed to speak freely about all aspects of their experiences, just as they occur to them in the counselling situation. It does not really matter how trivial or uninteresting some of these details seem to be on the surface; to the psychodynamic counsellor, all the feelings, thoughts, ideas and memories which the client expresses, are indicative of, or related in some way to, his major preoccupations and concerns. This free association by the client is not as easy as it sounds, for resistance to revealing any distressing or hurtful material is always strong. Over a period of time, however, the client will relax his vigilant censorship to some extent, so that long-forgotten memories and connections are revealed by him. Over this period of time also, the relationship between client and counsellor should have developed into a trusting and working partnership.

TRANSFERENCE

The development of the counsellor/client relationship is considered to be very crucial in psychodynamic counselling because in many ways it epitomizes or recreates, for the client, some of his early relationships, especially those with his parents or significant others in the past. It is a fact that people tend to transfer to new relationships many of the feelings and attitudes which they experienced in childhood. For a male client who has had a strict and punitive mother, for example, all subsequent relationships with women will tend to be influenced, to some extent at least, by the feelings which he had for her. This may well cause problems in adult life since the ambivalent combination of love and fear which he probably experienced in early life may make it impossible for him to respond in any other way to women generally. A focus of psychodynamic counselling would be to assist such a client to achieve a deeper understanding of his feelings for his mother, and then to analyse how these feelings may be influencing his relationships now. Only in this way can the client free himself from a negative response pattern which might make a fully adult partnership impossible for him. If the counsellor in this situation is a woman, it will probably become apparent at some stage during the counselling sessions that the client's ambivalent feelings are being transferred to her as well, for although the feelings which clients have for the counsellor are often initially positive, they may quickly become negative when the re-emergence of childhood emotions starts to occur. Without realizing it, clients tend to respond emotionally to the counsellor in the same way that they responded towards adults when they were children. This form of response invites a reciprocal one from the counsellor, for the client – again unconsciously – will try to elicit reactions similar to those he elicited from adults in the past.

The manifestation of these unconscious feelings, emotions and attitudes, which rightly belong to childhood, is seen as beneficial in psychodynamic counselling since it serves to bring into the open the client's usual way of functioning, especially when under stress. The insight gained when repressed feelings and emotions are thus revealed can be very great, but only when the counsellor works closely with the client in order to identify and understand them.

COUNTERTRANSFERENCE

If clients develop transference feelings for counsellors, then it follows that in what is, after all, a close working relationship, counsellors will inevitably experience feelings for their clients as well. The phenomenon of countertransference is another important dimension of psychodynamic counselling, and one which the counsellor needs to be constantly aware of in order to deal with it successfully. It is certainly not difficult to see that counsellors can also be influenced by unconscious material originating from their own past relationships. Clients may elicit from them feelings of inadequacy, anger, boredom or even hostility, and very often these feelings have very little to do with the therapy in progress, but are more directly linked to the counsellor's own complexes.

The emergence of strong emotions which are often difficult or impossible to explain, means that the counsellor needs to be in touch with a professional supervisor to whom she reports on a regular basis in order to monitor the quality of her work. In this way, feelings which rightly belong to the counsellor can be acknowledged and owned. The supervisor's function is to help the counsellor disentangle and make sense of any disturbing reactions which come to the surface during counselling sessions with clients.

It is not always the case, however, that the emotions and responses experienced by the counsellor are related to her own past experiences or complexes. They may actually be an indication of the kind of reaction that the client generally produces and expects from people, and if this is the case they can shed a great deal of light on his problems. For instance, the client whose mother was controlling may elicit a similar tendency to control from the counsellor, and if this is identified and highlighted in the counselling situation, it may help the client to change his dysfunctional behaviour in the future.

THE INTERPRETATION OF DREAMS

In 1900 Freud's book *The Interpretation of Dreams* was published, thereby establishing an interest in a subject which had previously been ignored by the scientific world. To Freud, dream interpretation was 'the royal road to a knowledge of the unconscious activities of the mind'. In psychodynamic counselling, clients are encouraged to become aware of their dreams in order to facilitate a deeper understanding of the unconscious forces which influence their lives. This attention to dreams and dreaming is not easy, especially at the beginning of counselling, when clients are often stressed, confused, and sometimes incapable of making sense of what probably is, a new and hitherto ignored dimension of their own experiencing. Counsellors can help by encouraging them to record their dreams and to recount these in the counselling sessions so that interpretation can take place. This interpretation can only be done by the client, since the images and symbols which occur in dreams are meaningful to him alone; with practice and experience it is possible for the client to establish coherent links between his everyday life and the experiences which he has during sleep. Even then the links can be tenuous because what is remembered of the 'manifest' dream is a censored version of what is actually contained in the 'latent' dream. Freud made a distinction between the manifest and the latent dream, and in doing so illustrated just how strong he believed the action of censorship by the mind to be. The associations contained in dreams are myriad and complex, so that time and experience are needed, not just by the client, but by the counsellor as well if the work required for dream interpretation is to be successfully undertaken.

The evolution of Freudian theory

Freudian theory continues to evolve, to expand and to attract attention from various people, many of whom do not subscribe completely to the classical or orthodox position. Right from the beginning, Freud's ideas caused controversy and dispute, and some of the most significant reactions came from people who had worked closely with Freud and who were impressed with his work, but not entirely satisfied with what he taught.

Among those who disagreed with Freud on several issues were his former associates Carl Jung and Alfred Adler. Freud did not seem to welcome dissenting opinion, and his reluctance to accommodate differing views led to a break between him and these two theorists. Jung and Adler developed their own personality theories, changing Freud's emphasis in several important areas.

CARL JUNG (1875–1961)

Jung disagreed with Freud on a number of issues and broke away from the original psychoanalytic school in 1913. After the break he formulated his own theories which he termed *analytical psychology*. The areas of disagreement with Freud included the subject of sexuality; in Jungian terms, this represents a small function of the mind and body, and is only one of a number of important drives. (Others include spiritual and cultural drives which are especially significant in the second half of life.)

CONSCIOUS AND UNCONSCIOUS

In Freudian theory, it is important to make the unconscious conscious if neurotic problems are to be effectively reduced. In Jungian terms, the activities of the unconscious and conscious minds should be coordinated as well as being made conscious. Fantasies of the unconscious should be highlighted so that they can be used to facilitate the development of the individual.

Analytical psychology does acknowledge that the unconscious contains much that is brutal and objectionable that people often want to forget, but it also emphasises the positive and life-enhancing possibilities of unconscious material. In Jungian psychology, the word 'psyche' is a broad term which encompasses not just the mind, but the soul as well. Psychic energy, referred to as *libido*, is viewed as a life force which flows between two opposite points creating tension and energy; it is constantly regulating itself in order to maintain the individual's equilibrium and sense of wellbeing.

THE COLLECTIVE UNCONSCIOUS

A concept which is unique to Jung is that of the collective unconscious. Jung clearly saw the influences of both evolution and heredity in forming the mind as well as the body. According to Jung's theory of the collective unconscious, we inherit characteristics which are manifest in our behaviour, especially in instinctive behaviour. In Freudian theory, childhood is the most important factor in shaping adult personality. Jung, on the other hand, puts less stress on the individual's past experiences, and places more emphasis on the way humans have developed historically. In his view, ancestral history has shaped the human brain, so that influences from the past are constantly with us.

ARCHETYPES

Jung referred to the universal ideas and images of the collective unconscious as *archetypes*. These are original forms which all human beings in all societies recognize. Certain images like water, fire and earth, for example, appear to have had the same symbolic significance throughout history, and are often used in classical and modern literature. Archetypes can also appear in shared emotional experience, and these unconscious ideas and patterns of thought are likely to surface during momentous human events such as birth and death. The people directly involved in such experiences often have similar dreams with similar recurring themes and symbols. This shared psychological experience was regarded by Jung as evidence of a collective unconscious.

DREAMS

A counsellor who is interested in analytical psychology will regard dreams as an important source of information and material which can be used by clients to develop self-awareness. Jung was especially interested in dreams and, in common with Freud, regarded them as the most significant manifestation of the unconscious. However Freud described dreams as wish fulfilment, whereas Jung believed that they represented a completion of the waking state. In other words, when something is neglected during the day, the dream will deal with it at night. Jung also regarded dreams as partly responsible for restoring balance and equilibrium, but he believed that in order to understand them, it was necessary to study a series of dreams instead of just one.

In Jungian psychology, dreams can have more than personal significance and sometimes the detail and symbols contained in them can only be deciphered through mythological and historical symbols. In other words, a person's dream may contain material which is not just relevant to the dreamer; it may also have something to say to, or about, other people. A *collective dream*, for example, may contain archetypes from the collective unconscious and, in this sense, may be of relevance to other people as well as to the dreamer. Biblical dreams provide some interesting examples of this last point.

MAJOR ARCHETYPES

There are four major archetypes of the collective unconscious:

- the persona,
- the anima/animus,
- the shadow,
- the self.

The word 'persona' means a mask and refers to the outward appearance which people use in everyday life. According to Jung, we are all expected to play the parts assigned to us by society, and this means that groups of people are assigned specific attributes and characteristics. In this way, the persona becomes a collective archetype. Policemen, for example, are meant to display attitudes of authority and reliability, while artists are expected to be colourful, bohemian and perhaps eccentric.

The word 'anima' refers to the unconscious female quality in the male, and the word 'animus' refers to the unconscious male quality in the female. According to Jung, we all have opposite sex qualities which we need to be able to express in order to feel well adjusted and healthy. The anima and animus are often repressed in Western culture, especially in societies

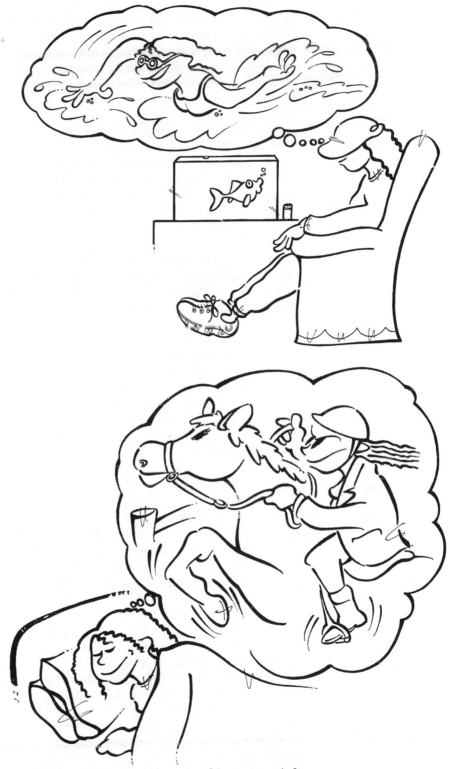

Fig. 1.2 *It is necessary to study a series of dreams instead of just one.*

where sex role stereotypes are encouraged. The feminine element which is contained in each man's unconscious is only one aspect of the anima, however; each man also carries with him an inherited image of women, and each woman carries an inherited image of men. These images are collective archetypes, and they are projected on to prospective partners and on to all the significant people with whom an individual comes into contact throughout life.

The *shadow* is the inferior being within us which is primitive and animal, as well as reckless and uncontrolled. It is also the personal unconscious, and is similar to Freud's concept of the id. The emotions and desires contained in the shadow are incompatible with civilized expectations, so people tend to conceal them as much as possible. The shadow is common to all of us, and in this sense can also be a collective phenomenon. According to Jung, it is useless, as well as harmful, to deny the existence of the shadow, since the shadow is not just destructive, but the source of creativity as well. When the shadow is severely repressed, it tends to grow in strength so that when it does eventually emerge, the individual feels overwhelmed by it. Its recognition, acceptance and integration is essential not just for the health of the individual, but also for the health of society as a whole.

The term 'self' describes a state of complete integration of all the separate elements of personality. This includes an acceptance of good and bad, of male and female, as well as a unity of conscious and unconscious. The process of reaching a state of self-hood can last for a lifetime, and very few people ever achieve it. The concept of 'self-hood' is similar to that of 'oneness', and it involves an awareness of the interrelatedness of all aspects of life, as well as an acceptance of the individual's uniqueness within the larger scheme of things.

JUNGIAN THERAPY

Counsellors who are interested in the Jungian approach view the client/ counsellor relationship as essentially cooperative. A central goal in therapy is the integration of all aspects of personality, including the anima, the Animus and the Shadow. The concept of personal unconsciousness does not, according to Jungians, adequately explain all areas of human experience. The human psyche is regarded as much more complex than this, and includes the important dimension of the collective unconscious which is present even before the individual has acquired any life experience. Dreams and their manifestations are especially significant in Jungian therapy, and the first dream that a client recounts is often taken as a starting point for the therapeutic process. Clients are often asked to read recommended books, and may even be given tasks to perform, including the illustration of dreams through painting or drawing.

The process of *individuation*, or the search for wholeness and wisdom, is a major goal of therapy, and although this may take different forms for different people, the client's spiritual awareness and development are considered and discussed. We saw earlier that the counsellor/client relationship is cooperative; it is also warm, relaxed and informal. The issue of transference is not regarded as particularly important, but when it does arise it is openly discussed between client and counsellor. Attention is paid, not just to the client's past, but also to the present, and to the future as well.

ALFRED ADLER (1870–1937)

Adler broke away from Freud's psychoanalytic school in 1911, two years earlier than Jung. Like Jung, Adler disagreed with Freud's insistence on sexuality as the major influence on personality development. He believed that Freud's emphasis on biological and instinctual drives was restrictive, although he did agree with him about the significance of the unconscious and the forces which it contains.

Following his resignation from Freud's circle, Adler set up his own school of *individual psychology*. The word 'individual' was deliberately chosen in order to highlight the distinctiveness or uniqueness of the human personality. Adler's view of human nature is optimistic, and emphasizes the importance of social interest, as well as integration and interrelation with the wider community in which a person lives. According to Adler, people who are not interested in others will experience great difficulty in life, and are bound to fail in their search for happiness. Although each individual is distinct and unique, all are members of the human race and dependent, to some extent, on other people. This makes social cooperation imperative, since it is based on fellowship and a willingness to contribute to the welfare of others. Each problem in life must therefore be seen in the context of the individual's association with other people, and emotional survival depends on the realization that total individualism can never lead to fulfilment.

THE INFERIORITY
COMPLEX

Adler described the concept of the inferiority complex as one of the key discoveries of individual psychology. The term refers to the feelings of inferiority which people experience when they find themselves in situations which they would like to improve. The origins of inferiority stem from early childhood when a state of dependence is commonplace. Adults are obviously much more powerful than children, and this fact alone can inculcate feelings of inadequacy and a subsequent determination to achieve superiority.

Every person experiences a sense of inferiority in childhood, but this varies in degree for each individual. Feelings of inferiority are always accompanied by stress, and this can have the unfortunate effect of propelling the person towards quick and easy solutions to problems. In other words, a person can try to achieve superiority through false means and selfish solutions. For instance, some people try to be superior through manipulation, illness, domination or bullying. By acting in these ways, they position themselves on what Adler described as 'the useless side of life' (*What Life Could Mean to You*, 1992). Since life continues to present people with problems, the final goal of superiority is never reached; what matters, however, is the striving towards perfection and improvement in our common social

Co-operation is based on fellowship and a willingness to contribute to the welfare of others.

situation. A person who is neurotic will always favour superficial solutions to life's problems, while a person who is healthy will learn from mistakes and difficulties and keep going courageously.

Adler pointed to several important factors which could affect the degree of inferiority a person might experience. These include birth order and the position of the individual within the family. Education, as well as social and economic factors, was also considered by Adler to influence a person's feelings of inferiority, and the drive towards a position of superiority. Any physical hardship or disability can lead to severe loss of confidence and hope, and thus heighten feelings of inferiority. Children who are neglected or spoiled are likely to suffer from low self-esteem, and those who are subjected to excessive parental pressure to succeed may suffer from anxiety and irreparable loss of confidence. Gender also plays an important part in the way that children view their positions socially. Adler was aware that sexual inequality exists in society, and he referred to what he described as the *masculine protest* which is expressed in a wide variety of behaviour, in boys as well as girls. Dislike of one's masculine or feminine roles arises when too much emphasis is placed on the concept of masculinity. This leads to denigration of their own femininity by girls, and to self-doubt and lack of confidence in their sexuality by boys.

LIFESTYLES

Early in life each child develops a strategy or 'lifestyle' in order to cope with feelings of inferiority. A child may try to change a weakness into a strength, or may overcompensate by trying too hard to reach goals which are essentially mistaken. An example of this is the cowardly person who becomes a bully.

Successful compensation, on the other hand, is constructive, and has positive advantages for society as well as for the individual. Artistic and intellectual achievement, for example, often compensate for deficiencies in other areas, and sometimes stem from feelings of inferiority which originated through lack of physical or athletic prowess.

Some children simply decide to opt out early on, and may develop symptoms of illness which serve to deflect attention from their fear of failure. Other children learn to approach things in an extremely casual way, so that their abilities are not really tested, and failure never becomes a reality.

When a lifestyle has been adopted, it becomes the individual's theme or pattern, and determines the kind of behaviour used to pursue personal goals. In individual psychology, it is assumed that all human behaviour has a purpose. The decisions which a person has made are based on their own unique experiences within the family, the community, and the present situation in which they are living. Striving for superiority is seen as innate, but the word superiority - as used in this context - refers to the attainment of one's potential, the development of competence, and the pursuit of perfection. The goal of superiority is therefore a legitimate and healthy one, and does not include the idea of power or domination over others.

INTERPRETATION OF PAST EVENTS

In individual psychology, it is not a person's literal past which is important but the way each person interprets past events, and the meanings which are given to experiences. A person who had an unhappy childhood may be traumatized and crushed by it, while another person with similar experiences may transcend them and plan a better future for himself and his family. Each person is *self-determined* by the meanings they give to their experiences, and in this sense, individual psychology is quite different from Freudian psychoanalysis with its influence on instinctual determinism. Adler did, however, concede that there were certain situations and conditions which could predispose some people to failure and lack of courage. These include physical disadvantage, spoiling and neglect.

ADLERIAN THERAPY

The Adlerian approach to therapy and counselling emphasizes the client's subjective reality, and in this respect it is often described as 'phenomenological'. Attention is paid to the way individual clients perceive their reality, and we will see later that other approaches to counselling, including person-centred and Gestalt, have extended this position.

The relationship between the Adlerian counsellor and the client is based on collaborative efforts and cooperation. The counsellor's role is, among other things, a teaching one, with the emphasis on re-educating clients whose life goals and assumptions may be dysfunctional and mistaken. The means which clients have chosen to achieve superiority may be unhealthy, and may work against them, so a basic aim of counselling is to help them understand their own thinking, and to identify more constructive ways of making progress. This approach includes encouraging clients to develop social interest and commitment, so that attention is focused not just on self, but on the needs of others and society as well.

The Adlerian counsellor also provides interpretation for clients which should help them to identify faulty motivation and to gain insight. This, in turn, should provide the impetus for change in lifestyle, and a deeper awareness of individual and societal needs. In individual psychology, failure to relate to, and to show interest in other people and society is regarded as a fundamental cause of human failure and difficulty. Because of this, attention is directed in counselling towards encouraging clients to relate more effectively to others. This is certainly a goal of all forms of counselling, but individual psychology places a great deal of emphasis on it.

Adlerian counsellors are interested in the client's position within the family, and often clients are asked to complete questionnaires which detail this kind of information. This also helps clients to identify any mistaken views of the past which they may hold. Faulty thinking is also identified, and irrational beliefs, which often lead to behavioural and emotional disturbance, are discussed and analysed. (*Rational-emotive therapy*, developed by Albert Ellis and described in a later chapter, is influenced by Adlerian psychology, and is also concerned with clients' irrational beliefs.)

Both client and counsellor work towards agreed and specific goals in the Adlerian model of counselling, and a contract is often made between them. Clients are encouraged to recount their dreams, and these are discussed during sessions so that current preoccupations can be identified. Clients' priorities are listed, so that these can be reassessed (by the client) if necessary. Throughout the course of counselling, encouragement is continually given by the counsellor to the client, and the cognitive emphasis of the model also encourages clients to think for themselves. The issue of transference is not regarded as significant in Adlerian counselling, and the general view taken is that it is unlikely to be a problem when clients are treated as equals in the therapeutic relationship.

THE NEO-FREUDIANS AND OBJECT RELATIONS THEORISTS

It is not within the scope of this chapter to discuss the work of all those theorists whose ideas have stemmed from Freudian psychoanalysis. Over the years, many of Freud's students and disciples went on to make careers for themselves, and these *Neo-Freudians* – as they came to be known – accepted some of his ideas and rejected others. Sometimes it was simply a case of greater emphasis being placed on one particular aspect of Freudian theory, but in general the Neo-Freudians tended to stress the role of social experience, and to de-stress the importance of sexual and aggressive impulses. Among the list of Neo-Freudian names are those of Karen Horney, Eric Fromm, Erik Erikson, Clara Thompson and Harry Stack Sullivan. The Neo-Freudians adopted many of Freud's basic theories concerning human personality, but they added new concepts of their own, and suggested change in other areas.

Object relations theorists, including Klein, Fairbairn and Winnicott, focus on the importance of very early relationships in shaping personality. From a counselling viewpoint, object relations theory enables counsellors to look at clients' problems relating to intimacy, dependence and identity in a different light and from a different perspective from that afforded by a purely Freudian viewpoint. The theory deals with the infant's relationship with its mother or primary care-giver, and pays special attention to the first weeks of life when a strong bond should be forming between infant and parents. The infant's relationship with parts of the mother's body (part objects) and with non-human objects is of special interest. Object relations theory has helped to influence the way that children's problems of separation are dealt with by hospitals, for example, and has focused attention on the need to encourage contact and bonding between babies and parents.

The ideas expressed in object relations theory are complex and cannot be adequately covered in an introductory text, but students who are especially interested in psychodynamic counselling should be prepared to read extensively if they wish to understand it fully.

CASE STUDY: SARAH

Sarah came for counselling because her boyfriend, with whom she had lived for the past two years, had just broken off the relationship. Although she suspected that he had been unfaithful to her once before, Sarah had no idea that he had recently become involved in a serious relationship with someone else. In her own words, her 'whole world had fallen apart' since Philip had spoken to her two nights previously, and she had thought about nothing else in the intervening time. She was unable to sleep properly and had started to diet and binge again - a habit she had managed to stop six months before all this had happened.

During her first meeting with the counsellor, Sarah was distressed and agitated. She wanted to talk at length about Philip and about the happiness she had shared with him while they had been together. The counsellor listened to her attentively so that she would be encouraged to talk at her own pace, and to examine all the aspects of the broken relationship. Sarah and Philip had met just after she had broken off with a previous boyfriend who had been a heavy drinker, and who often abused her verbally. Philip had seemed to be different, kind and conscientious, and they had liked each other from the very beginning. Six months after their first meeting they decided to share a flat, and at that time, Sarah said, she couldn't have been happier. She was aware that Philip was attractive to other women, and at first she was pleased by this, although deep down she was a little unsure of her own ability to hold his attention. Sarah mentioned several times to the counsellor that she considered herself to be 'plain' and that in view of this she had been very surprised when Philip had asked her to live with him.

Sarah was twenty-eight years of age. She was a trained nurse who worked in an intensive-care unit where the level of responsibility which she held was very high. Throughout the first and second counselling sessions, she referred to her work many times, saying how much it meant to her and how much she enjoyed the hospital atmosphere, the sense of community which she had with her colleagues, and the personal satisfaction which she derived from her position in the unit. In contrast, her home life had been almost a disaster as far as she was concerned. Her previous boyfriend had been unpredictable because of his drinking, and he had been unreliable with money. Philip was unpredictable in some ways too, and occasionally he had forgotten important events like her birthday, and overspent so that she had had to help him out financially. Anger was discernible in Sarah's voice when she mentioned this last fact, although at other times she seemed to be at pains to think only the best of her ex-boyfriend. She went on to say that her mother had often warned her about the general unreliability of men. However, it was clear from the tone of her voice, and her general demeanour, that Sarah did not happily subscribe to these views expressed by her mother.

Because she needed to talk at great length about the recent stressful events in her life, it was some time before Sarah was ready to look back to her childhood and her early relationship with her parents. Later, when she was more composed, she welcomed the opportunity to consider her past and the people who were important to her within it. The counsellor encouraged Sarah to recall as much detail as possible and to talk freely about issues which seemed to her to be important or significant.

Free association is a basic principle of the psychodynamic approach to counselling, and through its use clients are encouraged to recollect past experiences which may, at times, evoke intense emotional feelings. This release of suppressed emotion in the safety of the therapeutic environment, does not in itself eliminate conflict and distress, but it often leads to further exploration of repressed feelings and experiences. In Sarah's case, *insight* was achieved when she recalled some events in her childhood which had been particularly traumatic for her. Her parents had not been happy together, and her father left home for another woman when Sarah was fifteen. There had been a pattern in her parents' married life; her father had occasional affairs with other women, while her mother, although not happy with the situation, had tolerated it. Her mother had also denigrated Sarah's father, in his absence, and as far back as Sarah could remember, this bitterness was a constant refrain in her childhood. During the counselling sessions Sarah herself sometimes made disparaging remarks about men in general, and when the counsellor drew her attention to this, she was surprised, but quickly made the connection between her mother's attitude and her own.

Helping clients to understand the origin of their beliefs, attitudes and behaviour is one of the most important contributions which the psychodynamic counsellor makes, and this can be accomplished through the use of appropriate *interpretation*. Often this means clarifying and translating what the client is saying, so that the process of making connections and uncovering new material is facilitated. In this respect, interpretations should only be made when the client is ready to accept and assimilate them, otherwise they will simply be rejected outright.

Sarah went on to talk about her relationship with her mother which she described as an 'ambivalent' one. She loved her mother and still kept in daily contact with her, but she also felt controlled by her, and unable to free herself and become independent. Her mother had been domineering and had often put Sarah down; this had resulted in Sarah feeling inadequate, especially in the presence of older women. She had become particularly aware of these feelings when she started to work with older colleagues at the hospital. She was also aware of them – once the discussion focused on this area – in her relationship with the counsellor who was an older woman as well. This meant that in some ways Sarah tended to react to the counsellor as she might have done to her mother. Once these *transference* feelings were highlighted and discussed, Sarah was able to re-experience and express a range of feelings which she had for her mother. She also gained new insight into the way that her past was continuing to influence her present. Even though she loved her work and was good at it, she often felt inferior and lacking in confidence in the presence of older women colleagues. The insights that Sarah gained were extremely important to her, and as a result of them she decided to work towards greater independence and improved self-esteem.

On the subject of her father, Sarah showed a great deal of *resistance* and, from the outset, talked much more about her mother. During a later session, the counsellor referred to Sarah's father, and this prompted some discussion about him. He had been a handsome man, and as a small child, Sarah had adored him. By the time she was six years old though, she was aware of the tension between her parents and felt that she had to side with one of them. She opted to side with her father, but this decision caused her a great deal of guilt because she could see quite clearly the way he was treating her mother. As she talked about her father, Sarah became quite distressed. She knew he had always been unfaithful to her mother, and in fact, had left her in the end. Sarah referred to him as 'unpredictable' and 'unreliable', and even as she used these terms, the counsellor could see that she was becoming aware of the emerging parallels between her mother's relationship with her father and her own recent relationships with men. Sarah recalled how Philip had put her down and had criticized her appearance and her weight. She recalled that her father had been similarly critical of her mother. She referred again to the fact that she perceived herself as plain, and that Philip had picked this up and used it to control her. Sarah identified her own past *denial* of the way that Philip, and other boyfriends, had treated her. This, she said, had led to an increase in her eating problem which was always worse when she was under stress.

When Sarah had worked through her distress, and the angry feelings which began to emerge, she went on to explore, in subsequent sessions with the counsellor, possible ways of moving forward. Sarah was concerned to look at ways of improving her overall confidence, since she now saw this as a fundamental issue which had a great deal of bearing on future relationships, and on all aspects of her life generally. Throughout the sessions with Sarah, the counsellor was supportive in her interventions, and framed them in a way which would facilitate insight and understanding. Sarah was encouraged to talk about her childhood and to experience emotions which had been ignored for a very long time. She was then able to make important connections between the past and the present, and to identify ways in which early relationships were continuing to exert an influence on her.

FURTHER READING

ADLER, A., *Understanding Human Nature*, One World Publications Ltd, Oxford, 1992.

ADLER, A., *What Life Could Mean to You*, One World Publications Ltd, Oxford, 1992.

BROME, V., *Jung – Man and Myth*, Paladin, London, 1991.

BROWN, D. AND PEDDER, J., *Introduction to Psychotherapy*, Tavistock/Routledge, London, 1991.

DRYDEN, W. (ed.), *Individual Therapy in Britain*, Harper & Row, New York, 1984.

FORDHAM, F., *An Introduction to Jung's Psychology*, Penguin Books, London, 1991.

HUGHES, J. M., *Reshaping the Psycho-Analytic Domain*, University of California Press, Los Angeles, 1990.

JACOBS, M., *Key Figures in Counselling & Psychotherapy – Sigmund Freud*, Sage Publications, London, 1992.

JACOBS, M., *Psychodynamic Counselling in Action*, Sage Publications, London, 1990.

McGUIRE, W. AND HULL, R.F.C. (eds), *C. G. Jung Speaking – Interviews and Encounters*, Picador/Pan Books, London, 1980.

NELSON-JONES, R., *The Theory and Practice of Counselling Psychology*, Cassell, London, 1990.

CHAPTER 2

Person-centered counselling

The historical background

CARL ROGERS (1902–87)

Person-centered, or client centered, therapy was developed by the American psychologist Carl Rogers who was born in Illinois in 1902. His early background was a lonely and repressive one, as his parents, who held rigid fundamentalist beliefs, did not encourage the kind of emotional atmosphere which is conducive to childhood spontaneity and freedom of expression. He was brought up in the country where he spent most of his time in solitary pursuits, and since his parents did not want much contact with outsiders he had very little chance to mix with other young people or to become involved in social events. This lack of contact with other people had a profound effect on Rogers who, in later life, identified his poor self-confidence and social skills as having their origin in his childhood and teenage years.

Like most other children, the young Rogers was influenced to some degree by his parents' views, and this influence was responsible for his later ambition to become a minister of religion. As a preparation for his vocation, he enrolled to study history at the University of Wisconsin where he met a group of students whose home and religious backgrounds were similar to his own. At the age of twenty, he went to China along with them to take part in a Christian conference, and this visit had the effect of awakening strong feelings of independence within him, so that for the first time in his life he found himself questioning his parents' values and beliefs. This move towards independence was the starting point for further developments in his career, and although he did go on to attend a theological seminary to study for the ministry, he abandoned this two years later and went to Columbia University where, in 1928, he completed his Master's degree. After this he worked for two years at a Child Guidance Clinic in New York and later received his PhD from Columbia University. In 1940 Rogers became Professor of Psychology at Ohio State University and from 1945 to 1957 he held the position of Professor of Psychology at the University of Chicago. Later academic appointments included Professor of Psychology and Psychiatry at the University of Wisconsin (1957) and Fellow at Stamford University (1962). In 1964 he became Resident Fellow at the Western Behavioural Science Institute at La Jolla, California, where he subsequently formed the Centre for Studies of the Person.

Throughout his academic career, Rogers was also gaining a great deal of personal experience as a therapist. As well as this he wrote several important books including *Counselling and Psychotherapy* in 1942, *Client-Centered*

Therapy in 1951 and *On Becoming a Person* in 1961. The central theme in all of Rogers' later writing is the importance of the individual as a competent architect of his own destiny. Even though this competence is occasionally disturbed by the vicissitudes of life, Rogers nevertheless believed that each person has sufficient innate resources to deal effectively with whatever traumas, conflicts or dilemmas are experienced by them. This belief in the strength and integrity of human beings is a fundamental tenet of person-centered counselling. Even when an individual's resources are latent or hidden, they are always acknowledged as being present and having potential for growth and development.

There seems to be no doubt that Rogers' early childhood and teenage years had a great deal of influence on the subsequent formation of his ideas about psychotherapy and human relationships. While meaningful communication with his parents had been impossible for him as a child, as an adult he became an ardent exponent of clear communication between people, particularly between the two people who are engaged in the therapeutic or counselling relationship. This clear communication was to Rogers not just something which is expressed verbally; he also meant it to refer to the total relationship between client and counsellor, a relationship which he believed should be based on acceptance, respect and trust. These and other attitudes are transmitted to clients even when the counsellor is unaware of having expressed them. This makes it imperative for the person-centered counsellor to be in touch with her own inner feelings which she can then monitor and identify. It is also seen as important in the person-centered model for the counsellor to place a great deal of value on herself, for in Rogers' opinion it is only through a proper appreciation or love of self that true acceptance of and respect for clients can develop.

The emphasis on the person-centered model of counselling is placed, therefore, on the relationship between the client and the counsellor, and on the therapeutic changes which can take place for the client when there is an atmosphere of warmth, respect and acceptance. It was Rogers who first used the word 'client' as opposed to the word 'patient'. He did this in order to highlight the necessity of moving away from a purely medical view of people towards one which views individuals as responsible, self-sufficient and ultimately capable of organizing their own lives.

Person-centered theory grew in popularity in Britain during the 1960s when its main influence was initially in the field of education. More recently, however, it has become widely accepted in many other areas, including social work, health care and, of course, psychotherapy and counselling.

KEY WORDS

CONGRUENCE

Carl Rogers believed that a truly therapeutic relationship between client and counsellor depended on the existence, within the counsellor, of three important or 'core' conditions which he referred to as *congruence, unconditional positive regard*, and *empathy*. The word 'congruence' refers to the counsellor's ability

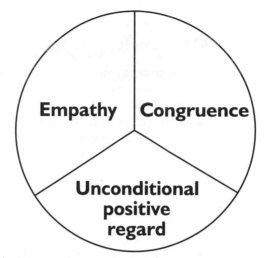

Fig. 2.1 *Rogers' three core conditions.*

to be a real or genuine person in the counselling situation, a person who has no need to act as an expert, to feel superior or to pretend in any way. Because of this lack of pretence or superiority, the counsellor who is congruent or genuine will encourage the client to seek the truth within himself, and thus identify the very core of his problem more effectively. Rogers used the word 'transparent' to describe the truly congruent or genuine counsellor, and by this he meant that the counsellor's openness should be such that the client is able to see right through to the real person beneath. A counsellor who is a real person will never attempt to deceive the client or to offer empty platitudes, nor will she try to hide or disguise her own sincere reactions and feelings. This means, for example, that even when a client behaves in a difficult or inconsistent fashion, the person-centered counsellor is willing to bring her perception of his behaviour into the open and to discuss it supportively with him. When this true sharing of perceptions takes place between counsellor and client, there is a greater chance that the client will be encouraged to become more open with himself, and this openness should in turn lead to deeper insight, healing and progress.

UNCONDITIONAL POSITIVE REGARD

The phrase 'unconditional positive regard' refers to the respect or valuing which the counsellor feels for the client. This should be given to the client without any conditions attached, for in the person-centered model the client is seen as a unique person who, regardless of his problems or difficulties, has a right to be accepted for himself. Rogers sometimes used the word 'prizing' to describe this attitude, and he believed that this prizing is necessary if the client is to feel safe within the counselling situation. Feeling safe also implies that the client knows that he is not being judged by the counsellor, even though the counsellor may very well have a value system which is different from his own. The client further needs to feel that the counsellor appreciates him as a person, regardless of his behaviour or the attitudes which he may be expressing at any given time. Within the person-centred model of counselling, the client's behaviour may be viewed as something quite separate from or even alien to him, since behaviour is, in any case, contingent upon the current circumstances or difficulties which a person is experiencing. Very often people respond to life events in ways which may be negative or counterproductive but which, nevertheless, seem to be the appropriate or only solution at the time. It is the counsellor's willingness and ability to see behind the client's behaviour and to come closer to the real person that is essential if therapeutic movement is to take place.

EMPATHY

The word 'empathy' is used to describe a particular characteristic which the counsellor should possess in relation to the client. When a counsellor is empathic it means that she is capable of understanding the client in the very deepest sense, that she can, when necessary, stand in the client's shoes and perceive things as the client perceives them, and that she can also transmit this deep understanding back to the client who will be encouraged and supported by it. This ability to enter into the true spirit or feelings of another person's world is sometimes referred to as being within the client's 'frame of reference'. It is quite different from sympathy because sympathy is concerned with feelings of pity, compassion or tenderness towards another person, whereas empathy requires much more effort, concentration and discipline. In order to develop true empathy, a counsellor needs to strive constantly for a clearer awareness of all aspects of the client's feelings, and then to experience his private world with him, as if it were her own. This is extremely difficult to accomplish and sustain, not least because it involves a continuous and intense active listening, not just to words but also to the feelings expressed and conveyed when no words are spoken.

The Model

In the person-centered model of counselling the personality of the counsellor is regarded as being of paramount importance, for it is impossible, according to Rogers, to separate the personality of the counsellor from the work that she does. In order to be effective, she needs to hold certain philosophical beliefs and attitudes which uphold the worth, dignity, significance and value of each individual. A counsellor who pays lip service only to the idea that each person is unique and valuable will, in the end, prove ineffective as a person-centered counsellor since her true inner beliefs will ultimately be transmitted to clients who will then be adversely affected by them. Most practitioners, using various models of counselling, would probably claim to value each individual in the way described by Rogers, yet very often this is not reflected in the kind of work they do. They may be directive or controlling in their attitudes towards clients, an orientation which is often due, in part at least, to having neglected their own personal growth and development. It is impossible, according to Rogers, for any person to value others unless that person is ready to value and care for their own identical needs.

Believing in the worth and the ability of individuals to direct their own lives implies that the person-centered counsellor is willing to allow clients to move at their own pace and to choose their own values and standards even when she does not necessarily agree with them. The belief that clients have the innate potential for self-direction and the motivation to achieve insight into their own problems is not one that all counsellors automatically hold. It is possible to subscribe to the belief at an intellectual level without really feeling it to be true, deep down. This is not to say that it is impossible for some counsellors ever to become person-centered in their approach because they do not have this deep conviction. They may actually acquire it through even limited experience of using the model, which then enables them to see how effective it can be. Once clients become aware that another person believes in their capacity to cope and to manage their own problems, they have a remarkable tendency to do just that.

A significant criticism which has been levelled against the person-centered model of counselling is that the counsellor who uses this approach is in danger of becoming merely passive or *laissez-faire*. This is, in fact, a misconception since a truly accepting and interested counsellor would never lapse into passivity. Interest and passivity are mutually exclusive attitudes; the first involves a great deal of concentration and attention, while the second requires no effort at all. Although the person-centered counsellor is not concerned to evaluate, diagnose or even guide the client, she is nevertheless engaged in the more difficult tasks of active listening and responding in a way which conveys deep understanding and acceptance. These attitudes need to be sincerely felt by the counsellor in order for them to be experienced by and helpful to the client.

Since the ability to step inside another person's frame of reference is not something which we all spontaneously possess, a focus of training for person-centered counselling is that practice of therapy should form an integral part of every training programme. Practice of therapy is quite different from the learning of specific techniques, because it concentrates on encouraging trainees to provide helping relationships with and for each other, as well as encouraging them to gain further experience of working with clients under the direction of a supervisor. Although it is not always available, another important element of training is the provision of personal therapy for counsellors, not with the expectation that this will solve all their personal problems, but rather in the hope that it will facilitate a deeper understanding of their own feelings, beliefs and attitudes. The development of this understanding should, in turn, increase the counsellor's awareness of the feelings, beliefs and attitudes of other people. It is the quality of the relationship between counsellor and client which is the most important element in the person-centered approach, and this deep awareness of self and others cannot be overestimated.

THE ACTUALIZING TENDENCY

Rogers put forward the view that each individual has within himself a strong tendency to grow, to develop and to reach the maximum potential of which he is capable in life. This *actualizing tendency*, he believed, was common to all living things, but he noted it particularly in human beings who, from the moment of birth onwards, possess an active drive or motivating force whose purpose is to enable them to achieve wholeness. The concept of the actualizing tendency is crucial in the person-centered model of counselling because it places a firm emphasis on the innate ability of people to improve and to regulate their lives, if external forces allow them to do so. Often a person's actualizing tendency is inhibited or obscured because of adverse circumstances such as emotional deprivation or trau-

The Actualizing Tendency. Each person has a strong tendency to grow, develop and reach maximum potential.

matic experiences in childhood. In Rogers' view, however, it is always possible to reactivate the actualizing tendency no matter how latent it has become, and this can be achieved in counselling when the core conditions of congruence, unconditional positive regard and empathy are present.

The concept of the actualizing tendency is also important for a much more fundamental reason, and this concerns the idea that if we, as counsellors, believe that people possess a drive towards growth and wholeness, then we must accept them as being intrinsically 'good' and therefore worthy of our deepest respect.

THE SELF-CONCEPT

An understanding of the self-concept is important in person-centered counselling for it relates to the individual's perception or image of himself which is based on his life experience and the way he sees himself reflected in the attitudes expressed by his family and friends. People acquire their self-concept very early in childhood and it is continually reinforced by ongoing interactions with other people throughout life. When an infant begins to interact with his environment, he simultaneously starts to build a picture of himself in relation to it, and if early experiences are bad or negative, then the subsequent development of the self-concept will also be negative. Thus, an individual who has received very little love and a great deal of criticism from parents in early life will, in all probability, grow into adulthood with a poor self concept.

The problem is compounded when teachers, and other significant people in a child's life, are also critical and unsupportive, for this combination of censure and criticism is instrumental in lowering even further the individual's belief in his own judgement, and his ability to direct his own life. Clients who come for counselling are often so used to being judged and directed by other people that they believe themselves incapable of making choices or decisions. Frequently, they turn to the counsellor for expertise and advice, as they did to so many other people in the past, hoping that she too will tell them what to do. This turning to the counsellor for advice and 'expert' help is not done because clients are lazy or unwilling to tackle their own problems; on the contrary, it is a direct result of their conviction that they do not themselves have the resources necessary to do so. The person-centered counsellor's task is to encourage such clients to get in touch with their inner resources, and show them that all people possess them, no matter how self-rejecting they have become.

It is not always the case, however, that clients who seek counselling are suffering from a severely-diminished self-concept. Many people are lucky enough to reach adult life with their self-concept, if not intact, at least not irreparably damaged. If people are brought up among family and friends who give them positive regard – which in turn enables them to regard themselves positively – then their self-concept will become what Rogers regarded as healthy and self-actualizing.

Fig. 2.2 *The self-concept and the organismic self.*

THE ORGANISMIC SELF

As well as the self-concept, each individual also possesses, according to Rogers, an *organismic self* which is essentially the real inner life of the person. This organismic self is present from birth and consists of the basic force which regulates each person's physiological and psychological growth. The central and most important aims of the organismic self are to grow, to mature and to achieve self-actualization. This instinctive movement towards harmony and integration is present in everyone, but because conditions of worth are often imposed early on in life, the organismic self can become obscured or even lost. Conditions of worth are those strictures which are directed towards people almost as soon as they are born, and they include rules to govern behaviour, along with disapproval and rejection when those rules are broken.

Because each child needs to feel loved and accepted, and to receive positive regard from parents and others, the oganismic self is neglected in favour of building a self-concept based on the internalized rules which other people have made. If this attempt to please others is continued throughout life, then the individual is not living according to his own inner beliefs, needs and inclinations, but according to an externally imposed concept of how he really should be. Quite frequently people go through life convinced that their self-concept is the only possible truth, and often it is only in times of crisis or bereavement that they manage to get in touch with their inner feelings, needs and capacities. This probably explains why some people suddenly and unexpectedly change their whole lifestyles once they have worked their way through a major life event or crisis.

Clients sometimes come for counselling because they have started to sense, for the first time ever, a vague unease or disquiet with the way their lives are progressing, and this is often related to changes which have taken place for them recently. A focus of the person-centered model of counselling is to encourage and support clients who wish to delve beneath the

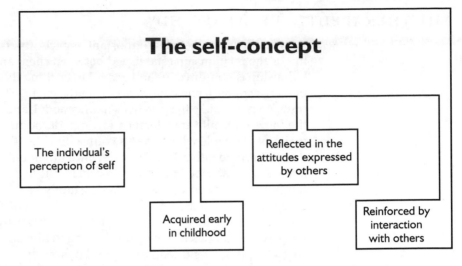

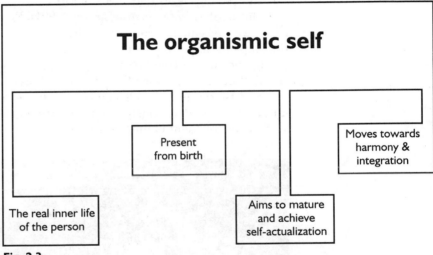

Fig. 2.3

concept of self which has largely been imposed by outside influences, and who wish to find instead the real or inner organismic self. It is impossible to do this, however, unless the counsellor is also committed to the idea that each individual has the inner potential and resources necessary for growth and improvement.

The desire for a deeper awareness of self is very strong, according to Rogers. He also believed that exploration and clarification of a person's current life situation would invariably lead towards growth and healing. This exploration and clarification can be achieved with the help of a person-centered counsellor who is willing to give the client plenty of time, as well as the respect and empathy which he probably failed to get in the past.

THE THERAPEUTIC RELATIONSHIP

As stated earlier, the most important aspect of person-centered counselling is the relationship established between client and counsellor. This relationship is non-directive and geared to eliciting the maximum amount of personal strength and confidence from the client. There is no emphasis on transference, unlike the psychodynamic model, and although Rogers took the view that mild transference feelings do occur to some extent in the majority of people who come for counselling, he did not believe that these would become either hostile or dependent enough to cause major problems. Rogers ascribed this lack of problematic transference to the fact that the person-centered counsellor is constantly striving to understand and accept everything about the client. When the client becomes aware of this acceptance, he gains clarity and insight, and this in turn encourages him to identify the feelings which rightly belong to him and not to the counsellor. As well as this, clients tend to respond positively to counsellors who interact with them on an adult-to-adult basis, so the possibility of neurotic or infantile feelings is lessened considerably.

In his book *Client-Centered Therapy* (1991), Rogers also makes the point that the terms which clients frequently use to describe the counselling relationship are 'impersonal' and 'secure'. The word 'impersonal' is an interesting one since it could easily be thought to imply that person-centered counsellors lack true warmth and feeling. It is, of course, exactly the opposite because these clients also perceive themselves as having very important and helpful relationships with their counsellors. What seems to be significant for them is the counsellor's ability to avoid intrusion of her

Every child needs to feel loved and accepted, and to receive positive regard from parents and others.

personality into the relationship, so that the client's personality is the only one which is highlighted during the counselling session. This ability of the person-centered counsellor to lay aside her own 'self' in order to participate more fully in the client's experience, is what gives person-centered counselling the secure and impersonal qualities which clients value so much. When clients realise that they are not being judged or evaluated, and that they are accepted for what they are, a feeling of security will inevitably follow; it then becomes possible for them to look at feelings and experiences which were once denied or hidden from awareness.

As a conclusion to this section on the therapeutic relationship between counsellor and client, it is worth mentioning that the concepts of the actualizing tendency, the organismic self and the self-concept are, in some ways, analogous to Freud's theory of the structure of personality. It is possible to see some parallels between, for example, the id and the organismic self, since both are meant to represent that part of the individual's psyche which is often neglected, repressed or ignored. The self-concept and the super-ego are similar too, for both describe the internalized rules, moral values and strictures which are largely laid down by other people, including parents and educators. The actualizing tendency appears to echo the functions of the Ego; these are concerned to mediate between the id and the super-ego, and in so doing to provide balance, harmony and true insight. In psychodynamic theory the strengthening of the individual's ego is regarded as the most important aim, while in person-centered theory it is the individual's actualizing tendency to grow towards wholeness and integration which is seen as the main focus for encouragement.

Abraham Maslow (1908 - 70)

Abraham Maslow is another theorist whose contribution to the person-centered approach to counselling is very significant. In 1958, he introduced the idea of a third force in psychology, the first two being psychoanalytic theory and behaviourism. Like Rogers, Maslow is usually referred to as a *humanistic psychologist*, since both their approaches emphasize the uniqueness of human beings, and both are concerned with subjective experience and human values. Their position is quite different both from that taken by the Behaviourists, who are concerned to focus on overt behaviour, and from psychoanalytic beliefs, which emphasise unconscious motives and the strong irrational forces which are said to drive the individual.

Maslow's view of the human person is essentially positive and optimistic, and is concerned to direct attention to the 'healthy' tendencies which he believed to be present in everyone. These include the search for knowledge and understanding, as well as the search for satisfying relationships and the development of rich emotional experience. He did not subscribe to the view that psychology can be general in its application, but believed that it should mainly concentrate on the study of individuals and their unique experiences. Maslow's positive evaluation of nature, and his stress on the uniqueness of human experience, reflects the philosophy underlying the person-centered model of counselling, and in this respect upholds and corroborates the views expressed by Rogers.

THE HIERARCHY OF NEEDS

In 1954, Maslow proposed a hierarchy of needs which he believed were responsible for human motivation, drive and initiative (see Fig. 2.4). Included in this hierarchy, and fundamental to it, are the basic *physiological needs* for food, water, oxygen and warmth, which are essential in order to maintain the biological wellbeing of the individual. When these needs are fulfilled, physical life is ensured; when they are absent, death is the result. Satisfaction of all the basic needs is usually regarded as essential before people can be motivated by higher-order needs, although history shows numerous examples of people who were prepared to sacrifice some - or even all - of these basic needs, so that higher-level needs, related to idealism and principle, could be met. According to Maslow, however, needs at

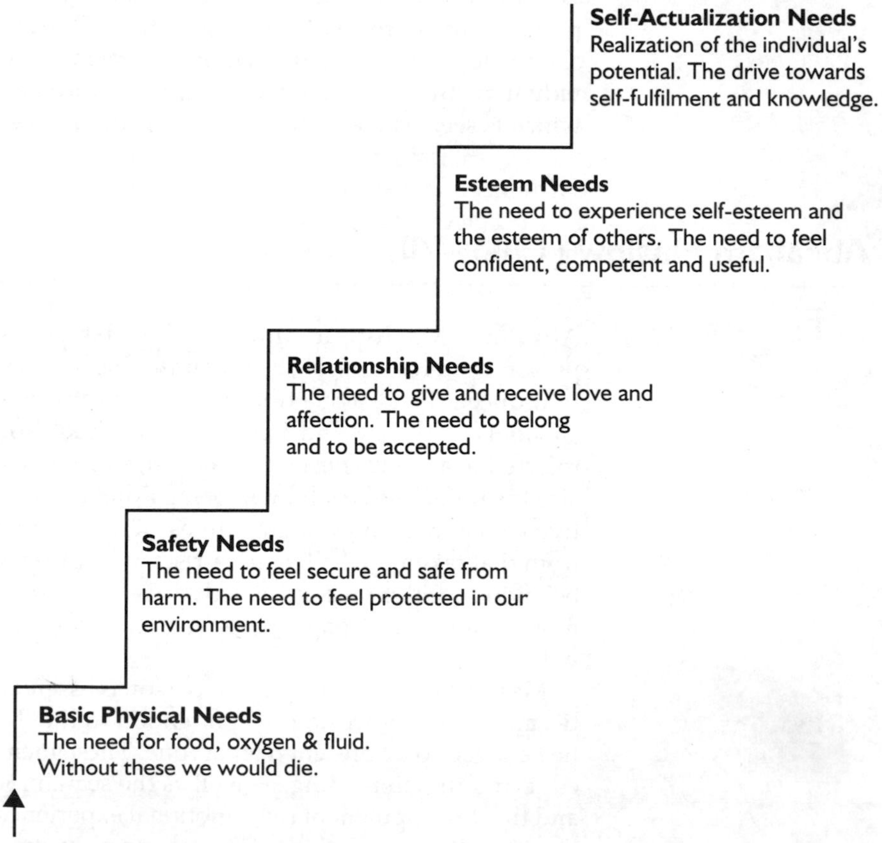

Self-Actualization Needs
Realization of the individual's potential. The drive towards self-fulfilment and knowledge.

Esteem Needs
The need to experience self-esteem and the esteem of others. The need to feel confident, competent and useful.

Relationship Needs
The need to give and receive love and affection. The need to belong and to be accepted.

Safety Needs
The need to feel secure and safe from harm. The need to feel protected in our environment.

Basic Physical Needs
The need for food, oxygen & fluid. Without these we would die.

Fig. 2.4 *Maslow's hierarchy of needs (adapted).*

the lower end of the hierarchy tend to take priority over those higher up, and must be at least partly met before others can be reached.

The next set of needs, according to Maslow's hierarchy, are those relating to *safety*. These are not exclusively related to physical safety, but encompass psychological and security needs as well. Protection from illness, threat and violence are also included here. Safety needs are quite evident in small children, since they require obvious protection and guidance, but these needs also continue throughout the lifespan. When an individual's psychological safety needs are threatened, emotional disturbance usually follows. This can be seen quite clearly in clients who come for counselling, for often their problems are related to vulnerability in this area, especially when family problems and financial difficulties figure largely in their lives.

Relationship needs are concerned with the giving and receiving of love, affection, acceptance and trust. Neglect of these needs, or disturbance of the balance required to maintain them, will also result in trauma and emotional disturbance. Quite often these are also referred to as 'social' needs, a term which places them in a much wider context and includes the daily social contacts which people require in order to give a sense of belonging and purpose to their lives. Clients whose relationship needs are disrupted or unmet, are often disoriented and lacking in self-confidence, and in more extreme situations, depression is the result. In a supportive therapeutic environment, however, some progress can be made by clients towards a fuller understanding of the factors which underly their relationship and social deficits. With increased understanding, clients frequently gain access to their true potential and are then able to deal successfully with problems which may, at first, have seemed insurmountable.

The need to feel competent and confident about one's own ability to solve problems is implicit in the next set of needs which Maslow describes. These are referred to as *esteem needs*, and they encompass all those areas of human requirement which are linked to concepts like self-respect, self-esteem and personal endeavour. The need to be respected by others, as well as self, is also included in this category, for respect from others is essential if people are to feel motivated to participate in communal and social activities. Self-esteem and esteem from others are in many respects inseparable, since they tend to enhance and to generate each other. A basic objective in the person-centered model of counselling is to help clients develop and increase their sense of personal worth, ability and competence. This can be accomplished when Rogers' core conditions of congruence, unconditional positive regard and empathy are genuinely used by the counsellor in order to facilitate the client's progress and growth. Esteem needs are also linked to people's need for status, appreciation and achievement, and in this respect are similar to Adler's concept of the innate drive for superiority and recognition.

THE NEED FOR SELF-ACTUALIZATION

At the top of Maslow's hierarchy is the need for self-actualization, and the drive towards knowledge and self-fulfilment. These concern the individu-

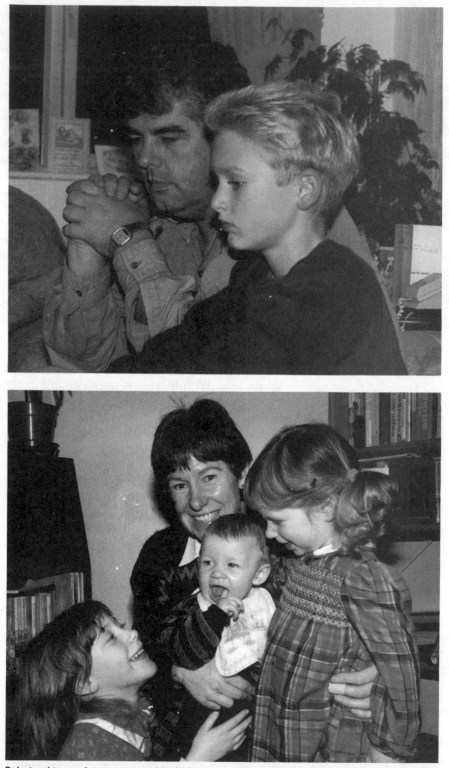

Relationship needs are concerned with the giving of love, affection, acceptance and trust.

al's search for meaning and for the development of his full potential. Although everyone is theoretically capable of achieving self-actualization, the majority never reach this position (Maslow, 1968, 1970). Maslow was interested in the personality traits of famous people who had, in his opinion, achieved self-actualization, and he described some of the characteristics which they had in common. These include:

- The ability to tolerate uncertainty.

- The ability to be objective and to perceive reality clearly.

- Spontaneity of expression, thought and action, as well as a sense of humour and openness.

- Acceptance of self and of others, including strengths and weaknesses.

- The ability to look outside 'self' to the problems of the wider world.

- The ability to resist pressure without being deliberately unconventional.

- The capacity to be more autonomous and self-reliant than other people.

- The ability to establish deep and satisfying interpersonal relationships.

- An appreciation of nature and basic life experiences, including everyday events.

- Interest in social issues and the welfare of others in the community.

- Originality and creativity, and a willingness to experiment with new approaches.

- A capacity for heightened or transcendent experience.

It can be seen from the above list that the majority of ordinary people are probably deficient in a number of them. In contrast, the historical figures examined by Maslow included, among others, Beethoven, Einstein and Spinoza, and what they all had in common was some claim to greatness or accomplishment. However, implicit in the theories of both Maslow and Rogers is the firm belief that it is possible to help people work towards self-actualization, even when their self-regard is low. Rogers, in particular, believed that growth and progress can be achieved through the experience of a warm and empathic therapeutic relationship. (Counselling and therapy are not the only routes to self-actualization, and many people realize their potential through education, religious experience, sporting endeavour or love, all of which are capable of affecting us profoundly.)

Deprivation of lower needs will obviously have a direct bearing on a person's ability to strive for self-actualization. Clients who come for counselling are often in a position where their relationship, security and esteem needs are not being met, and in this respect their journey towards self-actualization may be severely impeded. According to Maslow, it is possible for people to work towards self-actualization by practising behaviours which encourage the development of confidence, openness and spontaneity. These include:

- Developing a willingness to try new experiences and to change.

- Developing a capacity to listen to and to trust one's own feelings, instead of relying on others for guidance, instruction or advice.

- Striving to be honest, avoiding pretences and game-playing.

- Assuming responsibility and working hard.

- Risking unpopularity when personal views are not the same as those of the majority.

- Identifying personal defences and having the courage to give them up.

- Experiencing life as fully as a child does, with concentration and interest.

APPLICATION TO PERSON-CENTERED COUNSELLING

What is striking about the above list of behaviours, is the similarity between them and the self-management skills which are fostered in the person-centered model of counselling, and which should lead eventually to the development of individual autonomy. When clients first come for counselling, they are often reluctant to change, no matter how distressing their current situation is. New experiences appear threatening and unpredictable, and it may seem preferable to stay in a bad situation rather than risk the unknown. In a therapeutic situation where they experience the counsellor's unconditional positive regard, however, there is a real possibility that clients' confidence will increase, so that change will eventually seem less daunting.

The development of a capacity to listen to and trust one's own feelings, is also something which clients, initially at least, may be reluctant to do. Excessive reliance on the opinions of others, especially on the opinions of those in authority, is also typical of many clients whose self-esteem is low. A helping relationship based on Rogers' core conditions will encourage clients to trust their own judgements and opinions, and to question judgements and views which may have caused them unhappiness in the past.

The avoidance of pretence and game-playing is not something which can be accomplished easily, especially when they have become an established pattern of general communication. Many people learn in childhood to relate to others in these ways. Only when more positive forms of communication are experienced – as they should be experienced in the person-centered model of counselling – can clients begin to see how effective they can really be. It is not just the effectiveness of clear communication which clients can learn, however; they should also learn what it feels like to be valued and respected by counsellors who are consistently congruent or genuine with them.

Fear or avoidance of responsibility can also be linked to poor self-esteem, and when clients make progress in counselling, confidence and energy often return in equal proportions. Clients are often fearful of making mistakes and taking risks, but when a supportive environment is provided for them, the idea of responsibility for self can become a challenge and not a chore. In a similar way, the risk of unpopularity among family, friends and acquaintances becomes less ominous when clients experience acceptance in the counselling situation, even when they express views which do not necessarily coincide with those of most people.

The concept of client defences is generally associated with the psychodynamic model of counselling, and is not usually discussed in the context of the person-centered approach. This does not mean that defences do not exist; it simply means that in person-centered counselling the emphasis is primarily on the client as an unique person. The ways in which that person chooses to relate to the counsellor are accepted, even when defences are part of the communication. In the long term, defences should become less important to the client once he has sensed the counsellor's unconditional acceptance of him. The realization that acceptance can be gained without defences can act as an incentive.

When clients are preoccupied with practical, personal and emotional problems, it is difficult for them to experience life to the full and to be deeply absorbed and appreciative in the way described by Maslow. But it is possible for them to work towards this position, and it often follows when other, more pressing problems have been solved. Again, counselling may be the client's first experience of looking at things in new and fresh ways, and it sometimes happens that this first experience is a catalyst for even greater change.

Although deprivation of Maslow's self-actualization need does not lead to death, physical harm or discomfort in the way that deprivation of lower-order needs would do, lack of fulfilment does create other problems which are less obvious, and which may be difficult for even the individual to identify. It is commonplace in contemporary society to view people whose physical and material needs are catered for, as well-off or lucky, but often there is a deficit which only they themselves are aware of. Both Rogers and Maslow have identified this deficit, and related it to a fundamental and continuous human need for emotional, intellectual and spiritual growth.

CASE STUDY: ROBERT

When Robert first came for counselling he was anxious and unhappy about the GCSE examinations he was about to sit. His anxiety had started a few weeks earlier, and had been heightened by recent rows and tensions within his family. He had been uncertain, he told me, about coming for counselling, but had decided to do so in the end because he felt he was no longer 'able to cope'. He also added that he knew if he did not get help he would simply opt out of the exams and leave home.

My first impression of Robert was that he was physically ill at ease and very unsure about what kind of reception he might get from a counsellor. He was clearly suspicious of adults in general and seemed to believe that I might take the same line as his parents and teachers who were constantly telling him what he should do. A friend had suggested counselling to him, but Robert had come along reluctantly, determined to leave at once if he felt that any more pressure was being exerted upon him. For the first twenty minutes of our meeting, he talked at length about his fears concerning counselling while I listened attentively and encouraged him to voice all the worries which he felt. I told him that I understood why he had these concerns and afterwards went on to describe the counselling process, stressing that I was interested in and willing to listen to whatever he wanted to tell me. I added that I would not attempt to give him advice, or try to impose any of my own opinions or views upon him. He seemed disinclined to believe this at first, but I noticed that after a while he became visibly relaxed and adopted a more comfortable, open sitting position. Along with this, he started to give me more eye contact when we spoke, and even smiled occasionally, although his overall demeanour remained sad at times and strained.

I was concerned to get inside Robert's frame of reference and to understand what he was saying from his point of view alone. In order to do this, I continued to listen to him attentively even though this was sometimes difficult since his story was often disjointed and slightly confused, reflecting in many ways the state of events in his life at that particular time. I did not want to ask him too many unnecessary questions because I felt that it was important that he should proceed at his own pace and not feel himself hurried along by me. Occasionally I would paraphrase and summarize what he had been saying in order to clarify - for his sake and mine - some of the issues which he talked about. This seemed to encourage him to continue and explore further many of the problems which had been worrying him for some time. During our first session together, he talked about his college work, his parents and family, and the career choices which he was currently having to make.

Robert was sixteen years of age, the youngest of a family of three. He had an older brother and a sister who was ten years his senior to whom he was emotionally very close. His parents were the working proprietors of a small hotel, an occupation which absorbed virtually all their time and energy. Robert lived at the hotel with them, and in the evenings and at weekends he worked in the kitchen and helped serve at tables, tasks which he disliked intensely. Because he was the youngest of the family, he had always been regarded as the baby, and he had been more or less treated as such for as long as he could remember. This was a situation which had gradually become intolerable for him even though he admitted, with a wry smile, that he had often enjoyed his status in the past. More recently, however, he had experienced a strong desire to assert himself, to get away from home and to follow a career quite different from the one his parents expected him to choose.

Robert described himself as artistic and interested in literature and drama. He did not immediately describe himself in this way, but instead talked about his parents' ambitions for him. They wanted him to pursue a business course with a view to inheriting and managing the hotel when they retired. It was only when I encouraged Robert to focus on his own feelings and needs that he was able to identify his true ambitions and talents. He remarked that nobody had ever really expressed this kind of interest in him before and that he found it unusual and almost embarrassing to talk about himself in this way. We laughed about this, and Robert gradually and visibly became much more at ease with me. When we met for the second time, I was aware that we had established a good relationship, that he trusted me, and more importantly that he was beginning to get in touch with his own opinions and feelings, something which he had constantly been discouraged from doing by his parents, his older brother and especially by his sister. Robert was particularly close to his sister but she was inclined to smother him with affection, to treat him like a child and to disregard his views. She wanted him to go and stay with her for an extended holiday when he had finished his exams, so that he could have a break from his parents and the hotel, but Robert was beginning to sense that he would have no more freedom with her than he did at home.

In common with many clients who come for counselling, Robert was concerned with a much more fundamental issue than the one which initially preoccupied him. During our third counselling session he told me that he was gay. It was clearly very difficult for him to discuss this with me since he had only recently acknowledged the possibility to himself. He had not been able to talk about this to anyone else, and he felt that his parents would be 'horrified' if he told them. He was unsure what his sister's reaction might be, but felt instinctively that she could be supportive once she had recovered from the initial shock. I got the impression that Robert was testing my reaction to what he had said, and that he was very relieved when I responded in a totally accepting way. Clients must experience unconditional positive regard from counsellors, and they can only really experience this if it is actually and discernibly present. It is not something which can be simulated or feigned. This is a point worth emphasizing, because in order for Robert to make progress towards self-actualization he needed some evidence that I, at least, valued him exactly as he was. All the other adults in his life had been authoritative or patronizing in their attitudes towards him: his parents wanted him to study business, to have a girlfriend and to settle down eventually to manage the hotel. His sister wanted him to remain a little boy so that she could mother him and tell him what to do, while his brother was habitually critical of his clothes, his friends and his lifestyle in general. At the same time all of the family were, as he put it, 'more than good' to him, often giving him money and helping to finance holidays abroad.

Robert admitted ruefully that although he often found his family oppressive and their behaviour irritating, he nevertheless enjoyed the perks which they lavished on him. In talking at length about all these issues, Robert came to see that if he was ever to achieve independence and freedom he might have to forfeit some of the family benevolence. He came to this conclusion through his own efforts and I was careful not to influence him one way or the other. It continued to be difficult for him to identify his own opinions because he had been so used to capitulating to the opinions of others. Conditions of worth had been so strongly imposed on him since early childhood, and he had received so much adverse criticism that he found it difficult to disentangle his own needs from those of his parents and family. As a consequence of this, his self-concept was at variance with his real inner needs and inclinations. By encouraging Robert to become more in touch with his innate resources and strength, I was able to help him to make some tentative moves towards independence and assertiveness. In order to help him in this way, I had to ensure that I gave him sufficient time and space to try out new ideas, to reject them if he felt they would not work and to try again if necessary. While conveying my respect for him and his ability to plan his own future, I was conscious of my role as a totally objective sounding board, something which Robert needed to help him make sense of his own immediate circumstances.

Person-centered counselling was certainly not the answer to all of Robert's problems. What it did do, however, was to give him enough confidence to make plans for the future, plans which were based largely on his own needs and not on those of other people. He decided to tell his parents that he wanted to study drama at college, and that he was not interested in business or management of the hotel. After some initial dismay they accepted his decision and later developed a new respect for his ability to stand up for himself. This, in turn, gave Robert further confidence, and he subsequently felt strong enough to confide in his sister about his homosexuality. She was supportive and accepting, and although he felt it would be some time before he could trust the rest of the family to respond in a similar way, Robert believed that he had, at least, made a positive start towards independence and growth.

FURTHER READING

EGAN, G., *The Skilled Helper*, Brooks/Cole, Monterey CA, 1986.

GOBLE, F. G., *The Third Force*, Pocket Books, New York, 1975.

MASLOW, A., *Motivation and Personality* (2nd edn) Harper & Row, New York, 1970.

MASLOW, A., *Towards a Psychology of Being* (2nd edn) Van Nostrand, Toronto, 1968.

MEARNS, D AND THORNE, B., *Person-Centered Counselling in Action*, Sage Publications, London, 1988.

ROGERS, C. R., *Client-Centered Therapy*, Constable, London, 1991.

NELSON-JONES, R., *The Theory and Practice of Counselling Psychology*, Cassell, London, 1990.

CHAPTER 3

Gestalt counselling

The historical background

At the beginning of this century a group of German psychologists, including Max Wertheimer, Kurt Koffka and Wolfgang Kohler, founded a branch of psychology which came to be known as the Gestalt School. The word 'Gestalt' is a German one which in translation means either 'pattern', 'shape', 'form' or 'configuration'. The subject which most interested Wertheimer and his colleagues was the organization of mental processes, and in particular the importance of perception in determining each individual's view of reality. Based on their research and experiments, they formulated a number of theories which dealt with the way people organize stimuli into patterns and shapes.

One of the most significant of these theories concerns the idea that the whole pattern of a person's sensory experience is more important than the individual parts of that experience, in deciding meaning. What this really implies is that when we look at a watch, for example, we do not see all its individual working parts. Instead we see a whole timepiece which we perceive as a watch. The same principle of perceptual organization applies when we listen to music; we do not hear all the individual notes which comprise a harmony. What we perceive is the totality of the music which is, in effect, the tune. Gestalt psychology holds, therefore, that *the whole is greater than the sum of its parts*, for when we perceive things we are aware of a structure, form, configuration or pattern which is interpreted as a whole and not as a random group of separate items. To some extent this branch of psychology came into being as a reaction against what some people considered to be the limitations of other schools, including behaviourism, which is concerned to break up complex human behaviour into simple conditioned reflexes.

The emphasis on 'wholeness' was a significant influence on the formation of the Gestalt school of therapy. Another important influence was the philosophy of existentialism, which states that human beings cannot escape the necessity of dealing with, and making sense of existence, and that only when we address these important issues can we become free to make choices and to organize our world in a way which best suits us individually.

The word 'phenomenology' has also been used in connection with the origin of Gestalt therapy, and this too stems from philosophy and refers to the way in which individuals experience the environment and reality. According to the phenomenological perspective, the way in which each person perceives and interprets the world is entirely unique to that person.

Another important assumption is the belief that human beings are motivated by a strong, innate drive towards growth, self-actualization and the total fulfilment of their potential. From this description it can be seen that Carl Rogers' person-centered therapy was also greatly influenced by Phenomenology, since he too emphasised the innate tendency towards growth which motivates human behaviour.

LAURA AND FRITZ PERLS

Developed in the 1940s by Laura and Frederick (Fritz) Perls, Gestalt therapy is indebted also to the psychoanalytic tradition from which Perls came. Although they rebelled against what they considered to be the intellectualizing tendency of the psychoanalytic school, they were nevertheless influenced by certain aspects of Freudian theory. The structure of personality which Freud outlined, for example, was later translated by Perls into his topdog/underdog description of the intrapsychic conflict which people suffer when they continually try to please others at the expense of their own needs.

It is interesting to note that Fritz Perls is usually credited with all the important developments of Gestalt therapy, even though his wife was equally involved and certainly contributed an enormous amount of time, energy and expertise in order to increase interest and awareness among psychotherapists generally. The fact that he was a colourful and sometimes controversial character has secured him the more prominent position of the two, and has led to the mistaken belief that Gestalt therapy originated through his efforts alone.

Fritz Perls was born in Berlin in 1892. During the first part of his professional life, he trained as a psychiatrist and psychoanalyst in the Freudian tradition and, as is customary practice, underwent analysis himself as part of his training. Perls was influenced by some of the major figures in psychoanalysis, including Jung and Rank, and during the 1920s he worked at the Institute for Brain-Damaged Soldiers in Frankfurt where he met Dr Kurt Goldstein. Goldstein was a neuropsychiatrist who had developed what was known as the 'organismic' approach in therapy, an approach which emphasizes each individual's innate drive towards wholeness. This association with Goldstein and his work had a profound effect on Perls' subsequent development as a therapist. It was during this time also that he met his wife Laura, who was a Gestalt psychologist as well as a talented musician and scholar. Both Laura and Fritz Perls were Jewish, and during the 1930s they left Nazi Germany and went to South Africa where in 1935 they founded the Institute of Psychoanalysis. Their work at this time was moving increasingly away from the traditional medical theory of personality which tended to view human problems as evidence of pathology or illness, in favour of a more positive understanding of personality based on the assumption that people have all the resources for change within themselves.

Fritz and Laura Perls moved from South Africa after World War II, and emigrated to the USA. In the 1960s Fritz Perls held the position of psychologist-in-residence at the Easlen Institute in Big Sur, California, and it was during this time that Gestalt became widely recognized as an important development in therapy. It was during this period also that other movements such as meditation, flower power, the cult of the guru figure, and even to some extent the drug culture, were beginning to emerge. Perls himself underwent a period of training in Zen Buddhism in Japan, and there can be no doubt that his ideas and his work were influenced by all the contemporary trends. As mentioned earlier, Perls was at times a controversial figure, often shocking people by his language and his use of drugs. He often dressed in flamboyant hippy clothes, wore his hair long and clearly thought of himself as an important innovator and leader.

It is evident from his autobiography (*In And Out Of The Garbage Pail*, Real People Press, Lafayette, CA 1969) that his childhood was in many ways an unhappy one, his father often being violent towards his mother and verbally abusive towards Fritz Perls himself. His eldest sister died in a concentration camp, and his relations with his own daughter and grandchild were never completely happy. These personal details about Perls and his life are included here to give a more comprehensive, holistic and balanced picture of the man generally. The experiences of his childhood, his relationship with his parents and the era in which he lived, all had a bearing on his subsequent involvement with psychoanalysis, and later on his own Gestalt school, the central aim of which is, after all, to encourage people to fully experience their totality, wholeness and the integration of all aspects of their being. Fritz Perls died in Chicago in 1970.

KEY WORDS

THE HERE AND NOW

According to Gestalt theory, life and change take place in the present. It follows, therefore, that the focus of this particular model of counselling is on what the client feels, thinks and does at this particular moment of his existence. There is no emphasis on the client's past or childhood experience, except in so far as this experience is manifesting itself at the present time in therapy. It is possible to anticipate what may happen in the future, but again this anticipation is firmly rooted in the present. This concentration on the 'here and now' of the client's experience is clearly quite different from the focus of psychodynamic counselling which is more concerned to bring past experience into awareness.

WHOLENESS

In Gestalt counselling, the client's total participation - physical, emotional, intellectual and spiritual - is stressed throughout therapy. As well as this, there is a corresponding acceptance of the need to integrate all the different dimensions of each individual in order to achieve a healthy wholeness. Essentially this means that no aspect of the client is neglected in counselling, so the counsellor needs to be attentive not only to what the client is saying, but also to his appearance, body language, tone of voice and mannerisms. The client is similarly encouraged to become more aware of 'self' and to strive towards behavioural integration. A person may, for example, express one ideal intellectually, while at the same time expressing the opposite view with his body. Thus the client who says 'I am not depressed' in a sad tone of voice, while slumping dejectedly in the chair, may be unaware of the evident discrepancy between what he says and how he actually looks. In such a situation, the counsellor would aim to draw the client's attention to the sadness and to the dejected way he is sitting. Alternatively, the counsellor might encourage the client to exaggerate his tone of voice and his posture in order to bring their message more clearly into awareness. The client is thus encouraged to be more himself in a way that perhaps he has never done before.

The Gestalt approach encourages clients to be more self-accepting, to recognize and integrate all aspects of their nature, including the anger, hatred, jealousy and irrationality which is present in all of us. A basic premise in Gestalt theory is that in order to work more effectively towards self-actualization, we need to become more aware of all our human dimensions.

FIGURE AND GROUND

The principles of perceptual organization which were first described by the Gestalt school of psychologists at the beginning of the twentieth century have been assimilated into Gestalt therapy and are used to describe the way people perceive themselves, their bodily sensations, their feelings and their emotions. Whereas the Gestalt psychologists were concerned with external perceptions and the way, for example, people deal with sensory experience, especially visual and auditory experience, Gestalt therapy is concerned with the more complex issue of how people become aware of their own needs in relation to their total environment.

The word 'figure' in Gestalt theory refers to an individual's need at any particular moment. This may be a simple physical need such as hunger or thirst, or it may be an emotional one, such as the need for love, affection or praise. At any given time there will be several needs present which have to be met, and when a person is functioning well in relation to the environment (which includes other people), his needs are clearly seen against the 'ground' or background of the person's awareness. The task for each individual is to select the most important figure or need as it arrives, and to satisfy this need so that it can fade into the background. When this is successfully achieved the person is free to deal with the next most pressing figure. Together, figure and ground form a whole or pattern which is known as a 'Gestalt'. The process whereby each need or figure emerges and is dealt with, is referred to as the 'formation and destruction of Gestalts'.

The Model

Regardless of which model of counselling is being used, the working relationship between client and counsellor is of fundamental importance to the success or otherwise of the therapy in progress. Perhaps what distinguishes Gestalt counselling from other models is the degree to which the counsellor is prepared to be herself, to be open about her feelings and experiences, and to be willing to share these with the client when necessary. The relationship is often described as one which is based on free dialogue between client and counsellor, and this often means that the counsellor may be quite confrontational in what she says to the client.

When Gestalt therapy was at the height of its popularity this use of confrontation was sometimes abused by therapists, but in Gestalt counselling, a proper use of confrontation should never involve inappropriate pressure on the client. A counsellor can, for example, use confrontation in a positive way when she draws attention to the discrepancies existing between what the client says and how he actually appears when he is speaking. The client who looks habitually bored, but who insists that he enjoys his counselling sessions, is probably unaware that his physical appearance is a clear indication of the true state of his feelings, and he is likely to benefit from having this pointed out to him. In another example, the counsellor may also feel bored because the client has transmitted this feeling to her, and in the Gestalt model of counselling she would share this with him in order to highlight what is actually happening at that particular moment. Above all, the counsellor is concerned to encourage the client to take responsibility for himself, and to get in touch with his innate ability to solve his own problems. This is similar to the client empowerment implicit in person-centered counselling, but in the Gestalt model the counsellor's approach is much more active, for she may use specific directions to facilitate awareness and change in the client during therapy.

THE CLIENT–COUNSELLOR RELATIONSHIP

Since the central focus of Gestalt counselling is on the totality of the client's immediate experience, techniques such as role-playing, which are designed to elicit spontaneous feelings and self-awareness, are often applied. This means that the Gestalt counsellor needs to be a person who is creative and innovative in her work, and is also prepared to improvise, to experiment and to invest a great deal of personal energy and commitment to each session. However, it would be wrong to suggest that a successful Gestalt counsellor is one who is primarily concerned with the use and development of novel therapeutic techniques. On the contrary, each client is viewed as a unique individual who will require a correspondingly individualistic approach from the counsellor. What is suitable for one client is not necessarily suitable for another, so although techniques and experiments are used in Gestalt counselling they are always designed and adapted to meet personal needs. This adaptation to personal client needs is important since the client can change emotionally in the course of a counselling session. A client who has been severely inhibited and overly restrained, may, for example, become extremely angry or sad so that the therapeutic climate is changed from a static to an emotionally charged one. The counsellor must be able to respond to such a development as it arises. Each therapeutic encounter provides a unique opportunity for client and counsellor to work together in order to understand every event which takes place, as it takes place.

THEORY OF PERSONALITY

A useful starting point for the study of any counselling model is the theory of human personality from which it is evolved. As stated earlier, Gestalt is derived from several sources, including existential philosophy, phenomenology, the findings of the original Gestalt psychologists, and psychoanalysis (in which Fritz Perls trained). The phenomenological approach is also sometimes referred to as a 'humanistic view' of personality, and person-centered and Gestalt counselling come under this heading.

Before 1940, most therapists were influenced in their approach by psychoanalysis, and it was not until some of them trained in the phenomenological approach that an alternative became available for clients. Proponents of the humanistic/phenomenological perspective regard each person's way of perceiving and interpreting the world as unique. For example, when two people witness an accident, the individual accounts which they give of this will be different, not because there were two separate incidents, but because each person's interpretation of events is personal and therefore different.

Another assumption stemming from this approach and incorporated into Gestalt therapy is the idea - already stated - that the most important

Each person's way of perceiving and interpreting the world is unique.
Courtesy: Andrew Stewart

human motivation is an innate drive towards growth which, if unimpeded, will lead people to fulfil their potential. Clients are seen, therefore, as capable of improving on their own when the counsellor creates the right conditions for this to happen. The ideal conditions to facilitate the client are those which promote awareness, expression of feelings and perceptions, especially when these have previously been hidden from awareness, thereby inhibiting growth. The main difference between the person-centered and Gestalt models of counselling lies in the ways in which this awareness and expression of feelings and perception are achieved.

BODY LANGUAGE

In the Gestalt model the counsellor is much more likely to 'direct' the client's attention towards aspects of himself or his behaviour which he had hitherto ignored or dismissed. Very often it is body language which is highlighted, especially when it conflicts with what the client is expressing verbally. Gestalt counsellors frequently ask clients to focus on what they are experiencing 'here and now', and this focusing on the immediacy of experience often enables clients to become more aware of 'self'.

In the following example, a client has been talking for some time about the death of his wife, an event which occurred some years previously.

CLIENT: It's been almost five years now and I feel that I've got over it at last.

COUNSELLOR: Yet you seem to be on the verge of crying. Your eyes are full of tears at this moment.

CLIENT: (hesitantly) I do feel like crying, sometimes.

COUNSELLOR: What is it that your eyes are expressing?

CLIENT: That I want to cry. That I never really cried properly before.

COUNSELLOR: So you need to cry now, because all that emotion has been building up in you.

With this kind of direct attention on what is happening to him, the client is enabled to see what he needs in order to complete an important, and neglected, stage of mourning for his wife.

OTHER SKILLS

Another technique sometimes used in Gestalt counselling involves the client in a kind of one-person drama, using imaginary dialogue which may be with different parts of himself or it may be with other people either living or dead. The purpose of this kind of dialogue is to give clients an opportunity to get in touch with and express feelings which may have been suppressed or ignored for a very long time. In a similar way, clients are sometimes asked to play various parts of a dream in the hope that this will make the dream's imagery and symbolism more meaningful for them. The following dialogue, which took place between a counsellor and a young woman named Susan, illustrates how effective this way of working with clients can be. Susan had frequently referred to her inability to 'feel' deeply and to express her emotions adequately, especially anger. She described a recurrent dream in which she was locked in a room with a small child. The walls of the room were made of steel, and in the dream she tried desperately, but unsuccessfully, to find a way out for the child. She was not too concerned for herself in the dream, but she knew she must find a way out for the child who was with her.

COUNSELLOR: Let yourself go back into the dream now and *be* that small child.

SUSAN (*after a pause*): Yes, I'm back in it.

COUNSELLOR: Be that small child. Say what you feel right now.

SUSAN: Well, I'm very small, very timid. I'm frightened. I want to get out, but I don't know how.

COUNSELLOR: You want to get out of the room but you don't know how. What might help you to get out?

SUSAN: I want someone to help me get out.

COUNSELLOR: Who is the someone who might help you get out?

SUSAN: People outside the room.

COUNSELLOR: Talk to them now. Ask them to help you get out.

SUSAN: (*becoming angry and talking in a loud voice*) Let me out! Let me out!

Fritz Perls believed that when clients dwelt on past or future experiences, they were avoiding the present and escaping reality. In Gestalt counselling, the client's dream world is regarded as a powerful and immediate way of focusing on what has previously been disguised or hidden. The model is less concerned to emphasize change than it is to emphasize heightened awareness of what choices the client is making. Dreamwork is used quite extensively in Gestalt counselling, and unlike psychodynamic therapists, Gestalt counsellors are not concerned to interpret what their clients recount. Indeed, interpretation would be regarded as totally inappropriate, since the dream belongs to the dreamer alone, and only he can decide which elements of it are meaningful to him. The way the client comes to express this meaning can be facilitated or helped by the counsellor, but this must be done in a sensitive and tactful way.

ARE THERE ANY TECHNIQUES?

The word 'technique' has been used to describe some of the work which Gestalt counsellors do with clients, but, as already indicated, it would be misleading to regard Gestalt therapy as simply a repertoire of techniques to be selected and applied when necessary. In fact there are no prescribed techniques in the Gestalt model; each counsellor is free to use any process which will help the client and increase his awareness. In the above example, the client (Susan) was able to gain insight into a part of herself which she had previously denied or had been unable to express. As soon as she started to articulate her anger in the counselling situation, she knew that it was possible to do so since she had now experienced it. Another counsellor might have employed a different technique to achieve the same level of self-awareness and integration.

A fundamental focus of the Gestalt model of counselling is exploration into the ways in which people stop themselves from functioning properly, and in order to further this exploration, free association - which stems from the psychoanalytic tradition - is used. This encourages clients to bring into awareness any information which will clarify the present situation for them. Active use of imagination is also encouraged, and this is an idea which is associated with the Jungian tradition in therapy. Clients are also sometimes asked to exaggerate body movements which the counsellor has noticed.

JOHN

An example which illustrates this last point concerns John, a young man who during the course of his first counselling session talked at length and in abstract, intellectual terms about a family dispute which was taking place at that time. Like many people who rely a great deal on their intellect, John also seemed to be out of touch with his emotions, and had great difficulty in identifying his own feelings regarding people and events. As well as this, he seemed to be unaware of his own body sensations and expressions, and frequently exhibited restless behaviour, moving about in his seat and often giving the impression that he was in a ferment of confusion nearing despair. A focus of the counselling session was to help him identify his true feelings and the cause of his extreme restlessness. At one point, the counsellor noticed that John frequently used a gesture with his hand which involved smoothing the fabric of his jacket as he spoke. When she drew his attention to this, he quickly identified the feeling which went with it.

COUNSELLOR: What is that you are doing with your hand? Can you do it again, more slowly?

JOHN: (surprised) Yes, I'm smoothing it over. That's what I want to do. I want to smooth things over in the family as well.

This was just a starting point for further exploration of the various issues which concerned this particular client at the time. As a result of the counselling sessions he was able to look more closely at his feelings, at the language that was implicit in his body gestures, and to integrate these more fully with the strong intellectual side of his nature.

INTELLECTUALIZATION Fritz Perls believed that many people compensate for their inability to 'feel' deeply or express emotions by overintellectualizing, a tendency which he regarded as an obstacle to self-awareness. Allied to Perls' belief is a corresponding one also central to Gestalt therapy, which affirms the client's innate knowledge of what he himself needs to deal with his own situation. It may be that he is temporarily unaware of this knowledge existing within himself, but it is nevertheless always there and he can be helped to find it. When John's attention was drawn to his hand gesture he knew at once what he was trying to express. Gestalt therapy has occasionally been criticized for its anti-intellectual stance, a stance which seemed, at least, to denigrate the intellectual experience in order to promote the importance of feelings and emotions. Certainly, in the early days of its popularity, Gestalt therapy was anti-intellectual for the reasons stated, but there are clear indications that this situation is changing and that intellectual experience is being reintegrated in order to preserve the holism which Gestalt values so much.

GROUPWORK

So far the Gestalt model of counselling has been described as taking place between counsellor and client in a one-to-one situation. However, this format is not always used and in the early days Fritz Perls was himself more in favour of the group setting as a forum of counselling. He subscribed to the view that groups are, on a purely practical level, more financially attractive, and on a human/personal level, more conducive to development and learning through participation. He proposed a set of rules which were meant to act as guidelines for any group, especially one which was being conducted without a leader. Perls felt it was more important that group members should agree to the rules beforehand, and that pressure should never be put on members to speak if they were unwilling to do so. Along with this, he advised against talking within the group about people who were not within it, and he elaborated this point by saying that absent people could be made present in the group by having the person who was speaking play dual roles. In the following example Nia is talking to the group about her feelings of frustration and anger against her sister with whom she has had several acrimonious rows. The root of the problem, as far as Nia is concerned, is her sister's unwillingness to share the burden of caring for their elderly incapacitated mother with whom Nia lives. Instead of castigating her sister to the group, Nia is encouraged - in this case by the group facilitator - to play the roles of both her sister and herself, and to engage in a dialogue between them.

NIA: I wish you would come to visit us more often, even once a month would be great.
SISTER: You don't understand how difficult it is for me to get away.
NIA: What is it that stops you?
SISTER: The children. And not being able to drive. Also, Ron works shifts.
NIA: You could get a babysitter and come by bus.
SISTER: Well, I could, I suppose. It's just that I don't always feel welcome, so it doesn't seem worth the effort.

At this stage Nia paused to consider the remark about not feeling welcome, which she - as her sister - had expressed. It occurred to her that she had sometimes criticized her sister for interfering when she visited, for making suggestions about practical aspects of caring for their mother. Because of the immediacy of this particular technique, Nia was able to see that part of the problem was attributable to her attitude, and she identified this herself, which was much more effective than having someone else 'interpret' the situation for her.

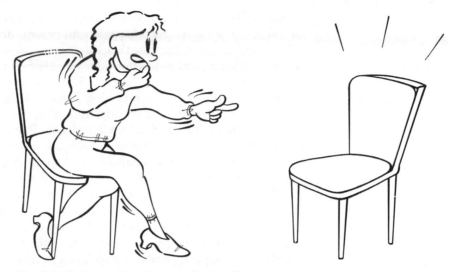

Fig. 3.1 *'Stop pretending, I know you're there!'*

THE EMPTY CHAIR

Conducting a dialogue with an absent person is much more effective when the 'empty-chair' technique is used. When Nia addressed her sister, she sat in her own chair, and when she 'replied' as her sister, she did so by switching to an opposite chair. The two-chair technique can also be used to represent two sides or aspects of the same person, so that, for example, a shy, retiring client could use it to get in touch with the more outgoing or gregarious part of his nature which he may have split off. In the same way, two elements of a dream can be re-enacted by the client. Susan, whose experience was described earlier, 'became' the small child of her dream, but she could have explored the symbolism and meaning further if she had chosen to become another of the images which the dream contained, for example, the steel walls of the room. She could then have conducted a dialogue between the walls and the child, and in doing so it is possible that her interpretation of the dream would have been more complete. Because the two-chair technique, like many other Gestalt techniques, tends to be very powerful and effective, it is not something which can be instigated without a great deal of thought and expertise on the part of the counsellor. This means, in effect, that the Gestalt counsellor should be adequately trained in the skills which underpin the model, (i.e. the skills of listening, observing and responding when appropriate).

TOPDOG/UNDERDOG

These are terms which Perls used to refer to the conflicting parts of an individual's personality which are constantly fighting for supremacy and control. In many ways this concept is similar to Freud's theory of the ego/super-ego, which again represents intrapsychic conflict. Perls' topdog represents that part of an individual's psyche which is always righteous and concerned with order and control. Topdog achieves this through bullying and 'shouldism', that is by frequently reminding the individual that he 'should do better', 'should be intelligent', should never be angry', and so on. These 'shouldisms' are inherited from parents and from each person's cultural background. They are then internalized and accepted as absolutes by the individual, and exert enormous moral pressure to conform. Underdog, on the other hand, is insecure, lacking in conviction and incapable of the kind of aggression which topdog possesses. Instead of straight confrontation with the bullying topdog, underdog prefers to procrastinate, to whinge and to use rationalizations in order to allay the sense of guilt which arises as a result of his inability to meet topdog's demands.

People can expend vast amounts of energy in trying to please their topdog persona, while simultaneously hoping to escape its strictures through the use of underdog tactics. A focus of Gestalt counselling is the integration of these two opposites within the individual, and this means encouraging the client to accept that they are both valid parts of himself which can coexist quite comfortably side by side. In this way the pressure of conflict is reduced and the topdog/underdog split is lessened.

USE OF LANGUAGE

A very important aspect of Gestalt counselling is the consideration of the way people use language. It is an interesting fact that quite a few clients who come for counselling display a certain amount of alienation from themselves in the way they speak. This is highlighted by frequent references to

Fig. 3.2 *Topdog/underdog.*

'it' rather than to the personal pronouns 'I' or 'me'. Thus a client may say, for example, 'It was awful', instead of 'I felt awful', when he is describing the pain he felt after an operation; in speaking this way, he is effectually distancing himself from the traumatic feelings he wishes to convey. Language can be limiting in the counselling situation, since people very often use it to shield their true feelings. As well as this, words are sometimes used without sufficient thought given to their selection beforehand. Generally there is too much emphasis on language as a means of communication, and people forget that there are other ways of expressing themselves.

In the Gestalt model of counselling art work, including drawing and painting, is sometimes used to facilitate those clients who have difficulty in expressing themselves verbally. When Brian, a sixteen-year-old client who was fairly inarticulate, wanted to describe the muddle he felt himself to be in, the counsellor encouraged him to try to draw the way he felt. Brian did this successfully from his own point of view, because once he saw what he had depicted he then found himself able to select the words to go with it. Another way of focusing on language is to ask the client to repeat more slowly, more loudly or more carefully, as the case may be, what it is he has just said. This has the effect of concentrating the client's attention on himself, thereby enabling him to get in touch with his deeper emotions and feelings.

INCOMPLETE GESTALTS

At the beginning of this chapter an outline was given of the principles of Gestalt formation and destruction which are central to the Gestalt school of therapy. According to the theory, people are constantly experiencing needs which have to be met if psychological (and physiological) health is to be maintained. These needs include the ordinary physical ones, like the need for food, but they also include relationship and self-fulfilment needs as well. When a person is in a state of equilibrium in relation to his total environment, needs or 'figures' emerge continually and are clearly perceived against the 'ground' or background of his awareness. These emerging figures, distinctly visible against their background, are known as *Gestalt formation* (*Gestalten* in the plural) and the process whereby they are dealt with is known as Gestalt destruction.

This formation and destruction is an ongoing process which, if unimpeded, will ensure that the individual is functioning well, is healthy and usually happy. But if needs are not met they cannot be successfully destroyed or dealt with, so they clutter up the person's perceptual field and further emerging needs become muddled, difficult to identify or indistinguishable from one and another. This means, for example, that a person who has been unable to resolve a problem, conflict or traumà, will have difficulty in coping with other pressing needs as they inevitably present themselves. In this situation, the Gestalt counsellor would be concerned to encourage the client to identify clearly and to deal with the issues which have been left unresolved. This is usually an intensely emotional experience for the client, so the counsellor needs to be skilful and sensitive in the approach which she uses.

The case study which follows gives some examples of the ways in which the client identifies her unfinished business from the past, and subsequently sets about the difficult task of resolving some other issues which had been problematic for her.

CASE STUDY: MAIRI

Mairi was a client who decided to come for counselling six months before she actually made the first appointment. During those six months she had done extensive research in order to help her select the model of counselling which she felt would be most appropriate for her individual needs. Because of this research, she was well acquainted with Gestalt principles, and was aware that the counselling sessions were likely to be emotionally-charged situations for her. However, she felt that this was the right approach and the one which would benefit her the most. She stated these views to the counsellor when she attended for her first appointment.

Mairi was forty-six years of age, a slim, attractive woman who obviously took great pride in her appearance and dress. She was bright and cheerful when she first met the counsellor, and she described in great detail the number of books she had read prior to the visit. Her speech was articulate and voluble, and at times she talked so quickly that it seemed she hardly paused for breath. There was so much information she wanted to convey, but in particular she wanted to talk about her husband who had died six years previously. They had, she said, been very close to each other, and unlike many couples she knew, their marriage had been happy and stable. The biggest disappointment for them was the fact that they had never had children.

The counsellor listened to Mairi carefully, taking in the details of everything she said, but also observing her body language, her mannerisms and the tone of her voice as well as the speed at which she was talking. When Mairi paused after her description of past events and the relationship with her husband, the counsellor focused at once on the immediate situation and the manner of her speech.

COUNSELLOR: There is so much you want to say. It all seems to come rushing out at once.
MAIRI: Yes, I feel I ought to put you in the picture straightaway.
COUNSELLOR: The picture of how you are right now?
MAIRI: Yes.
COUNSELLOR: Would you say more about that, about the picture of who you are right now?
MAIRI: (slowly) Well, I live on my own and I don't get an opportunity to talk about personal things to anyone. That's why I feel I've got to say as much as I can now, while I have the chance.

As soon as her attention was focused on the immediate situation, Mairi's speech slowed down and became much less urgent. She seemed to relax visibly, although she continued to 'hug' herself occasionally, a gesture which the counsellor noticed was more pronounced when she talked about the happiness she and her husband had shared.

COUNSELLOR: Tell me what you are doing with your arms.
MAIRI: (Surprised) I'm holding them around myself.
COUNSELLOR: What do you experience when you do that?
MAIRI: I feel comforted.
COUNSELLOR: Comforted?
MAIRI: Yes, as I did when my husband used to hold me.

Mairi started to cry when she said these words. She then went on to explain that for years she had been unable to express her sorrow properly. Her family, although supportive in many ways, were nevertheless appalled by excessive displays of emotion. The counsellor encouraged her to experience in full the grief which she had buried so long, and Mairi cried for quite some time. After this she became less agitated.

COUNSELLOR: How do you feel now?
MAIRI: Relaxed. Much better.

Mairi wanted to talk about another relationship in which she had become involved during the previous year. This relationship was with a man who worked as a lecturer at the college where she herself was teaching. Mairi talked warmly about the man when she first mentioned him, but after a while she stopped suddenly and became silent.

COUNSELLOR: You seem lost for words now.
MAIRI: Yes, I suppose I have a block about Alan. I feel guilty because of Hugh (i.e. her dead husband).

The counsellor went on to explore with Mairi this feeling of guilt which had inhibited the growth of her new relationship. Early in their married life, Mairi and Hugh had made a pact with each other that neither would remarry in the event of the other's death. This promise had been made when Mairi was very young, but she still felt obliged to adhere to it at all costs. Anything else would have seemed like a betrayal of her husband. However, because of her developing love for Alan she had decided she could no longer tolerate these feelings of guilt, and this had prompted her to seek help through counselling.

COUNSELLOR: You don't want to feel this guilt any longer?
MAIRI: No.
COUNSELLOR: Where is this guilt? Which part of your body do you feel the guilt in?
MAIRI: (indicating her chest) It's here near my heart.
COUNSELLOR: Say that again, but instead of saying 'It's here', try saying, 'My guilt is near my heart'.
MAIRI: (becoming agitated and restless) Heavy. It feels heavy and suffocating. I feel heavy and suffocated.

COUNSELLOR: What would take your suffocation away?
MAIRI: If I could talk to Hugh, I suppose if I could explain to him, that would take it away.

The counsellor asked Mairi if she would like to try the empty chair technique in order to talk to her husband. Mairi was doubtful at first, but later on she brought up the subject herself and expressed a wish to engage in the kind of dialogue which the counsellor had suggested. This proved to be emotionally taxing for Mairi, and the counsellor was careful not to push her in any way, but to allow her to conduct the dialogue at her own pace. At first Mairi protested that she did not know how to start.

COUNSELLOR: May I suggest a sentence for you?
MAIRI: Yes.
COUNSELLOR: Say to your husband, 'Now I have found someone I love and want to marry him.'

The purpose of suggesting this sentence to Mairi was not that she should simply repeat what the counsellor had told her to say, but that she should try the sentence out for herself, test its meaning and appropriateness, and then use it if it suited her to do so. In the event, it proved effective in concentrating Mairi's attention on what exactly it was that she wanted to say to her husband, and once she had started on the dialogue she absorbed herself in it totally. This had a cathartic effect on her emotionally, and when she attended for her next session she said that she felt much better about her relationship with Alan, and that she no longer felt her husband's disapproval. Mairi attended for eight counselling sessions altogether, and during the time she spent with the counsellor (and in between) she worked very hard and with a great deal of courage and tenacity in order to resolve some of the other issues which had caused her problems.

FURTHER
READING

CLARKSON, P., *Gestalt Counselling in Action*, Sage Publications, London, 1990.

DRYDEN, W. (ed.), *Individual Therapy: A Handbook*, Open University Press, Milton Keynes, 1991.

FAGAN, J. and LEE SHEPHERD, I. (ed.), *Gestalt Therapy Now*, Penguin Books, Aylesbury, Bucks, 1972.

HOUSTON, G., *The Red Book of Gestalt*, Rochester Foundation Airlift Book Co., London, 1990.

CHAPTER 4

Transactional analysis

The historical background

ERIC BERNE (1910–70)

Transactional analysis (TA), which was first developed by Eric Berne and described by him in 1961, is a theory of personality as well as an analysis of the ways in which people communicate and interact with each other. Berne, whose original name was Eric Lennard Bernestein, was born in Montreal, Canada, in 1910. He became a qualified doctor and completed his medical training at McGill University. In deciding to follow a medical career, Berne was probably influenced by his father who had also been a doctor. As a small child, he had been close to his father, and had taken a keen interest in the work which he did.

There are indications in Berne's writings, although not explicitly stated, that he shared his father's sense of altruism towards the people in his care. Doctor David Bernestein, had been a general practitioner whose daily work had brought him into contact with the poorest people in the community which he served; unfortunately, he died at the early age of thirty-eight when his son Eric was just eleven years old. When, many years later, Eric Berne wrote his best-selling book, *Games People Play*, he too was addressing the needs of people who were 'less advantaged', this time in his own specialized area of psychotherapy. This specialized area had previously been obscured by esoteric language which was difficult for anyone, except initiates, to understand. One of Berne's greatest achievements was that he translated the terminology of psychotherapy into a language which was accessible, and easy for any intelligent person to grasp.

On completion of his medical training in 1935, Eric Berne went on to study psychiatry at Yale University, and later on he took up a psychiatric post in New York. During the 1940s he underwent training as a psychoanalyst at the Psychoanalytic Institute of New York, but when in 1956 he applied for membership of the Institute, his application was turned down. It is possible that Berne was rejected by the Institute because he had become increasingly critical of traditional Freudian psychoanalysis. While completing his US army service as a psychiatrist during the 1940s, Berne was given an ideal opportunity to work on the development of his own theories. He took advantage of this opportunity while doing research into the phenomenon of intuition, a subject in which he was particularly interested. His research involved extensive work with individual soldiers, and the outcome of this was that Berne acquired sufficient knowledge and data to form the basis of his future work on transactional analysis. At the same time, he was working with civilians as well as with soldiers, and he was becoming interested in group psychotherapy, and this too was a formative influence on TA theory and practice.

In the post war period, Berne worked as a psychiatrist, serving various establishments, including the Mount Zion Hospital in San Francisco. As well as this, he founded a private practice and continued to write books – something he had started to do during his service in the army. One of his most significant contributions to the development of fresh thinking within his profession, was the establishment of regular seminar meetings at which people could discuss various issues and topics. It also afforded opportunities for people to present papers which they had written, and to discuss their ideas with colleagues.

When his application to the Psychoanalytic Institute was rejected in 1956, Berne was disappointed, but he proceeded to channel his energy into the work which he was already doing on TA. In 1961 *Transactional Analysis in Psychotherapy* was published, and in 1964 *Games People Play* was also published. Although the latter is probably the more widely read, the former contains a more detailed exposition of the theory and practice of transactional analysis. Both books, however, succeed in demystifying, to some extent at least, the concepts and language applicable to psychotherapy and its practice.

THE NEED FOR AN ACCESSIBLE LANGUAGE

The language of TA has been both praised and disparaged since it was first outlined by Eric Berne, but very few people would dispute the fact that its basic principles are fairly easy to grasp. Psychotherapy had in the past been available only to people who could afford it, or to people who were ill and institutionalized. One of Berne's major contributions was his presentation of psychotherapy as something which could be clearly understood, not merely by therapists, but by patients and clients as well. In stripping the psychotherapeutic language of its technical jargon, he succeeded also in showing that psychotherapy need not be elitist or inaccessible. On the contrary, Berne believed that it should be available to those who needed it or wished to avail themselves of it, and that it should, moreover, be presented in such a way that the client is enabled to participate in a clear exchange of information with the therapist. In order for clients to participate in this exchange, the structure of personality and the principles underlying TA need to be clear to them, and Berne achieved this clarity through his use of simple language. Since its introduction, however, the theory of TA has become progressively more elaborate and complex; different schools have come into being, although they all subscribe to its basic principles.

RECENT DEVELOPMENTS

The influence of transactional analysis has become widespread in other fields too, not just in America, but internationally. These include education, management, industry, health care and communications. It is certainly not exclusive to the psychotherapeutic situation, for courses in transactional analysis are frequently attended by people who wish to develop better communication skills with colleagues at work, or with friends and family at home. There are many TA organizations in existence now all over the world, but the most important and influential of these are the International Transactional Analysis Association (ITAA) and the European Association for Transactional Analysis (EATA), both of which provide a framework for training and accreditation. Short and long courses are available for counselling students who wish to undertake training in TA therapy, and further details about these are easily obtainable through direct contact with either of the above organizations.

Eric Berne died suddenly in 1970 at the age of sixty. His influence in the field of psychotherapy, as well as in the other areas mentioned above, is increasing all the time.

KEY WORDS

EGO STATES

The idea of *ego states* is central to TA theory. Eric Berne described three ego states, or states of 'self', which he referred to as Parent, Adult and Child; he spelt these with initial capital letters in order to differentiate between the meaning which he gave them and the meaning usually associated with these words. The three ego states are, according to Berne, common to all of us and govern our thoughts, feelings and behaviour. In order to explain what he meant more fully, Berne used a series of diagrams to illustrate each aspect of his theory. The most basic of these is a structural diagram as illustrated in Fig. 4.1.

The principle of ego states is that each person carries within his/her individual personality three separate ways of thinking about, and reacting to, the external

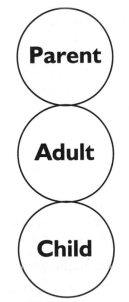

Fig. 4.1 *Structural diagram of personality.*

world. These states of thinking, feeling and reacting are not just roles which can be adopted in different situations; they are, in fact, actual psychological states which have been formed in the individual from infancy onwards.

THE PARENT EGO STATE

The *Parent* ego state is like a recording of all the instructions, socialization and nurturing which is passed on from parents and parental figures to the child during the first five or six years of life. Much of this information is absorbed without question, since the small child is unable or too young to challenge parental guidelines. All the parents' actions and pronouncements, along with the example which they gave, are recorded in the Parent ego state, and although much of this is negative a great deal is positive as well.

Since the socialization process is an important part of learning in early childhood, children are frequently, and of necessity, given restrictive commands like 'don't do that', 'stop that', or even more frequently 'no'. These instructions are accumulated and recorded by the child, so that eventually they become internalized as part of his own personality. It is important to remember that information is passed on to the child from both parents, so that where there is acrimony or serious discord between parents, negative influences will predominate in the formation of the individual's Parent ego state.

In adult life, the Parent ego state, which carries so much information from the past, enables the individual to cope with various aspects of living. These include all those skills and tasks which by their nature have to be learned. Some examples of these are the skills that people need in order to socialize with others, or the basic skills essential for crossing the road safely. People use their Parent ego state continually, without ever having to think about it. This last point identifies the reason problems arise, however, because people often go into their Parent ego state when it is inappropriate or counterproductive for them to do so. Thus, for example, a fifty-year-old man might still think, feel and behave according to a set of rules for living which he absorbed in early childhood and which are no longer useful or applicable for him today. If he has difficulty at work because he is domineering and dictatorial towards junior members of staff, then he is probably operating in his Parent ego state, and this will not be conducive to harmony with his colleagues. The Parent ego state is divided into *Critical* or *Controlling Parent* and *Nurturing Parent,* and represents both aspects of parental influence on the individual.

THE CHILD EGO STATE

Like the Parent ego state, the *Child* ego state derives its impetus and meaning from the past. In a sense it is like a second recording which is being made alongside that of the Parent. The difference is, however, that the Child ego state represents the actual reactions of the small child to the people and events in his life. These *emotional* responses are carried on into adult life and can be evoked at any given time, again often outside the person's awareness. The

Child ego state remains with us all throughout life, and encompasses not only emotional responses but creativity and freedom as well.

When referring to the Child, Eric Berne emphasized that he did not intend it to mean 'childish' or 'immature', and since these two words are often derogatory, he stipulated that they should never be used in transactional analysis.

When in the Child ego state, people can express themselves in either of two main ways. For this reason, the model is further divided into *Adapted Child* and *Free Child*, which describe these differing aspects (see Fig. 4.2). In early life children quickly learn to adapt to the expectations of parents and parental figures. Small children soon sense when their parents are pleased or displeased, so they adjust their behaviour accordingly in the hope that they will win parental acceptance and approval. Often, what works with one parent will not succeed with the other, so different responses are developed to suit the child's relationship with each parent.

A small girl might learn that her father is pleased with her when she is quiet and passive, whereas her mother prefers her to be more outgoing and active. Years later, in adult life, the young woman is likely to respond in the ways that her parents preferred, even when her responses are no longer appropriate, and may even, in fact, be dysfunctional. If she finds herself at a boardroom meeting where, for example, the other members present are predominantly male, she may again become quiet and passive since that was the expectation which the most important male figure in her early life had of her. In this case she is responding in her Adapted Child ego state. She may later on attend another meeting where the members are predominantly female, in which case she may become more cheerful, vocal and outgoing and at the same time hold herself back from serious participation in the debate taking place. In this second

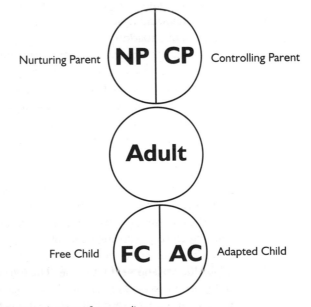

Fig. 4.2 *Descriptive diagram of personality.*

example, she is also responding in her Adapted Child ego state, since she is yet again experiencing the feelings and exhibiting the kind of behaviour which used to please a parent, this time her mother.

The feelings and behaviour characteristic of the Adapted Child are therefore still under the control of the parents or parental figures; however, the feelings and behaviour of the Free Child are different in the sense that they are spontaneous, having escaped the inhibiting influence of parents. In their Free Child ego state, people re-experience the strong feelings they had in childhood, feelings like rebelliousness, anger, joy and a sense of fun. Repression of the Free Child in adult life can lead to diminished enjoyment, a lack of creativity and curiosity, and inability to express emotions. Inappropriate expression of the Free Child, at the wrong time and in the wrong place, can also cause problems.

THE ADULT EGO STATE

When a person is thinking, feeling and behaving in a way which represents a realistic response to others and to the environment, that person is said to be in the *Adult* ego state. The Adult is capable of objective appraisal of the environment and can make decisions and judgements accordingly. A person who is functioning in the Adult ego state is likely to think and act in a logical and natural way, and is not going to be overwhelmed by strong emotion from the Child ego state, or by out of date information and rules emanating from the Parent. The example given earlier, of the young woman at the boardroom meeting, can be used again to illustrate this last point. If she had been in her Adult ego state, she would have been able to participate as an equal in the meeting, regardless of the sex of the other people present. In other words, her Adult would have looked more closely at the information coming from her Child and would have rejected it on the grounds that it was not applicable to her present situation.

The ongoing experiences which each person gains throughout life are stored as information and data in their Adult ego state; this is periodically re-examined and updated in order to meet changing situations or needs. The function of the Adult is not to obliterate the Parent and Child, but rather to look critically at the information contained in both, and then to make clear decisions based on its appropriateness or otherwise to present circumstances.

All three categories of ego states, Parent, Adult and Child, are present in children as well as in adults. Early in life children begin to question parental directives and to form their own opinions based on the information which they are absorbing continually from the environment. Thus a small child who has been told not to touch strange animals may do so because his *Child* is curious. He may then get scratched or bitten, and thereby discover that his parents' prohibition made perfect sense. The information which he has received from them becomes part of his own *Parent* ego state, and since he has tested it out, his own *Adult* ego state tells him that it is true.

Changes in ego states are not just experienced internally but can also be observed externally. There will be changes in a person's behaviour, appearance and tone of voice when he moves from one ego state to another. A client, whose name was Paul, went for his first job interview and was quite confident that he had all the necessary qualifications. He had checked all the details of the job and his Adult processing system assured him that his chances of getting the job were good. However, during the course of the interview, he was asked a particularly difficult question and this had the effect of pushing him without warning into his Child ego state. For what seemed like an eternity, Paul became silent and embarrassed, and worse still, he found himself laughing nervously just as he would have done when he was unsure of himself as a child. The point about Paul's discomfiture was that he not only felt it, but that it was perfectly obvious to the interviewers as well. Fortunately for him, he was able to regain his Adult composure, and to say outright that he did not know the answer to that particular question, so that he could then move on to the next point raised.

At first glance it might seem that the Parent, Adult and Child ego states which Berne describes are almost identical to Freud's super-ego, ego and id structure of personality. It is true that Berne was trained in the orthodox psychoanalytic tradition, and must therefore have been influenced, to some extent at least, by Freudian theory. There are several important points of difference, however, the most significant of these being that Berne's ego states are meant to refer to actual, discernible manifestations of each. For this reason, a person who is in a Child ego state, for example, will feel, think and act as he did when a child. In other words, he will become the child he once was, and will resume his childhood way of responding to a particular environmental stimulus. This Child ego state will be felt and experienced by him and can be observed by others as well. On the other hand, Freud's description of the id, which may look in some ways like the Child ego state, is different because it cannot be observed from the outside and cannot necessarily be directly identified by the client either, since it is — by definition — unconscious. In a similar way, the Parent ego state may look like Freud's 'super-ego', but the person who is in Parent will think in, feel in and, most importantly, manifest observable signs of that particular state. The influence which people feel when they are in Parent is not as generalized as that of the super-ego or conscience. What they do experience are the actual thoughts, feelings and attitudes of parents or parental figures. Berne emphasized that his ego states represent real people 'who now exist or once existed' for the client (*Transactional Analysis in Psychotherapy*, 1991).

The Adult, which is concerned with reality-testing, objectivity and making judgements, is similar to Freud's concept of the ego in many respects. The central concern for both the Adult and the ego is the development of autonomy within the individual. However, in the case of Berne's Adult, the definition is more precise and less theoretical than Freud's definition of the ego, and again, the Adult is clearly felt and experienced by the individual and is observable by others too. It should be added that Berne's model of the ego states was not designed to negate Freud's; rather, it was proposed as an alternative model which would be clearer and more efficient for clients and therapists to use.

The Model

The transactional analysis model of counselling takes as its starting point the view that most people have all the resources, including energy, intelligence and responsibility, necessary to solve their own problems. In this respect, it is similar to both the person-centered and the Gestalt approaches, but much of the theory of transactional analysis and the techniques used with clients are quite different from these other two. The term 'transactional analysis' encompasses both structural analysis, which is the theory of personality outlined in diagrammatic form in Fig. 4.1, and transactional analysis, which is a theory of communication. Other relevant terms are 'script analysis', which is concerned with the theory of early experience and its effects on present behaviour, and 'games analysis', which deals with the theory of ulterior meanings in communication.

TA counselling can take place either in a group setting or with an individual counsellor. When Eric Berne first developed his model of therapy, TA was commonly conducted in groups, and this is still the format for many TA therapists. There is, moreover, a great deal of evidence that transactional analysis is more effective in groups since there is, by definition, more communication taking place, more stimulation generally, and a better chance of people learning about themselves through interaction with others. This last point highlights a significant difference between Berne and other therapists, in that he was concerned to emphasize the importance of looking at social as well as personal psychology; in this respect, TA is a more comprehensive approach than the other humanistic models.

THE ANALYSIS OF 'TRANSACTIONS'

The theory of personality, or the ego-state model which Berne described and which was outlined at the beginning of this chapter, is the basic foundation on which the TA model of counselling is built. Following on from it, is the analysis of the transactions which take place between people. In other words, the first part - the theory of personality - refers to the individual, while the second part - the analysis of transactions - refers to people's social behaviour. With clients in the counselling situation, analysis of the ego state model should always precede the analysis of transactions, since it would be impossible to understand the second in full without a firm grasp of the first.

Berne used the word 'stroking' to describe the exchanges which take place between people; he then described a stroke as 'the fundamental unit of social action', and an exchange of strokes as a 'transaction' (*Games People Play*, 1968). People exchange strokes in various ways, either through physical contact such as kissing, hugging, or through touching in a non-intimate way. Non-verbal communication such as smiling – and even negative responses such as scowling and frowning – are forms of stroking too. Strokes are important for all of us, and even negative ones are preferable to no recognition at all, according to a child's perception. However, this perception can be changed later in life, through counselling, for example.

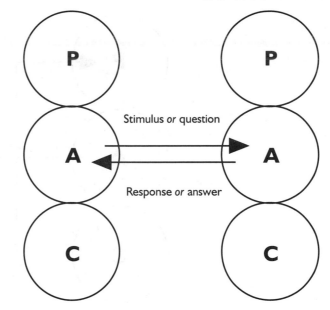

Fig. 4.3 *Complementary transaction.*

COMPLEMENTARY
TRANSACTIONS

When I communicate with another person, I can do so from either my Parent, my Adult or my Child ego state, and that person can respond to me in any of their ego states. If I address a colleague at work from my Adult ego state, and she responds to me in her Adult, then the transaction which has taken place between us is a *complementary* one. This is illustrated in the following example:

Question: Where are the files which we looked at yesterday?
     (*Adult to Adult*)
Response: They're in the top drawer of the filing cabinet. (*Adult to Adult*)

 If transactions continue to remain complementary in this way, then real communication can take place between participants. Another way of illustrating this point is to show it in diagrammatic form as Berne does throughout his writing (see Fig. 4.3).

CROSSED
TRANSACTIONS

If, however, I address the same question to my colleague and she responds from either her Child or her Parent ego states, then the transaction which has taken place is described as a *crossed transaction*.

Question: Where are the files which we looked at yesterday? (*Adult to Adult*)
Response: Why am I always expected to find things around here? (*Child to Parent*)

Again, this can be illustrated in diagrammatic form (see Fig. 4.4).
     If my colleague had answered from her Parent ego state, then the exchange might have been the following:

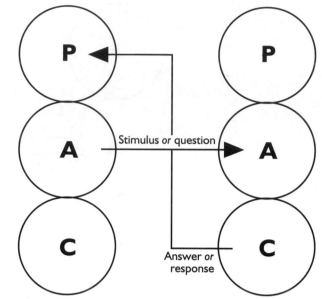

Fig. 4.4 *Crossed transaction.*

Question: Where are the files which we looked at yesterday? (*Adult to Adult*)

Response: You really must try to be more organised with your filing system. (*Parent to Child*)

Figure 4.5 shows this in diagram form.

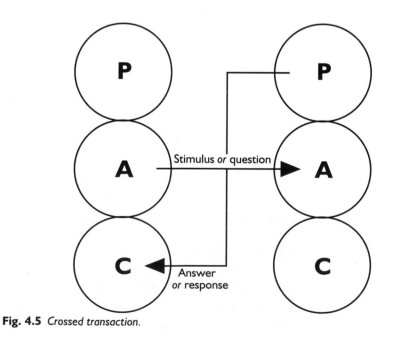

Fig. 4.5 *Crossed transaction.*

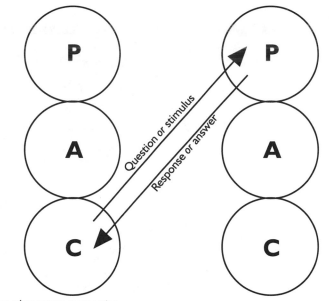

Fig. 4.6 *Complementary transaction.*

When crossed transactions take place in this way, real communication will break down and bad feelings may result as well. Of course it is not the case that complementary transactions only take place between people communicating from one Adult ego state to another. Complementary transactions will also occur when the response given is the one which the stimulus intended to elicit. The following exchange is an example of how this develops:

Question: I just can't find that file anywhere. What could have happened to it? (*Child to Parent*)

Answer: Don't worry. I'll find it for you. Just give me a minute. (*Parent to Child*)

In this case Fig. 4.6 illustrates the complementary transaction.

ULTERIOR
TRANSACTIONS

Berne described a third category of transaction which he referred to as ulterior because not one, but two messages are conveyed during it. One of these messages occurs at the social level, while the other takes place at the psychological level. The psychological message is always the stronger of the two and is conveyed non-verbally, while the social message is of lesser impact and is conveyed through the actual words spoken. The following exchange is an example of the covert and overt meanings contained in ulterior transactions.

NURSE: Your wound is really well healed now. It won't be long before you can go home. (*Adult to Adult*)

PATIENT: I'm still a bit sore, but yes, you're right. I'll soon be going home. (*Adult to Adult*)

At first glance this looks like a clear Adult-to-Adult exchange, and on the social level that is what it is. However, tone of voice and body language have a direct bearing on what is being said. Depending on the nurse's tone

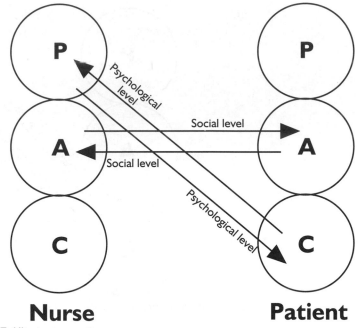

Fig. 4.7 *Ulterior transaction.*

of voice, general demeanour and other non-verbal clues, her words to the patient may convey the following, at a psychological level:

NURSE: Hurry up and get well. We need your bed for another patient. (*Parent to Child*)

And the patient's response at a psychological level may be:

PATIENT: OK, I'll be good and get well quickly so I can go home. (*Child to Parent*)

Fig. 4.7 illustrates the ulterior transaction.

GAMES

People often play psychological games which are extensions of ulterior transactions. These are frequently repeated in a recognizable way and on the surface appear to be straightforward transactions. However, what is expressed is not what is really felt, and this is especially true of the person who initiates the transaction. Although there are different types of games, some elements are common to all of them:

- There is a series of complementary transactions which appear straightforward.

- There is an ulterior transaction which is sometimes referred to as the 'hidden agenda'.

- There is a conclusion in the form of a negative payoff. This is the real reason for playing the game.

People sometimes have favourite games which they play over and over again in order to confirm their own OK positions or not-OK positions (which will be discussed later) or the positions they have assigned to others. As well as this, games help to pass the time and they ensure that people get attention – strokes – even though they may be negative. An example of a game often played by people who go from one friend to another, ostensibly hoping for help and advice, is the 'Yes, but' game. No matter what is suggested by the friend, the reply is invariably 'Yes, but'. Still the friend carries on trying to be helpful and says, 'Why don't you...?' and again receives the reply, 'Yes, but'. This is often followed by well-thought-out reasons why the suggestions which the friend is making will not work. In the end, the friend feels frustrated, ineffective and useless. This is the whole purpose of the game.

THE CLIENT/COUNSELLOR RELATIONSHIP

Many of the communication problems which arise between people can be explained by using Berne's ego state model and transactional analysis. This can be enormously helpful when working with clients in the counselling situation because most of the problems which people encounter in day-to-day living are directly related to the breakdown of effective and meaningful communication. For this reason, Berne was concerned to highlight the importance of good communication between client and therapist in the first place. In his view, therapeutic progress was facilitated when the client was familiar with the theoretical framework of TA and the terminology used to describe it. This means, in practice, that clients who come for counselling are encouraged to learn about the TA model, and this can be done either by explaining the fundamental principles to them, or by asking them to read about TA, or better still, both.

Some centres run introductory courses which clients are encouraged to attend, and when group work is the forum for therapy, the aims of the therapy are discussed in the group. At every stage, the client should know what is happening to him, and he should be clear about the progress he hopes to make, and is making. This clarity of purpose and progress can only be achieved and maintained when client and counsellor are both speaking the same language.

THE CONTRACT

To encourage the client's progress towards change and recovery, both he and the counsellor enter into a 'contract' which specifies all the methods which will be used during therapy, and this must be agreed to by both parties. This is quite different from the usual form of contract employed in other models of counselling. This latter form of contract deals mainly with issues such as the times when counselling sessions will take place, and the number of sessions likely to be needed in order to complete therapy. In TA counselling the contract is specific and is outlined in much more detail. It includes aspects of the business dimension such as payment, duration of therapy and timing, and a much wider agreement on the goals of therapy and the way these will be achieved as well.

This contractual relationship between client and counsellor implies true equality and sharing of information and, furthermore, gives responsibility to the client for much of the work which will be done during the counselling. Thus, the client is encouraged to say what it is that he hopes to achieve from therapy, and to confirm that he will work with the counsellor towards the attainment of those goals. The counsellor, in turn, confirms that she is willing to facilitate the client to the best of her ability. To demonstrate the openness between them, any notes which are written during therapy are available for the client to read if he wishes. Throughout the whole process of therapy, the emphasis is on the kind of positive change which will enable the client to develop a greater degree of autonomy in the future. The goals which he wishes to achieve are set out in positive terms too, so that attention is shifted away from mere problem-solving towards a wider and more constructive approach to his personal development.

Len was a client who came for TA counselling because he wanted to lose weight and to cut back on his drinking. As far as he was concerned, his weight and his drinking were the 'problems' which he had, and which needed to be dealt with. Instead of focusing exclusively on the negative aspects of his behaviour, the counsellor encouraged him to focus on more positive objectives, such as his ambitions to travel and to learn to swim. Once his goals were couched in more positive terminology (e.g. 'I want to travel and to learn to swim'), Len was able to see how his sedentary lifestyle and his drinking were impediments to the real pleasure he could derive from sport and travel.

THE OK POSITION

Transactional analysis views people generally in a positive light, and one of its basic assumptions is that people are OK. What this really means is that everyone is believed to have worth, value, dignity and importance. Young babies have no reason to feel anything other than OK about themselves, as long as their physical needs are met and their parents are caring and protective towards them. Problems can arise later on, however, when children receive negative or mixed messages from their parents which have the effect of making them question the OK position which they once had.

There are some fortunate people whose early-childhood experience gives them unqualified confirmation of their own self-worth, which is consistent and sufficient to enable them to retain their *I'm OK - you're OK* position for life. But many small children are subjected to the opposite approach by their parents, and their shortcomings or failings are habitually pointed out to them in various ways.

For example, parents may say to children 'You're too slow', 'You're clumsy', 'You're stupid', or 'You're silly', and children may accept the accusations literally and develop negative feelings about themselves. And because parents are all powerful, all good and all important, they are always 'OK' in the child's estimation. This means that the child's position in relation to his parents changes from its original 'I'm OK – You're OK' to 'I'm not OK – you're OK'. The 'I'm not OK – you're OK' position is very common and is probably experienced by the majority of people. This is not because the majority of parents are always negative and destructive, but because the whole experience of childhood and growing up is fraught with difficulty, disappointments and set-backs which are impossible to avoid. Children are, after all, small, helpless and at the mercy of the adults around them; and adults, who are bigger and can do so many things, are by definition 'OK'.

In some cases, children experience their parents as either absent or unloving, and when this happens their OK position will be 'I'm not OK – you're not OK'. In other instances, children may be cruelly treated by their parents in which case the position adopted may be 'I'm OK – you're not OK'. This last group of children learn quickly to take care and to rely on themselves, and to suspect and distrust other people.

As children grow up, the position which they decided upon early in life remains with them. All three 'not-OK' positions are dysfunctional to a greater or lesser degree in adult life, because they effectively preclude any real closeness with other people. Besides this, the early OK positions which people adopt are outside conscious awareness, and are therefore difficult to identify and to counteract. The position which people should ideally strive for is the 'Get well' – I'm OK – you're OK' position, because it indicates both self-acceptance and acceptance of others. A conscious decision can be made in later life to work towards the 'I'm OK – you're OK' position, and it can be successfully achieved by anyone who is interested in the process of self-actualization and the development of true autonomy, and who is also willing to examine in a critical way the circumstances of early childhood. It should be added that it is possible for people to move from one position to another, depending on circumstances, but the general tendency is for people to adhere to one main position.

LIFE SCRIPTS

The OK positions which people adopt in early life, therefore, can be changed when people consciously decide to change. What happens more frequently, however, is that people continue to live their whole lives according to the 'life script' which they decided upon in early childhood. In transactional analysis, the word 'script' refers to the individual's early conditioning and its effect on present thinking, feeling and behaving. Berne describes the 'script' as a 'preconscious life plan' (*Transactional Analysis in Psychotherapy*, 1991) in accordance with which people live out their daily lives, structuring their relationships and activities to suit its demands.

According to Berne each person decides in early childhood, 'how he will live and how he will die, and that plan which he carries in his head wherever he goes, is called his script'. This life plan is like a prophecy given to the child by parents or parental figures and is so definite that he subsequently feels obliged to honour it. He makes the decision that this is the best way to survive in the family. Even when people believe that they are behaving in an autonomous way, they are still very often acting according to the dictates of their script.

Examples of the predictions which are passed on from parents, and which often govern people's lives, are: 'You'll never be any good', 'You'll always have poor health', or 'You'll end up in trouble'. Berne referred to these as the script 'payoff' or 'curse', and these along with negative comments like 'Shut up!', 'Get lost!' or 'Drop dead!' are responsible for the initial phase of script programming. Later on, when the child is older, 'counterscript' messages are picked up by him and these often include family slogans like 'Work hard', 'Get a good education', 'Have some pride in yourself', and so on. The initial script messages may be given to the child verbally, or they may be passed on non-verbally or even indirectly. A child may be repeatedly told, for example, 'You're just like your grandfather', and the underlying message may be 'He was no good and he never got anywhere'.

The counterscript messages which come from the parents' Nurturing Parent are quite often in direct opposition to the script programming which the child has received earlier on. However, the counterscript does, according to Berne, determine each person's lifestyle, while the earlier programming will determine his 'ultimate destiny'. In every life-script there is also a 'spellbreaker', which represents either a time or an event which will effectively negate the script. Thus a person may be freed from his script after a certain length of time, or following a specific event like the death of his parents or, more tragically, his own death.

PERMISSIONS

Although Berne believed that the majority of children receive negative programming from parents, he nevertheless allowed for the fact that parents often give their children positive *permissions* as well. Since there is no element of coercion attached to them, these permissions represent areas of free choice for the child. A person who receives frequent permissions in childhood will develop more autonomy later on as a result. The giving of permissions has nothing to do with 'permissiveness', which refers to attitudes of indulgence, acquiescence or sometimes even the total abdication of parental responsibility.

In the TA model of counselling the concept of 'permission' can be used effectively when, for example, the counsellor gives the client permission to abandon self-destructive behaviour and encourages him to be kind to himself instead. These permissions can be stated explicitly by the counsellor, and may involve simply telling the client that he does not have to follow a particular course of action, the rationale for which has probably been passed to him from parental figures and is now stored in his own Parent ego state. Berne believed that it was possible, and quite often necessary, to help people in this way, so that the negative instructions which they received during childhood were reversed during therapy. A person who is slowly killing himself through drug or alcohol abuse, for example, may respond to the counsellor's permission to stop, rather than to a stark injunction to stop. The reason for this is that the counsellor is taking upon herself the responsibility for switching off the parental recording which has governed the client's behaviour to date. In doing so she is also offering the client the most important permission of all, which is the permission to think for himself. This last permission is the one which the client needs most of all, if he is to develop autonomy and freedom from his script.

POTENCY AND PROTECTION

In order to be effective, the counsellor must also be able to offer the client what Berne referred to as 'potency' and 'protection'. The word 'potency' is used here to describe the counsellor's vigour and self-assurance when dealing with the client's Parent ego state which is usually very strong. For a counsellor to give a client permission to disobey his Parent, she must also be in a position to offer him protection from the consequences of exercising his newly-established autonomy. This offer of protection may be simply a matter of telling the client that he can contact the counsellor when and if he needs to. It can be seen from all this that the TA model of counselling is different in many respects from other models. In the first place, the TA counsellor is prepared to tell the client what to do when necessary. In the second place, it is not the relationship between client and counsellor which is the most important factor (unlike the person-centered approach); what is important is the fact that the counsellor's task is to 'cure' the client, in much the same way as a doctor would cure a patient. The word 'cure' is used, in this context, to refer to the development and full realization of client autonomy.

At the beginning of this chapter we mentioned that Berne's father was a doctor, and that, as a child, Berne had been very close to him. There is evidence throughout his writings that Berne's approach to therapy was greatly influenced by the medical model which he clearly admired. The therapist as a person who 'cures' is further emphasized by Berne's frequent references to the 'diagnosis' of ego states, and the shifts which occur in

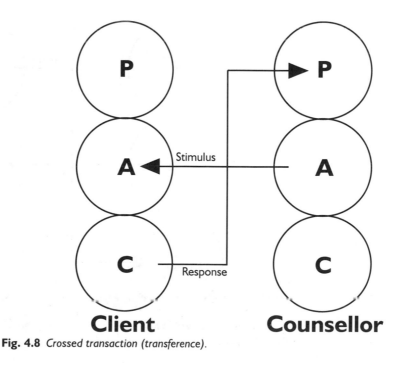

Fig. 4.8 *Crossed transaction (transference).*

them. He believed that the therapist should be trained to observe and to diagnose ego states, and in order to do this she needs to have appropriate training, supervision, and ideally, therapy herself. This training should not be a narrow one, and should include a firm grounding in psychodynamic theory, and group practice as well. At all times the counsellor should remember that she and the client are different; her function is a professional one, while the client is there to receive help.

TRANSFERENCE

According to the psychodynamic definition, transference refers to the phenomenon of transferring to new relationships many of the feelings and attitudes which we had in childhood. These feelings and attitudes were mainly for parents or parental figures, and they are carried into adult life and unconsciously influence the way we view and relate to other people. A child who had a strict and punitive mother, for example, may later on in adult life view other women in positions of authority with suspicion or apprehension.

Berne believed that transference was a common cause of problems, not just in the therapeutic situation, but in everyday life as well. The way that transference reactions occur can be illustrated by reference again to his ego state model (see Fig. 4.8).

The diagram shows that the stimulus or question is directed from the counsellor's Adult to the client's Adult, but that the response is given from the client's Child to the counsellor's Parent. In this way the client is relating to the counsellor as if she were a parent or parental figure.

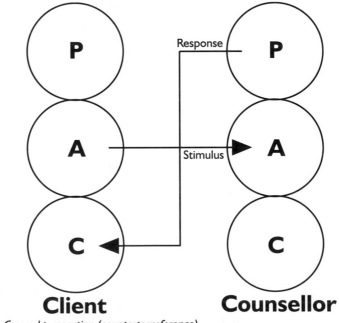

Fig. 4.9 *Crossed transaction (countertransference).*

COUNTERTRANSFERENCE

The word 'countertransference' refers to the feelings which are transferred from the counsellor's past to the present situation with the client. In the example illustrated in Fig. 4.9 the counsellor is responding like a parent to the client. This response from the counsellor has come from her Parent ego state which, in turn, is a compilation of all the parental influences she has absorbed as a child. The stimulus is the client's question which is directed from his Adult to the counsellor's Adult.

CASE STUDY: PHIL

Phil was thirty-five years of age and lived alone in a council flat where he had been for over ten years. His parents were relatively young, both in their sixties, and when he first came for counselling he described the family as 'very close'. Later on, in a subsequent counselling session, he reversed his original description of them and expressed a great deal of anger against what he called 'the stifling atmosphere at home'. Phil had one sister who was two years younger than him; she had returned to live with her parents after the break-up of her marriage, but for various reasons this arrangement was not a happy one, either for her or for the rest of the family.

Some time before he came for counselling, Phil had started an education course in the hope that this would increase his future chances of getting a job. At first, he found the course difficult, but as time went on he gathered confidence in his ability to study and to pass exams. His confidence was further boosted when he gained distinction grades in several of the engineering exams at the end of his first term of study. Phil's financial situation was precarious since he was not in full-time employment and the grant which he received was inadequate to meet his needs. As well as this, the evening work which he had done for the past few months was now over. Phil's rent was in arrears, he owed money to the bank, to the College Student Services Department, as well as to his parents who had been giving him financial assistance at regular intervals for over a year. As a consequence of all this, he was perpetually worried, lonely, unable to socialize and increasingly subject to lengthy periods of depression.

Phil had stated that he was close to his family, and it was certainly the case that they all spent a great deal of time together. Their home was just two streets away from his flat, and Phil spent at least three evenings a week there with his parents and his sister, largely, he said, because he did not have the money to do anything else. Although he had never married and did not have a steady girlfriend, Phil was engaged in a sporadic affair with a woman he had met some years previously. She was now unhappily married, and Phil's current practice was to meet her whenever she got the opportunity to come to his flat at weekends. The relationship was unsatisfactory for Phil since it involved a great deal of secrecy and increased the feelings of tension and guilt which he already had. As a consequence of this, he had started to drink a lot at weekends, and this, combined with his heavy smoking, was a further strain on his limited financial means.

Phil's father, now retired, suffered from diabetes, and the state of his health was a major consideration in the family household. Whenever anything went wrong, he had a diabetic attack which threw everyone into panic. Afterwards there were feelings of guilt for having upset him, and as far back as Phil could remember his father had used these attacks in order to exercise 'control' within the family. Phil's mother, who was clearly in awe of her husband, always capitulated to his wishes. She felt that her children – even though they were now adults – should also defer to him, and she often accused them of 'slowly killing' their father because they had failed in their adult lives and had thus proved to be a disappointment to him. Phil's mother was conscious of her social position, and was acutely embarrassed that her son was currently unemployed. She felt that this reduced her standing with friends and relatives, and in fact, Phil had only recently discovered that she had lied to some of his relatives by saying that he still worked in the evenings. Phil was aware that she did not understand or value the course which he was doing, and this worried him considerably. Recently, there were more frequent rows within the family, and these were nearly always related to money. It seemed there was a great deal of resentment – frequently expressed – against Phil for the fact that he had borrowed money from his father, thereby exposing him to worry and further diabetic attacks. Phil, in turn, expressed his resentment against his sister for what he regarded as her sponging attitude to his parents, and her decision to make her home with them since the break-up of her marriage.

Since the principle of 'contractual agreement' is a fundamental one in the transactional analysis model, Phil's counsellor explained this to him when they first met. At this early stage she did not ask him to detail his problems, but used the first part of their initial session to talk about confidentiality. In relation to this, she told Phil that she might use some of the information from their counselling sessions, later on, in discussion with her own supervisor. After some explanation about this, Phil agreed that she could do so. The counsellor then asked him for background details about himself and his lifestyle. This included details about his present state of health and whether he had ever suffered from any major illness, either physical or mental. Phil was not receiving any medical or psychiatric treatment, nor was he taking any non-prescribed drugs. He did not usually drink throughout the week, but during the weekend his intake was substantial, although variable, depending on his financial situation. He smoked about ten cigarettes a day, but said he would certainly be tempted to smoke more if he had the money to do so.

Having checked all these details, the counsellor then went on to draw up a business contract with Phil. This included mutual agreement about their dates of meeting, along with mutual decisions concerning the frequency and length of counselling sessions and the way these sessions might be structured. Together they agreed to meet once a week for the following six weeks and to allocate fifty minutes to each session. During the next stage of working together, they devised a treatment contract. According to this, Phil said clearly what it was he hoped to achieve through counselling, and the counsellor agreed that these were feasible goals which would move him closer towards autonomy.

In view of the fact that Phil had referred to his weekend drinking and the depression that accompanied it, the counsellor was aware that he might harm himself by attempted suicide. Although the thought had occasionally crossed his mind, Phil had, nevertheless, made the decision that this was something he would never do. He agreed to make the decision yet again in the counselling situation, and was emphatic and genuine in his Adult commitment to it. In transactional analysis, clients are frequently asked to make this kind of commitment, especially when it appears that their life-script may be one which dictates a tragic outcome, like suicide, severe mental illness, or harm directed towards others. A threefold decision is therefore made which rejects all these tragic outcomes. This is an important aspect of counselling in TA terms, and is called *closing the escape hatches*. The treatment contract which Phil made with the counsellor was phrased in a positive way. There were major changes which he wanted to make in his life and these were outlined as follows:

- To improve the state of his health.
- To achieve financial independence.
- To develop a wider social network.
- To develop a better, less dependent relationship with his family.

Phil discussed these objectives with the counsellor and was encouraged to be more specific about their actual meaning. When asked, for example, what he meant by the state of his health, he mentioned that he wanted to stop smoking and to cut down his drinking, as he felt that in doing so he would feel better physically and also gain in personal confidence. He found it much more difficult to address the matter of financial independence, but was eventually able to do so. He identified this as a central issue in his life, upon which many of the other problems were contingent. Phil understood the principle of game-playing very well, and could easily recognize those which were going on amongst his family members. In particular, he could pinpoint his own contribution to them, especially to the games which his father habitually played with him. Thus the guilt which he felt about his father's illness was seen in a new light by Phil. He was able – through structural analysis – to look more closely at the events of his past and at the dynamics of his present family interaction.

During the time which she spent with him, the counsellor was in a position to observe Phil's ego states, and she was concerned to focus attention on his Child in order to help him identify the original scenarios from which some of its present manifestations stemmed. In the safety of the counselling situation, he experienced the intense feelings of anger, sadness and depression which, as a child, he had often felt when his father berated him for failing exams or for mixing with the wrong kind of friends. As well as this, he was also able to re-experience the resentment and guilt which he felt towards his father, who had often been absent through illness during the course of his childhood. In focusing on and staying with his Child ego state in this way, Phil discovered that he could look at his childhood experiences and see them more clearly. This, in turn, reminded him of the patterns or life-script which he had earlier discussed with the counsellor, and he now became aware of the possibility that this was a Never script, which dictated that he should never get the job which he wanted, nor the permanent girlfriend, nor the financial and familial independence which he longed for so much. It seemed to him that no matter what he set himself up to do, his script behaviour made sure that he failed to achieve it. Although the counterscript messages which he received in later childhood had exhorted him to 'work hard' and to 'get on in life', the original script messages were more influential. Because of them, Phil had decided very early in life that he was a failure and did not deserve his father's time, support or love.

Since individual autonomy is the opposite of script attachment, a focus of the ongoing counselling sessions with Phil was intervention by the counsellor inviting him to look at his script beliefs, and to question them in the light of present reality. Over a period of several counselling sessions, he was then able to change some of his earliest childhood decisions which had laid the foundations of his script. This re-decision process was completed by Phil while in his Child ego state, immediately following re-experienced scenes from his early childhood. This helped him to identify and feel the links between past and present, and to look more closely at the wider range of options which were available to him now as an adult. After this, in his Adult ego state, he reaffirmed his decision to change and examined the practical implications of what this would involve for him. This reappraisal of his life prompted him to stop drinking heavily at weekends and to give up smoking. These basic changes left him better off financially, as a consequence of which he was able to socialize more. He did not borrow money again from his father, and he paid back what he owed to him as soon as he was in a position to do so. In the longer term, Phil was successful in establishing a relationship with an eligible girlfriend, and since he had achieved independence from his family he was able to devote time and attention to her and to himself.

The counsellor congratulated Phil for the changes which he had accomplished, and she continued to recognize and to reinforce the progress he was making. As his physical health improved, he felt better emotionally as well, and this in turn made him much more optimistic about the possibility of getting a job. During their last session together both client and counsellor re-examined the contract which they had made at the beginning of their work together, and it was clear to both that Phil was achieving the goals which he had set himself.

FURTHER READING

BERNE, E., *Games People Play*, Penguin Books, London, 1968.

BERNE, E., *Transactional Analysis in Psychotherapy*, Souvenir Press, London, 1991.

BERNE, E., *What Do You Say After You Say Hello?*, Corgi Books, London, 1992.

STEWART, I., *Eric Berne – Key Figures in Counselling & Psychotherapy*, Sage Publications, London, 1992.

STEWART, I. and VAN JOINES, *TA Today: A New Introduction to Transactional Analysis*, Lifespace Publishing, Nottingham, 1987.

STEWART, I., *Transactional Analysis Counselling in Action*, Sage Publications, London 1989.

CHAPTER 5

Rational-Emotive Counselling

The historical background

ALBERT ELLIS

Albert Ellis was born in Pennsylvania in 1913 and moved to New York with his family when he was four years of age. His father was frequently away from home on business, and when Ellis was twelve years of age his parents divorced. After that time he saw even less of his father. His mother spent a great deal of time with her friends, so that Ellis, his younger brother and his sister, were in many respects neglected. Ellis cooked for himself and the other children, and generally took care of the household while his mother went out in the evenings, or socialized with her friends who had come to visit.

From the age of five onwards, Ellis suffered a series of illnesses, including severe tonsillitis followed by acute nephritis. As a result of this, he spent long and frequent periods in hospital and was unable to take part in sports and other childhood activities. In addition, he was shy and introverted, and suffered bouts of deep anxiety whenever he was asked to participate in classroom or school activities. During the depression of 1929, Ellis's mother lost all her savings, and the family was reduced to poverty. In spite of all these handicaps, he refused to become depressed; he worked hard at school, and from a very early age made a determined effort to understand and get on with other people. Later on, in adult life, Ellis developed diabetes, but he never allowed this to hamper his style in any way, and always maintained an energetic, hardworking and enthusiastic approach to life.

From the age of twelve, Ellis had an ambition to become a writer. He took a business degree at the Baruch School of Business and Civic Administration of City College in New York and studied accounting as his main subject. At an early stage, he considered teaching as a career, but his childhood experiences had left him with a phobia about public speaking (later on he cured himself of this phobia through the use of desensitization), and instead of teaching he continued to write, so that by the age of twenty-eight he had completed twenty full-length manuscripts. Unfortunately, these were not published. As well as writing, Ellis was reading widely at this time. His main areas of interest were psychology, sexuality, love and marriage. He began to act as an unofficial counsellor to his friends who confided in him, and this prompted him to study for an MA degree in Clinical Psychology. Later on he completed his PhD at Columbia University, and went on to write numerous professional and popular articles and books on sex. He also became a pioneering marriage, sex and family therapist, and was the first president of the Society for the Scientific Study of Sex. As well as this, he championed the rights of homosexuals and continued to write prolifically.

Although his original training was in the area of family and marriage counselling, Ellis believed that it had shortcomings in that it did not adequately address the *individual* needs of the couple in a relationship. As a consequence, he decided to train as a psychoanalyst, and during this training he underwent the customary periods of analysis himself. When this was complete, Ellis went on to practise classical analysis and psychoanalytically orientated psychotherapy for several years. However, he never claimed to be an orthodox Freudian in the strict sense, and from early on in his career he questioned what he regarded as some of Freud's more contentious theories and unscientific views, especially those regarding sex.

By 1953, Ellis had become disillusioned with psychoanalysis as a form of therapy, mainly because he viewed it as an inefficient use of both the client's and the analyst's time. Some of the techniques which are used in psychoanalysis – such as free association and dream interpretation – he considered to be time consuming and limited in the results which they produced. There were many aspects of psychoanalysis which Ellis did enjoy. In particular, he liked the 'detecting' part of the work (*Reason and Emotion in Psychotherapy*, 1990), and was very interested in what his clients told him. But over a period of time, he found himself abandoning the use of classical analysis and reverting instead to other methods of psychotherapy.

It was during this time that Ellis became interested in behavioural learning theory. He realized that psychoanalysis and behavioural learning theory had something important in common in that both emphasized the significance of conditioning in early life. Ellis arrived at the conclusion that people could be helped to overcome their problems through action as well as through insight. Indeed, he believed that this action was necessary if clients were to become 'deconditioned' from their early conditioned responses and thus free themselves from their own emotional problems.

Ellis gradually realized, however, that it is not just early conditioning which can impede the process of growth and maturity; allied to the conditioning is the client's own negative and self-destructive reinforcement of early disturbing or traumatic experience. It occurred to him that people often cling tenaciously to outdated feelings of depression, anger, guilt and hostility which are no longer applicable to the present situation. The key to this tenacity, he decided, is language which is uniquely human and separates human beings from all the lower animals. Through language, people continue to reinforce their own outmoded thinking and in doing so, perpetuate their own suffering. Much of this negative thinking is a direct result of what people have been *told* by others in early life, and the information received in this way has become accepted as absolute truth. In other words, many of the fears and anxieties which people experience, are defined in the first place by others, and are subsequently reinforced by the individual's internal soliloquy.

This new focus on language and thinking had a profound effect on Ellis's work and led him further away from psychodynamic theory; by 1955, the theory and practice of *rational-emotive psychotherapy* was beginning to evolve. Ellis had always been interested in philosophy, and this too became a definite influence on his work. Of particular importance are the ideas of the Stoic philosophers, including Epictetus, whom Ellis has frequently quoted as saying:

> Men are disturbed not by things, but by the views which they take of them.

Ellis often refers to philosophy and literature in his writings. His interest in creative writing is obvious from his style which is lucid, interesting and a pleasure to read. Although unable to fulfil his early ambition, he nevertheless utilized his writing talent in the service of psychotherapy and teaching. Ellis regards the therapist's task as a teaching or re-educating one. More precisely, he defines the job of the therapist as that of an effective *emotional re-educator* (*Reason and Emotion in Psychotherapy*, 1990).

Ellis was a prolific writer throughout his career, and in 1956 he read his first paper on Rational-Emotive Therapy to the American Psychological Association in Chicago. The Institute for Rational Living, an educational establishment, was founded in 1959 and has now been incorporated into the Institute for Rational-Emotive Therapy which is based in New York, although branches of it have been established throughout the world. Ellis previously held the posts of Chief Psychologist at the New Jersey State Diagnostic Center (1949-50) and Chief Psychologist of the New Jersey Department of Institutions and Agencies (1950-52). He also served as Consultant in Clinical Psychology to the New York City Board of Education and he was Adjunct Professor of Psychology at Rutgers University, at the United States International University as well as at Pittsburg (Kansas) State University.

The neglect which Ellis suffered in his childhood does not appear to have had any lasting or damaging effects on his personality. His own view of the matter is that he developed habits of self-reliance early on, and that this self-reliance and determination not to be miserable about anything enabled him to achieve a great deal, both in the fields of therapy and writing. He continues to work as the President of the Institute for Rational-Emotive Therapy in New York. His most important contribution to psychology has been the establishment of rational-emotive therapy as the first of the modern cognitive behavioural approaches.

KEY WORDS

RATIONAL-EMOTIVE

Ellis originally called the therapy which he had developed 'rational psychotherapy'. Later on, however, he changed this when he realized that critics believed he was concerned only with clients' thinking, and not with their emotions or their behaviour. In order to define his work more precisely, and to distinguish his position from that of other therapists who were using a purely 'rational' approach, Ellis finally decided to use the term 'rational emotive' to describe the therapy which he had pioneered. The double term serves to encompass the cognitive aspects of the approach, and to focus on the emotional dimension as well. Rational-emotive therapy is concerned, therefore, not just with clients' thinking, but also with the emotions and the behaviour which follow on from these. The principal aim of therapy is to help clients to change their irrational patterns of thinking, *and* to show them how these dysfunctional patterns can lead to emotional disturbance and counterproductive behaviour. In his book *Reason and Emotion in Psychotherapy*, Ellis makes the point that the theory of Rational Emotive Therapy '...holds that human thinking and emotions are, in some of their essences, the same thing, and that by changing the former one does change the latter.'

The irrational patterns of thinking which clients steadfastly adhere to are reinforced by their internal language or self-scolding. This self-scolding is a direct result of childhood experience, and is derived from largely negative information passed on from parents and from society in general. Ellis is more concerned with the ways in which people cling to negative and unrealistic thinking than he is with the origin of this thinking. This does not mean that he sees no value in tracing this illogical thinking to its original source, or of helping clients to gain insight into distant or past events. What it means is that Ellis is concerned – unlike the purely psychodynamic therapist – with the way that clients perpetuate and compound the original problem through self-defeating verbalization and thought.

RATIONAL AND IRRATIONAL THINKING

One of the ideas frequently expressed by Ellis is that human beings have a basic tendency to be irrational as well as rational in their thinking. It is this tendency to be irrational or illogical that is the root cause of most human unhappiness and suffering. A central aim of rational-emotive therapy and counselling is to help the client identify the ways in which his irrational thinking causes his unhappiness, and to further encourage him to establish and maintain more rational and therefore functional ways of thinking. Rational thinking, according to Ellis, enables people to fulfil the twin goals of staying alive, and of achieving happiness and freedom from pain and suffering. The kind of emotional upheaval which causes unhappiness is linked to faulty or irrational thinking. When more rational patterns of thinking have been adopted and sustained, emotional experience becomes more positive as a consequence.

THE ABC MODEL

Ellis has described the relationship between thinking and emotion through the use of his ABC model of personality and emotional disturbance. According to the model, it is not what happens at point A which causes an individual to experience disturbance or discomfort; on the contrary, it is the individual's own self-talk or 'catastrophizing' which inflicts the damage, and this takes place at point B. Then at point C, the individual experiences the emotional disturbance or reaction which follows directly from his own negative self-talk. The mistake which most people make, according to Ellis, is that they identify the activating event at point A as the cause of their unhappiness, whereas in reality it is the way that they think about the event which causes the problem. It is worth including Ellis's quotation from Epictetus again in order to highlight what is meant by this last point.

Men are disturbed not by things, but by the views which they take of them.

There are many other quotations from philosophy and literature which could be used to support the view that people have the ability to choose whether or not they will become disturbed by events in their lives. In *Paradise Lost* Milton clearly makes the same point when he says: 'The mind is its own place, and in itself can make a Heaven of Hell, a Hell of Heaven'.

Figures 5.1 and 5.2 illustrate the ABC model or framework. In Fig. 5.1, Paul, who is eighteen years of age, fails his driving test. His immediate reaction to this event is to say to himself: 'It's awful that I failed the test and I'm useless for having failed'. As a consequence of his belief and inference, Paul becomes unhappy and depressed and decides that he will not even try the test again.

In Fig. 5.2, however, Paul's belief and inference about having failed his test is much more moderate and realistic. His reaction is: 'Too bad I failed the test. It's disappointing. I'll have to take more lessons'. Obviously Paul feels regret, disappointment and some irritation, but nevertheless decides to take more lessons and to do the test again as soon as possible. Thus the activating event at A – i.e. failing his driving test – does not leave Paul devastated as it did in the first example because his emotional response at C has been mediated by more positive self-talk at B.

People can choose how they will respond to activating events, but they can only do this when they have identified the self-destructive beliefs which are the cause of emotional disturbance and unhappiness. Identifying self-defeating beliefs will also demonstrate to clients how it is that negative thinking often actually fulfils the predictions which an emotionally disturbed person makes. This point is illustrated by the following example which describes how Katie, a student, attends a tutorial appointment with her teacher and wonders why the assignment she handed in last week is not mentioned by the teacher.

A Activating Event – Teacher does not refer to or mention the assignment which Katie submitted last week.
B Belief and Self-talk – Katie thinks: 'The essay must be awful. She doesn't even feel it's worth mentioning. She probably thinks I'm not up to much.'
C Emotional Consequence – Katie feels depressed.
D Behavioural Consequence – Katie goes out of her way to avoid the teacher over the next few weeks. She fails to submit her next two assignments.

After a while the teacher notices that Katie seems to have lost interest and that her work is slipping. She interprets this as an indication that Katie is a poor student. This serves to reinforce Katie's belief that she is no good.

HEDONISM

Ellis uses the word 'hedonism' to describe the kind of pleasure and happiness which he believes is attainable by anyone who is prepared to work hard for it.

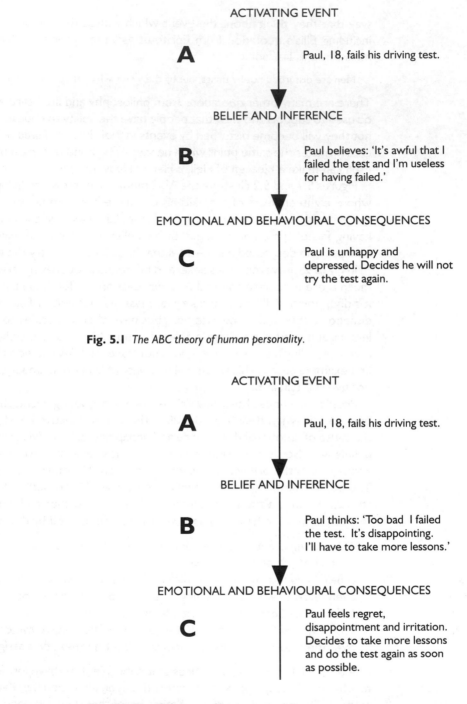

Fig. 5.1 *The ABC theory of human personality.*

Fig. 5.2 *The ABC theory of human personality.*

(NB: His is not a dictionary interpretation of this word.) He distinguishes between 'long-range' and 'short-range' hedonism, and views the former as a valid goal in rational-emotive therapy. In short-range hedonism there is an emphasis on immediate gratification and Ellis views this as counter productive since it usually involves excess, which is unlikely to be beneficial for either physical or psychological health. In long-range hedonism, however, gratification is deferred on the understanding that true happiness requires effort and planning. It is probably true to say that all theoretical models of counselling subscribe to the view that happiness requires some measure of planning, discipline and work, but Ellis expresses the view explicitly in order to underline the point that the rational-emotive approach is more than a purely cognitive one.

The Model

The rational-emotive model of counselling emphasizes an active, didactic and re-educative approach which is different from any of the other models described so far. Counsellors who use the rational-emotive approach are prepared to be directive and challenging in order to promote client self-awareness, and to help them achieve *intellectual* as well as emotional insight. Intellectual and emotional insight are not considered sufficient, however, for clients to overcome their problems. Action is required as well, and this is stressed through a programme of behavioural and emotive techniques designed to facilitate more rational and scientific ways of thinking.

Unlike psychodynamic theory, which underlines the importance of understanding the past and its influences, rational-emotive theory is more concerned with clients' present problems, and in particular, in the way that clients themselves perpetuate these problems. Ellis believes that many of the difficulties which clients experience do have their origins in the distant past, but he highlights the need to examine current manifestations of these, and the importance of working towards a more balanced, self-accepting and philosophical approach to living.

LANGUAGE

Ellis is interested in the way that people cling to assumptions which they acquired in childhood. These include unquestioned rules about relationships and life, which over a period of time become the bedrock of all their judgements, decisions and actions. A person's assumptions are seen as internalized ideas and theories which, in childhood, may have served the individual well, but which in adult life are often dysfunctional or anachronistic. It is the survival of dysfunctional or anachronistic thinking in the present that rational-emotive counselling aims to highlight and challenge. In particular, Ellis stresses the importance of language and underlines its significance in relation to human thinking. According to him, any feeling, gesture or attitude directed against us cannot in itself cause us unhappiness or harm; these things can only hurt us if we allow them to do so. When we tell ourselves how awful or terrible it is that someone has been unkind or unhelpful, then we make ourselves depressed and unhappy through our own *self-talk* and *reindoctrination* of negative attitudes expressed to us in the past. The interaction between thinking (self-talk) emotions and behaviour is a basic assumption of rational-emotive theory.

In the following example, Sean, who has recently been appointed to a university post, is just about to give his first lecture, on the subject of the Romantic poets. A couple of hours before going to the lecture hall, he starts to ruminate about the task ahead of him. His self-talk or thinking goes along the following lines:

> There will be a lot of students there. Many have studied the Romantic poets before. They are likely to know a lot about the subject. They may not appreciate what I have planned to say to them. Some might even leave the lecture hall in boredom. My God, it would be awful. I would just die – it would be terrible.

It is not difficult to see that if Sean continues in this vein he will become depressed, well in advance of his lecture. This heightened negative emotion will, in turn, affect the delivery of his lecture, which is bound to suffer as a consequence. On the other hand, Sean might very well approach his task from a very different viewpoint which, although expressing apprehension and a certain level of anxiety, is nevertheless realistic and unlikely to hamper his performance:

> There will be a lot of students there. Many of them have studied the Romantic poets before. They probably know a good deal about the subject, but it is not likely they will know as much as I do. After all, I have spent a lot of time in research. They may not appreciate what I have to say to them. But I have to start somewhere, and it is good experience, anyway. On the other hand, they might like my lecture. It is well prepared, and it is not the end of the world if it is not perfect. Yes, they might like it and that would be great.

In this second instance, Sean is placing himself in a better position to achieve success in his lecture, and even if his performance is less than perfect, he is not going to be devastated by it. It is his choice of internalized language that makes the difference between a potentially positive or negative outcome. Ellis explains the way that language has a direct bearing on people's behaviour, and in this respect rational-emotive therapy is different from both the psychodynamic and behaviourist approaches. Although language is what makes people human, it can also cause deep unhappiness since it can be used internally in a self-destructive way.

IRRATIONAL BELIEFS

Ellis has identified a number of irrational beliefs which he believes are responsible for causing a great deal of human suffering. These irrational beliefs are passed on from generation to generation via the family and society, and since they are part of our cultural heritage, they are seldom seriously questioned. They include views about education, family, politics, religion, freedom and a good many others. Ellis refers to these irrational ideas as 'societally inculcated superstitions and prejudices'. Since they are rarely questioned or examined, even in adult life, by those who subscribe to them, they frequently cause emotional disturbance.

Among the irrational beliefs which Ellis describes are the following:

It is absolutely essential that I am loved and approved of by everyone, not just for myself but for everything I do as well

This idea is obviously irrational since it would be impossible to have everyone love us, nor is it even necessary for them to do so. Believing that it is essential to be loved and approved of by everyone, and at all times, causes a great deal of self-inflicted suffering because such a belief generates high levels of anxiety. Besides, people who want to be loved and approved of at all times set impossibly high standards for themselves, since such an ambition requires continual hard work and expenditure of energy. Insecurity is also generated by this constant need for approval, and ingratiating behaviour is likely to follow. A consequence of all this is that valid individual needs will probably suffer. Indeed, people who spend a lot of time and energy trying to please others, often neglect their own needs and preferences, and frequently diminish even further their already impoverished confidence and self-esteem.

I must be good at everything and at all times. Otherwise I am not a worthwhile person

Again, it is obvious that this is an irrational belief since it would be impossible for anyone to be good at everything all the time. It is reasonable to want to succeed at work, and to have satisfactory and fulfilling relationships. It is also reasonable to want to achieve a comfortable standard of living, both for oneself and one's family, but it is not reasonable to demand a high degree of perfection in all areas of life, because placing such pressure on oneself will invariably lead to stress and illness. Another important aspect of the irrational belief that one *must* be totally competent in all areas of life is that it is bound to lead to excessively competitive behaviour since there will always be people who are better at certain things, no matter how hard one works to prove otherwise. Additionally, there will always be people who are better looking or more talented artistically. In any case, there are external attributes which are visible or demonstrable. The true inner worth, which each individual possesses, is not visible from the outside, and exists regardless of conventional definitions of success and achievement. Another problem arises when we neglect our true talents and interests in pursuit of conventional achievement, for this neglect of 'self' leads in turn to personal frustration, and further striving for the outward trappings of success.

Many people, including myself, are immoral, wicked and bad, and should therefore be castigated for our transgressions

Ellis identifies this belief as one which stems from religious teaching. According to the doctrine of free will, people can choose to behave well or badly. However, in the light of further knowledge – especially in the fields of psychology, sociology and psychotherapy – there is evidence to suggest that people are subject to outside forces which often impinge on, or even impede, their ability to make totally free choices. Nevertheless, many people continue to adhere to the notion that they, and others, *must* always act rightly, and that failure to achieve this absolute goal is evidence of immorality and weakness of character. The idea that oneself and others should *always* do the right thing is unrealistic because it does not take sufficient account of human weaknesses and individual circumstances. A much more realistic and human approach is one which acknowledges that we all make mistakes, and that though we can endeavour to reduce or overcome these, we should not expect perfection from ourselves or from others. Excessive self-blame produces guilt, anxiety and depression, while excessive criticism of others engenders hostility, pomposity, prejudice and bigotry. If we accept people as they are and try to understand them more fully, then we are unlikely to have unrealistic expectations of them. Ellis refers to the need to see things from the other person's 'frame of reference' and this is similar to Rogers' client-centered approach to people and their problems.

If things are not the way I want them to be, then it is absolutely awful

People often become extremely upset or frustrated when other people, situations and events are not exactly as they would like them to be. The irrational expectation that everything and everyone should be pleasant and congenial to us at all times, will inevitably lead to disappointment, frustration and anger, and will probably make us rigid and demanding in our approach to others. It is pointless to rail against heaven when, for example, the weather is bad or when the checkout assistant at the supermarket runs out of carrier bags just as our turn comes. Yet, there are many people who torture themselves with the unrealistic belief that the gods are against them because the weather and the checkout person are far from perfect. There are many situations in life which we can work to change, but there are many others which are immutable or beyond our control. The urge to *catastrophize* about the inevitable is a fundamental cause of unhappiness in clients and is also a waste of psychic energy. This is because such catastrophizing serves to direct attention and stamina away from those situations which can be realistically improved through time and effort, and substitutes feelings of impotence, anger and aggression in the place of enthusiasm and creative thinking.

My unhappiness is caused by other people and by events which are outside my control

According to this belief, people have no control over the circumstances of their own lives. This kind of thinking commonly leads to passive and ineffectual behaviour, and is a form of retreat from the more difficult business of acknowledging the part that we ourselves play in the shaping of our lives. Ellis believes that it is the way we *think* about other people, circumstances and events, that determines their potential to harm or upset us. People may sometimes physically attack or abuse one another, and thereby cause damage or harm. It is unlikely, however, that harm could be caused through thinking or even through spoken abuse. It is unlikely, but it is possible if the person who is the recipient of malign thinking or verbal attack is willing to be harmed by it. In other words, we all have control over our response to psychological attacks levelled against us. According to this theory, people disturb themselves by their own reactions to other people's attitudes. When other people are insulting towards me, I can learn to react by ignoring or discounting their behaviour, and in doing so I can control my own emotions and maintain my equilibrium and happiness as well.

It is a fundamental rule of rational-emotive theory that people are capable of changing the way that they view others, circumstances and events, and that even though this may take practice and effort to accomplish, it can nevertheless be done by any intelligent person. Again, language has an important role to play in the re-education process because it is through the internal use of language, or self-talk, that the individual becomes indoctrinated in the first place. It follows, therefore, that revised self-talk will help to change perceptions and responses. By carefully monitoring his own thoughts and internal language, the individual can effectively identify the part he plays in causing his own unhappiness. In particular, he can identify the adjectives he uses which are responsible for the way he feels *himself*. To say, for example, that it is 'upsetting', 'awful' or 'horrible' when friends fail to live up to our expectations, means that we are making ourselves feel 'upset', 'awful' or 'horrible'. We have the alternative of thinking that it is 'unfortunate' and 'inconvenient' that they have not done what we expected them to do, but we can still be tolerant of their fallibility, and kinder to ourselves in the process.

OTHER IRRATIONAL BELIEFS

Ellis describes several other irrational beliefs which he considers to be a basic cause of human unhappiness. Among these, for example, is the belief that whatever has happened in the past is still enormously influential and will continue to exert power over us in the present. Thus, a person who has had an emotionally impoverished childhood may come to expect less than satisfactory relationships in adult life. This belief has obvious disadvantages since it effectively precludes the possibility of ever achieving emotional fulfilment and stability. It is also evasive because it avoids the difficult task of dealing with and resolving past events, so that more adult ways of functioning in present relationships can be learned. It is obviously much more difficult to deal with emotional issues when one's emotions have been abused in childhood, but it is not impossible, especially when help is available through counselling or other forms of therapy.

Another irrational belief which Ellis highlights, is the idea that we should always be deeply affected or even extremely upset about other people's shortcomings, problems and actions. It is *sometimes* the case that we can help others who are experiencing difficulties or distress, but it would be impossible to take responsibility for all the ills of the neighbourhood. To try to do so would obviously lead to worry, depression or other illness. If we become upset because a neighbour has some obvious fault, or does not respond to us in the way we would like, it is a waste of time because no amount of anxiety or resentment on our part will ever change the situation, or the neighbour. What we can do, however, is to change the way we respond to other people so that we can cease to be upset by them.

Attending to their own needs and responses is exactly what people who subscribe to another of Ellis's beliefs do *not* do; this irrational idea is one which dictates that we need to rely on other people who are stronger and more capable than us in order to get through life. Although we are certainly dependent on others in various ways, excessive dependence will stifle initiative and growth. People often become dependent on others so that they will not have to take responsibility for their own mistakes, but such an approach to life is bound to inhibit learning, since it is mainly through trial and error that knowledge and skills are acquired. People do need to seek help from others at times, but since all of us are responsible for ourselves in the end, it is important that we should learn habits of independent thought and action.

CHANGING IRRATIONAL BELIEFS

In Ellis's view, most human disturbance is caused by irrational thinking, some examples of which were given above. It follows, therefore, that in order for people to grow and change, to become independent and psychologically healthy, the irrational views which they hold need to be identified and challenged. Even when a person's illogical thinking is deep-rooted from childhood, it is possible, according to rational-emotive theory, to change it. Quite often people spontaneously question their irrational beliefs at certain stages of life (for example, during teenage years, or later on during the so called 'mid-life' crisis). Spontaneous questioning can also occur following major events such as bereavement, loss or trauma.

For many, however, irrational beliefs continue throughout the lifespan, and cause a great deal of neurosis and suffering. Some of these people seek help through psychotherapy or counselling, and regardless of whatever model of therapy they come across or choose, the therapist's main task will be to help them see the illogical and dysfunctional nature of their thinking. In rational-emotive counselling, though, the emphasis will not just be on identification of irrational beliefs; it will also concern itself with the client's methods of sustaining and perpetuating these beliefs in the present. After this initial stage, the rational-emotive counsellor's task is to help the client to work towards changing his beliefs, and she does this through the use of vigorous persuasion and sustained challenge. The counsellor's attack on the client's irrational beliefs is designed to help him change his self-defeating ways of thinking so that he will learn to think and express himself in more rational and realistic ways.

THE THERAPEUTIC RELATIONSHIP

In common with other models of counselling, rational-emotive theory regards the relationship between counsellor and client as being very important. The rational-emotive model emphasizes the need to understand the client and his problems, and identifies a further need to communicate this understanding and acceptance to the client. However, there is less stress on empathy than in Rogers' model. The ability to enter into the client's world, which is sometimes referred to as *being within the client's frame of reference*, is a fundamental prerequisite of the client-centered model. According to the rational-emotive approach, the counsellor's ability to remain detached, though understanding, is preferable, for in this way she is less likely to become enmeshed in the client's irrational thinking. In other words, the counsellor needs to be clear in her own head that the client's thinking is irrational. Counsellor warmth towards the client is not regarded as a necessary component in the rational-emotive counsellor/client relationship and, in fact, too much warmth is regarded by Ellis as distracting and liable to sabotage the hard work which the client needs to do.

Transference, which is a central issue in the psychodynamic model of counselling, and is used as a means of looking more closely at the client's early relationships, especially with parents, is not deliberately evoked in the rational-emotive model. Instead, the counsellor's task is to observe and analyse all the client's irrational beliefs, including the irrational belief that he *must* be loved by the counsellor and other people in his life. In this way, much of what actually disturbs the client is brought out into the open, discussed and dealt with, so that his inclination to develop a transference attachment to the counsellor is lessened.

Whereas person-centered counselling is non-directive in its approach to clients, a view implicit in rational-emotive theory is that people who are emotionally disturbed need to be actively, and authoritively, taught to accept themselves and others. For this reason, the rational-emotive counsellor is more direct in her approach, and this directness may take the form of *persuasion, didactic teaching* and *debate*. Debate, in particular, is designed to encourage an open and honest encounter between the client and the counsellor, and to free the client from the restrictive and dysfunctional thinking which has inhibited his growth in the past. *Informality* and *humour*, in the counselling situation, also play a part in assisting the client to develop more discerning cognitive habits, and in helping him to become less rigid in his thinking generally. There should be nothing rigid either, in the counsellor's approach to the therapeutic relationship, and in fact, rational-emotive counsellors often vary their style according to the needs of different clients. Some clients may, for example, prefer the counsellor to be formal in the relationship, whereas others may value informality of style. These differences can easily be accommodated, so long as the main aims of rational-emotive counselling are not compromised. The central aim to eradicate the irrational beliefs held by clients can be accomplished regardless of whether the counsellor's style is formal or informal, but the techniques which she uses are always logical, directive, persuasive and essentially re-educative.

In common with other models of counselling, Rational-Emotive theory considers the relationship between counsellor and client to be very important.

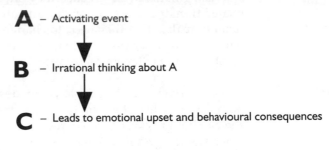

A – Activating event

B – Irrational thinking about A

C – Leads to emotional upset and behavioural consequences

Fig. 5.3

TECHNIQUES OF RATIONAL-EMOTIVE COUNSELLING

The ABC model (see Fig. 5.3) which Ellis uses to explain the relationship between thinking and emotion (referred to earlier) can be understood by nearly all clients who come for counselling. In order to use the model, however, it is important to start by looking at the *activating event* and the *emotional upset* which the client describes, and then to identify the *irrational thinking*, *beliefs* and *inferences* which the client experiences as part of the sequence.

The client needs to fully understand the connection between his thinking at B, and the emotions and behaviour which follow on at C. In addition, he needs to see clearly that his emotional upset and the accompanying behaviour are not directly caused by the activating event A, but are caused instead by his negative thinking and inferences about A. It is often the case that clients blame their emotional distress on the activating event, without ever considering the significance of their own thinking about

Fig. 5.4 *'Take me home now Jim – they're getting down to talk about us again.'*

it. When clients come to identify the connection between their thinking and their emotional disturbance, they can then understand just how closely related thinking and emotion actually are. After this, it is not difficult for them to realize that they need to change their own negative thinking, in particular their negative internal sentences or self-talk, in order to achieve emotional and behavioural balance.

AN EXAMPLE

Yvonne, a twenty-two-year-old client, describes what she calls her 'recent humiliation' when she went to a department store to return a dress which she had bought earlier. One of the seams of the dress had become undone when she tried it on at home, so she decided to return it and to ask for a refund. The shop assistant questioned Yvonne and asked her whether she had worn the dress since she had bought it. Yvonne became very angry, and even though she succeeded in getting her refund, her anger continued and later turned to depression. Yvonne's counsellor asked her to recall what it was she had been saying to herself just before she experienced her anger in the shop.

YVONNE: I can remember thinking, 'She doesn't believe me. God, I feel humiliated. How dare she question me!'

The counsellor then encouraged Yvonne to look again at her internal self-talk and to identify the irrational beliefs which prompted it. This was initially difficult for Yvonne to do, but after some time she outlined the beliefs as follows:

- People should always like me.

- People should always believe me.

- If they don't like me and believe me, it's awful, dreadful, and I can't bear it.

The counsellor encouraged Yvonne to look closely at these beliefs and to challenge them. In particular, she asked Yvonne to question the assumption that people *should always* like her and believe her. Yvonne was able to see that her disturbance and anger in the shop had been caused by her own thinking and self-talk about the event which had just taken place, and that it was possible for her to change irrational thinking by substituting rational beliefs. She was encouraged to tell herself that it is not essential to be liked and believed by everyone, and that even though it might be preferable to be liked by other people, she need not castigate herself when they disliked her. In this way she was also shown that it was possible to control her thinking and her emotions by changing the language with which she had consistently indoctrinated herself in the past.

THE CONTRACT

Before establishing this kind of working relationship with Yvonne, the counsellor was careful to discuss their contract for work together, and to outline the details of this in specific and clear terms. Thus the goals which Yvonne wished to achieve were clarified in advance, and in this respect long-term goals were seen as more desirable than short-term ones. Although Yvonne had wanted to rid herself of all negative feelings as quickly as possible, she gradually came to see that she needed to develop more assertive ways of coping with situations similar to the one she had encountered with the shop assistant, and that such a development would take time and effort on her part. She also learned that it would be inappropriate to feel no emotion in such situations, and that she could choose less devastating responses such as regret or concern.

HOMEWORK

In rational-emotive counselling, clients are frequently given homework assignments to complete. These are designed to correct the client's irrational beliefs and to help him replace them with more realistic and less disturbing language or self-talk. Clients need to be taught how to challenge their own illogical thinking. One way of doing this is to ask them to keep a *diary* and to record all their sabotaging self-talk over a period of time; after this, they can practise disputing their beliefs through further written assignments.

Bibliotherapy is another form of homework often used in rational-emotive counselling, and involves asking clients to read a selection of self-help books on the subject of rational-emotive theory. Quite often clients are encouraged to participate in an activity or task which has, in the past, been difficult for them to do. Since Yvonne had a special difficulty in dealing with shop assistants, the counsellor gave her an assignment which involved exchanging goods at the local store. One reason for giving this kind of assignment is that it helps clients to realize that even though some effort is required on their part, there is nothing catastrophic or terrible about it.

Exercises in *critical thinking and questioning* can also be given as homework, and these are especially useful because they encourage clients to identify and challenge their previously accepted assumptions, and to imagine and explore alternatives which offer greater and more liberating potential for them.

It is important that clients should understand why they have been given homework assignments, and that they can see their relevance in connection with the irrational beliefs they have held. It is also important that assignments are completed by clients, since the work done outside the counselling sessions will consolidate the progress being made during them. If homework assignments are not adequately planned and discussed, there is a greater possibility that they will not be completed. Clients should always be clear about targets, and about the nature of assignments to be used. When clients are asked to practise cognitive techniques to help them dispute irrational beliefs, they should be told exactly how this is to be done, and whether, for example, they need to write things down or record them on tape, or both.

Assignments can be discussed between counsellor and client during subsequent counselling sessions. Clients need to know what progress they have made, and to receive some positive reinforcement for success and achievement. Problems identified by the assignment can also be discussed, as can any reluctance on the client's part to actually complete assignments which were given.

HUMOUR

Humour is also frequently used in rational-emotive counselling, and is often an effective way of showing clients just how ludicrous or amusing their irrational beliefs really are. It goes without saying that humour should always be used *with* the client and never *against* him, and it is also important to judge accurately its appropriateness or otherwise with individual clients.

IMAGERY

Clients may benefit when rational-emotive imagery techniques are used to help them imagine various situations and how they might choose to respond to these. A client might be asked, for example, to imagine that he is in a situation which has previously prompted him to experience inappropriate and negative emotion, and then to further imagine himself responding in a more appropriate and less damaging way. An extension of imagery technique involves asking clients to project themselves into the future in order to test the validity of their fears about events which might occur later on. Imagery may also be used to encourage clients to practise coping strategies which they can visualize as often as they need to.

During counselling sessions the counsellor should continue to engage in forceful and vigorous *disputing* with the client in order to dismantle his irrational beliefs, and to substitute rational and less disturbing beliefs in their place. The client can also learn to internalize rational beliefs by practising disputation with himself, and he can extend this to discussing rational-emotive ideas with other people so that eventually he becomes not just a rational thinker, but an effective exponent of the theory as well.

ROLE-PLAY

Rational-emotive counselling is eclectic in that it draws on a wide range of skills and techniques, some of which have been developed by other theoretical models. Role-playing is sometimes used when clients are disturbed or apprehensive about a particular situation. For example, a client may be apprehensive about the prospect of a job interview, and he may be helped by role-playing the interview during a counselling session where he can confront his negative feelings about it, and the beliefs underlying his feelings. After this he can move on to explore more positive ways of responding, and in particular, more positive and realistic beliefs about the interview, so that even if he is unsuccessful, his sense of worth and self-esteem will remain intact.

GROUPWORK

Rational-emotive counselling can be used in a group setting and, quite often, fairly large groups of twelve to fourteen people function well together. Rational-emotive group counselling has certain advantages over individual counselling, the first and perhaps the most important being that it is efficient, since more people are present to receive therapy. It is also more economical for the same reason. All the members within the group are taught the principles of rational-emotive theory, so that each can assume the role of therapist, and work under the guidance of the group leader to help one another. This has the added advantage of giving participants a greater incentive to learn the theory as well as the social skills necessary for successful group interaction. Participants are also likely to benefit from the experience of hearing other people talk about their problems, for often a feeling of cohesion or solidarity arises when people realize that others have had similar emotional disturbances in their lives, which they have actually dealt with, or are dealing with successfully. Group interaction can also help those participants who are attending individual counselling sessions, but who need the additional reinforcement of group membership to help them tackle long-standing problems. The two forms which are included at the end of this chapter can also be used to help clients identify their irrational beliefs, to dispute them and eventually replace them with more effective rational thinking.

INSTITUTE FOR RATIONAL-EMOTIVE THERAPY
Personality Data Form

Instructions: Read each of the following items and circle after each one the word STRONGLY, MODERATELY or WEAKLY to indicate how much you believe in the statement described in the item. Thus, if you strongly believe that it is awful to make a mistake when people are watching, circle the word STRONGLY in item 1; and if you weakly believe that it is intolerable to be disapproved of by others, circle the word WEAKLY in item 2. Do not skip any items. Be as honest as you possibly can.

Acceptance

1. I believe that it is awful to make a mistake when other people are watching. — STRONGLY MODERATELY WEAKLY

2. I believe that it is intolerable to be disapproved of by others. — STRONGLY MODERATELY WEAKLY

3. I believe that it is awful for people to know certain undesirable things about one's family or background. — STRONGLY MODERATELY WEAKLY

4. I believe that it is shameful to be looked down upon by people for having less than they have. — STRONGLY MODERATELY WEAKLY

5. I believe that it is horrible to be the centre of attention of others who may be highly critical. — STRONGLY MODERATELY WEAKLY

6. I believe it is terribly painful when criticized by a person one respects. — STRONGLY MODERATELY WEAKLY

7. I believe that it is awful to have people disapprove of the way one looks or dresses. — STRONGLY MODERATELY WEAKLY

8. I believe it very embarrassing if people discover what one is really like. — STRONGLY MODERATELY WEAKLY

9. I believe that it is awful to be alone. — STRONGLY MODERATELY WEAKLY

10. I believe that it is horrible if I do not have the love or approval of certain special people who are important to me.

STRONGLY
MODERATELY   WEAKLY

11. I believe that one must have others on whom one can always depend for help.

STRONGLY
MODERATELY   WEAKLY

Frustration

12. I believe that it is intolerable to have things go slowly and not be settled quickly.

STRONGLY
MODERATELY   WEAKLY

13. I believe that it is too hard to get down to work at things it often would be better for one to do.

STRONGLY
MODERATELY   WEAKLY

14. I believe it is terrible that life is so full of inconveniences and frustrations.

STRONGLY
MODERATELY   WEAKLY

15. I believe that people who keep one waiting frequently are pretty worthless and deserve to be boycotted.

STRONGLY
MODERATELY   WEAKLY

16. I believe it is terrible to lack desirable traits that other people possess.

STRONGLY
MODERATELY   WEAKLY

17. I believe that it is intolerable when other people do not do one's bidding or give one what one wants.

STRONGLY
MODERATELY   WEAKLY

18. I believe that some people are unbearably stupid or nasty and that one must get them to change.

STRONGLY
MODERATELY   WEAKLY

19. I believe that it is too hard for me to accept serious responsibility.

STRONGLY
MODERATELY   WEAKLY

20. I believe it is dreadful that one cannot get what one wants wants without making a real effort to get it.

STRONGLY
MODERATELY   WEAKLY

21. I believe that things are too rough in this world and that therefore it is legitimate to feel sorry for oneself.

STRONGLY
MODERATELY   WEAKLY

22. I believe it is too hard to persist at many of the things one starts, especially when the going gets rough.

STRONGLY
MODERATELY   WEAKLY

23. I believe that it is terrible that life is so unexciting and boring.

STRONGLY
MODERATELY   WEAKLY

24. I believe that it is awful for one to have to discipline oneself.

STRONGLY
MODERATELY   WEAKLY

Injustice

25. I believe that people who do wrong things should suffer strong revenge for their acts.

STRONGLY
MODERATELY   WEAKLY

26. I believe that wrongdoers and immoral people should be severely condemned.

STRONGLY
MODERATELY   WEAKLY

27. I believe that people who commit unjust acts are bastards and that they should be severely punished.

STRONGLY
MODERATELY   WEAKLY

Achievement

28. I believe that it is horrible for one to perform poorly. STRONGLY MODERATELY WEAKLY

29. I believe that it is awful if one fails at important things. STRONGLY MODERATELY WEAKLY

30. I believe it is terrible to make a mistake when one has to make important decisions. STRONGLY MODERATELY WEAKLY

31. I believe that it is terrifying for one to take risks or try new things. STRONGLY MODERATELY WEAKLY

Worth

32. I believe that some of one's thoughts or actions are unforgivable. STRONGLY MODERATELY WEAKLY

33. I believe that to keep failing at things is to be a pretty worthless person. STRONGLY MODERATELY WEAKLY

34. I believe that killing oneself is preferable to a miserable life of failure. STRONGLY MODERATELY WEAKLY

36. I believe it is frightfully hard to stand up for oneself and not to give in too easily to others. STRONGLY MODERATELY WEAKLY

37. I believe that when one has shown poor personality traits for for a long time it is hopeless for one to change. STRONGLY MODERATELY WEAKLY

38. I believe that if one does not usually see things clearly and act well on them one is hopelessly stupid. STRONGLY MODERATELY WEAKLY

Control

40. I believe that one cannot enjoy himself because of his early life. STRONGLY MODERATELY WEAKLY

41. I believe that if one kept failing at important things in the past, one must inevitably keep failing in the future. STRONGLY MODERATELY WEAKLY

42. I believe that if parents have trained one to act and feel in in certain ways, one can do little to act or feel better. STRONGLY MODERATELY WEAKLY

43. I believe that strong emotions like anxiety and rage are caused by external conditions and events and that one has little or no control over them. STRONGLY MODERATELY WEAKLY

Certainty

44. I believe it would be terrible if there were no higher being or purpose on which to rely. STRONGLY MODERATELY WEAKLY

45. I believe that if I don't keep doing certain things over and over again something bad will happen if I stop. STRONGLY MODERATELY WEAKLY

46. I believe things must be in good order for one to be comfortable.

STRONGLY
MODERATELY   WEAKLY

Catastrophizing

47. I believe that it is awful if one's future is not guaranteed.

STRONGLY
MODERATELY   WEAKLY

48. I believe it is frightening that there are no guarantees that accidents and serious illnesses will not occur.

STRONGLY
MODERATELY   WEAKLY

49. I believe that it is terrifying to go to new places or to meet a new group of people.

STRONGLY
MODERATELY   WEAKLY

50. I believe it is ghastly for one to be faced with the possibility of dying.

STRONGLY
MODERATELY   WEAKLY

R E T SELF-HELP FORM (Sichel & Ellis 1984)

A ACTIVITING EVENTS, thoughts or feelings that happened just before I felt emotionally disturbed or acted self defeatingly:

....

....

C CONSEQUENCE or CONDITION – disturbed feeling or self-defeating behaviour that I produced and would like to change:

....

....

| **B** BELIEFS – Irrational Beliefs (IBs) leading to my CONSEQUENCE (emotional disturbance or self defeating behaviour). Circle all that apply to these ACTIVATING EVENTS. | **D** DISPUTES – for each circled Irrational Belief. *Examples:* 'Why MUST I do very well?' 'Where is it written that I am a BAD PERSON?' 'Where's the evidence that I MUST be approved or accepted?' | **E** EFFECTIVE RATIONAL BELIEFS (RBs) to replace my Irrational Beliefs (IBs). *Examples:* 'I'd prefer to do very well but I don't HAVE TO.' 'I am a PERSON WHO acted badly, not a BAD PERSON.' 'There is no evidence that I HAVE to be approved, though I would LIKE to be.' |

1. I MUST do well or very well.		
2. I am a BAD or WORTHLESS PERSON when I act weakly or stupidly.		
3. I MUST be approved or accepted by people I find important.		
4. I am a BAD UNLOVABLE PERSON if I get rejected.		
5. People MUST treat me fairly and give me what I need.		
6 People who act immorally are undeserving ROTTEN PEOPLE.		
7. People MUST live up to my expectations or it is TERRIBLE.		
8. My life MUST have few major hassles or troubles.		
9. I CAN'T STAND really bad things or very difficult people.		

10. It's AWFUL or HORRIBLE when major things don't go my way.

....
....
....
....

11. I CAN'T STAND IT when life is really unfair.

....
....
....
....

12. I NEED to be loved by someone who matters to me a lot.

....
....
....
....

13. I NEED a good deal of immediate gratification and HAVE TO feel miserable when I don't get it.

....
....
....
....

Additional Irrational Beliefs:

14.

....
....
....

15.

....
....
....

FEELINGS and BEHAVIOURS which I experienced after arriving at my EFFECTIVE RATIONAL BELIEFS:

....
....
....
....

CASE STUDY: ELEANOR

Eleanor, who was thirty-two years of age, had suffered from what she described as 'SAD syndrome', or Seasonal Affective Depression, for most of her adult life. Over the past two years, she had become increasingly miserable during the winter months and had visited her doctor on several occasions in the hope that medication would help her to cope with the condition. However, her GP was adamant that she did not suffer from true depression, and he consistently refused to give her drugs to alleviate her symptoms. Eventually, he suggested that she might benefit from counselling and Eleanor, who was reluctant at first to consider this, nevertheless decided to give it a try. Shortly afterwards, she made an appointment to see a counsellor who had been recommended to her, and whose approach she knew to be rational-emotive in orientation.

Eleanor was married and had two small children, both of whom at this stage were attending school. She had a part-time job as an administrative assistant which she enjoyed, and she hoped that eventually this would lead to full-time employment. During the initial session, the counsellor learned that Eleanor had spent the first eight years of her childhood living abroad with her parents, that her mother was French, and that Eleanor herself was bilingual, even though nowadays she hardly spoke French except to her mother when she visited. Eleanor's marriage had come under strain as a result of the depression which she suffered each winter, and it was this threat to her marriage which had prompted her to come for counselling. She said that her main problem was apathy and lack of confidence which seemed to be made worse by the darkness and cold of the winter; she also added that she did not believe herself to be a good mother, or much of a homemaker either.

The counsellor listened as Eleanor described her problem, and occasionally asked questions in order to clarify certain aspects of it. She then went on to ask Eleanor what she hoped to achieve through counselling and Eleanor was in no doubt that she wanted to regain more energy and confidence, and to feel more optimistic about life in general. The counsellor encouraged Eleanor to be specific in defining her needs.

COUNSELLOR: What is it you would like to start working on now?
ELEANOR: I would like to get through this coming winter feeling well.

The counsellor agreed with Eleanor that they would target this as her main goal in the initial counselling sessions. During the following session, she asked Eleanor for more details about her winter depression.

ELEANOR: I can't stand winter, not in this country, anyway. It always makes me depressed. I envy people who live in warm countries.
COUNSELLOR: Tell me about the depression. What happens to you when you feel that way?
ELEANOR: I get terribly tired and switched off. Then I eat more. When it's cold and dark I just want to stay in the house and eat chocolates in front of the fire. Then I put on weight and hate myself. (She laughs)

It seemed to the counsellor that Eleanor was experiencing an exaggerated and sustained negative emotion (i.e. depression) in response to her beliefs about the cold and dark of winter, and this was accompanied by dysfunctional behaviour in the form of overeating and extreme lethargy. The counsellor discussed this with Eleanor and showed her that her depression was directly caused by her *thinking about* the winter, and that she could replace this with a more appropriate emotional response like regret, sadness or disappointment, once she had succeeded in changing her beliefs and internal language. Like many clients in rational-emotive counselling, Eleanor was preoccupied with what she regarded as the cause of her depression (winter), which in the ABC framework is the *activating event* (see Fig. 5.5).

Activating Event –	Onset of winter with colder weather and darker evenings.
Belief and Inference –	Eleanor thinks 'I can't stand it. I should be in a warm country.'
Emotional and Behavioural Consequence –	Eleanor is depressed. She overeats and stays indoors every evening.

Fig. 5.5

Eleanor remembered the summers abroad when she was a child, and she spoke with anger and resentment against the British winter. People frequently become upset when situations and events are not exactly as they would like them to be and they often have the irrational expectation that *things*, as well as people, should be pleasant to them at all times. The counsellor worked with Eleanor on the ABC model to show her that her emotional problem (depression) was caused by her irrational thinking about winter and that her behavioural problems of overeating and hibernating were also linked to her illogical thinking. It was not long before Eleanor was able to see that her emotional upset, and the behaviour which accompanied this, were not directly caused by winter, but were prompted by her own internalized language instead.

COUNSELLOR: What is it you are thinking or saying to yourself just before the feeling of depression comes?

ELEANOR: (*pause*) I'm a prisoner in this cold and dark. I can't stand it. I should be somewhere warm.

The next step was to look more closely at Eleanor's internalized language and to help her identify the irrational beliefs which underpinned it. In the first instance, Eleanor's insistence that she *should* be in a warm country abroad, indicated that some of the irrational beliefs responsible for her emotional disturbance were the following:

● Things should always be the way I want them to be.
● I must get everything I want in life.

Through a process of *debate*, the counsellor challenged Eleanor to think more rationally, and to substitute more realistic, appropriate beliefs for the dysfunctional, inappropriate and negative beliefs she had experienced to date. Homework exercises were prepared and discussed, so that Eleanor would have the opportunity to work on her new rational beliefs and convictions, and generally put her new learning into practice. As it was now winter (December), the counsellor asked Eleanor to keep a diary and to record all her negative self-talk over the following week, and to practise disputing her irrational beliefs on tape. The belief that she *should* be in a warm country abroad was replaced with the more rational statement: 'It would be nice to live in a warm country abroad, but it isn't awful that I don't, and I can stand it.'

Eleanor was also asked by the counsellor to practise changing her internal language, so that her thinking would become less rigid and self-sabotaging. Thus, for example, when she once would have said, 'It will be terrible this winter', she now learned to replace this with: 'I don't like winter much, but I can accept it. It certainly won't kill me and I don't need to get depressed about it.' Eleanor soon became adept at conducting fairly forceful dialogue with herself as part of homework assignments, and she discussed her progress with the counsellor in follow-up sessions. She was, by this stage, very interested in rational-emotive therapy and had read several books on the subject. The counsellor gave her a behavioural assignment which involved walking each evening for a fifteen-minute period, and Eleanor enjoyed this, although initially she had been reluctant to do it. At about this time she decided that she wanted to further her education and perhaps go to university eventually to read French. Because she still lacked enough confidence to apply immediately, the counsellor persuaded her to attend assertiveness-training classes, where her newly awakened interests were given further encouragement.

Role-playing was also included in counselling sessions so that Eleanor could practise interview skills. She had made another decision, to work towards a long-term goal of spending more time with her relatives in France, once her financial position at home permitted her to do so. Along with this, she gradually adopted a much more philosophic approach to the British winter, managed to cut down on her comfort eating, and lost some weight as a consequence. In all, she felt more energetic and enthusiastic and finished her counselling sessions aware that she had made a great deal of progress.

FURTHER READING

DRYDEN, W., *Current Issues in Relational-Emotive Therapy*, Croom Helm, London, 1987.

DRYDEN, W., *Rational-Emotive Counselling in Action*, Sage Publications, London, 1990.

ELLIS, A., *Reason and Emotion in Psychotherapy*, Citadel Press, Carol Publishing, New York, 1990.

MURGATROYD, S., *Counselling and Helping*, The British Psychological Society & Methuen, London, 1988.

NELSON-JONES, R., *The Theory and Practice of Counselling Psychology*, Cassell, London, 1990.

CHAPTER 6

Behavioural counselling

The historical background

Behaviour therapy, or behaviour modification as it is often called, has evolved from that branch of psychology which is concerned with theories of human learning. *Classical conditioning* and *operant conditioning* are two major theories of learning, and both are based on scientifically tested principles which have been formulated as a result of laboratory studies and experiments. This is in sharp contrast to Freudian and psychodynamic theories which are unscientific in the sense that they have not been rigorously tested in order to establish their validity. There is, for example, no real scientific evidence to support Freud's concept of personality – the id, the ego and the super-ego – and the existence of the unconscious. This lack of scientific authority has often led to severe criticism and controversy.

There are some similarities between psychodynamic and learning theories of behaviour (both emphasize the importance of conditioning in early life), but learning theory does not claim that instinctive urges and repressed unconscious thought are the forces which regulate human behaviour. On the contrary, learning theory is concerned with actual observable behaviour. This approach stems from the work carried out by a number of psychologists at the beginning of the twentieth century who experimented with animals in order to formulate and validate their theories. However, it was not until the 1950s and 1960s that behaviour therapy started to emerge as a well defined therapeutic approach which could be used to treat a wide variety of behavioural problems. In the 1950s, Hans Eysenck began to treat people who suffered from phobias, and he based his work on the findings of earlier research done by Pavlov on classical conditioning. Similar work was being carried out by other psychologists in different countries, and Joseph Wolpe, who pioneered techniques of systematic desensitization, was also influenced by Pavlov's experiments. B. F. Skinner was working in the USA and developing further the work started by E. L. Thorndike on Operant conditioning, and as a result of his research, Skinner designed a model for controlling behaviour which is based on principles of reinforcement.

Since the 1970s the importance of thinking as well as behaviour has been incorporated into the behavioural approach, so that the cognitive aspect of human experience is now being given the attention which it previously lacked. This means that the term 'cognitive behavioural therapy' is now often used interchangeably with the original term, behaviour therapy.

Learning theories

The following is an abbreviated account of the way in which behaviour therapy has evolved from theories of human learning.

PAVLOV

Ivan Pavlov was born in Russia in 1849 and studied animal physiology at university. In 1904 he won the Nobel Prize for his work on the physiology of the canine digestive system. Later on, Pavlov switched his research to experimental studies concerned with the way animals learn. These famous studies are now termed *classical conditioning*. At the time of his original research with dogs, Pavlov had noticed that they would sometimes salivate when no food was present. This would occur, for example, when an assistant, who normally brought their food, approached with a container. Dogs usually salivate at the taste of food, and this response is known as an *unconditioned reflex*. However, the dogs which Pavlov was observing had started to salivate in anticipation of eating, and Pavlov reasoned that some mechanism in their brain was the cause. In order to find out more about this mechanism, he devoted the rest of his life to research on the subject.

It seemed clear to Pavlov that the dogs in his experiments had learned to associate the sight and sound of the approaching assistant with the expectation of food and eating, and this expectation, in turn, triggered the reflex of salivation. He devised an experiment which involved attaching a container to each of the harnessed dogs, so that the amount of saliva they secreted could be measured exactly. In the first part of his experiment, Pavlov confirmed that when food was placed in a dog's mouth the dog would salivate, but it would not salivate at the sound of a ringing bell, although it clearly heard the bell and showed some interest in it. In the second part of the experiment, Pavlov rang the bell first, and then placed some food in the dog's mouth. This pairing sequence was repeated many times. Finally, the bell was rung and the dog salivated in response, even when no food was presented. It thus became obvious that the bell alone was now capable of eliciting the response of salivation (*see* Fig. 6.1).

CLASSICAL CONDITIONING

What Pavlov demonstrated by his experiment was that the dogs he worked with had *learned* to associate the bell with food and this, in turn, caused them to salivate. This kind of learning is often referred to as *associative learning* and is present not just in animals but in humans as well. A small baby quickly learns when one event follows another. When, for example, a baby sees a bottle of milk she associates this with the taste of milk, and the subsequent satisfaction of drinking it. Many human responses can be classically conditioned, especially emotional responses, and again experimental evidence for this has been achieved through research with animals. If a cat is placed in a cage and subjected to mild electric shocks preceeded by the

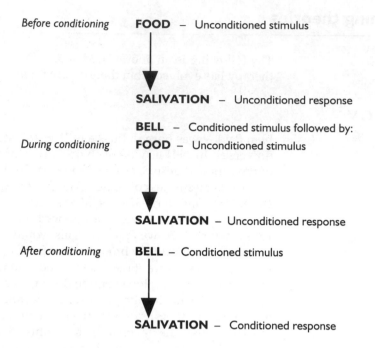

Fig. 6.1 *Classical conditioning.*

sound of a bell, one probable outcome is that the cat will demonstrate fear reactions as soon as the bell is rung. Repeated pairing of the bell with the electric shocks will condition the cat to fear the bell even when no electric shock is administered. The process whereby the *conditioned stimulus* (bell) produces the *conditioned response* (fear) in the cat is called *acquisition*. Conditioned responses may vary in strength and some are easier than others to acquire. Children often develop fear responses to dentists, for example, and the strength of the fear will be determined by the pairing of the conditioned stimulus (the dentist) and the unconditioned stimulus (discomfort or pain of treatment). If the discomfort or pain felt by the child is substantial, then the sight of a dentist is likely to lead to a fairly intense conditioned response of fear.

Pavlov believed that the association which occurs in classical conditioning, between the conditioned and the unconditioned stimuli, was related to the fact that they occurred in close juxtaposition with very little time lapse in between. What has been found through further research and experience, however, is that even when there is substantial delay between the two, conditioning can still take place. Taste aversion is one example of this phenomenon, when the conditioned stimulus (food) is followed, perhaps twelve hours later, by the unconditioned stimulus (nausea and vomiting). The person who suffers a severe attack like this may develop an aversion to the particular food which caused it, which indicates that stimulus proximity is not essential to produce classical conditioning.

VARIATIONS

Conditioned responses can change over time, and people (as well as animals) learn to react differently to their changing environment. The following are some of the ways in which conditioned responses vary.

Stimulus generalization refers to the way in which a conditioned response may occur when a stimulus, which is similar to the original one, is used. The strength of the conditioned response in this case will depend on the similarity of the new stimulus to the original one. This phenomenon has both advantages and disadvantages in terms of adaptive value; a person who becomes ill as a result of eating a particular kind of fish which is off, may steer clear, in future, of any fish which smells or tastes suspicious. This avoidance will ensure that a repeat attack of food poisoning does not occur, but carried to extremes, avoidance of food is clearly maladaptive in terms of human survival.

Stimulus discrimination is what enables both animals and humans to differentiate between one kind of stimulus and another. The person who avoids fish which smells or tastes suspicious, will not normally refuse all forms of protein as a result of a nasty experience. Similarly a mother who acts at once to comfort her crying child, will not usually extend her response to every crying child. Pavlov's dogs learned to discriminate between different bells, and they only salivated in response to the bell originally used to condition them.

Stimulus extinction. A response which is not at least occasionally reinforced will eventually stop. In one of Pavlov's experiments a bell was repeatedly sounded, but no food was given to the dogs. After a while, the strength of their conditioned response began to diminish, and later on salivation stopped. The amount of saliva had decreased steadily when the number of unreinforced trials was increased. The eventual elimination of response is known as *extinction*. However, it is possible to re-establish a conditioned response by once again pairing the conditioned and unconditioned stimuli, and this response is referred to as *reconditioning*.

Spontaneous recovery of a response can occur even when a learned response has been 'extinguished'. This happens when the conditioned stimulus is presented after some time. The dog whose response had disappeared will suddenly salivate when it hears the bell, and this would indicate that it still retains some residual expectation of food. An interesting point in connection with this is that the conditioned response will be stronger when there is a substantial time gap between extinction and the reappearance of the conditioned stimulus. Extinction will once more occur, however, unless the unconditioned stimulus is again paired with the conditioned stimulus.

J.B. WATSON

J.B. Watson, a US professor of psychology, is often referred to as the 'father of behaviourism'. This title is appropriate in many ways because his interest was focused on the study of pure behaviour, and not on mental processes. Watson believed that learning took place through the simple association of two things repeatedly occurring in sequence. In order for learning to occur, therefore, an association or connection must be made, and it must be renewed at intervals which are fairly close together. Watson and Pavlov were engaged in experiments at roughly the same time, one in the USA, the other in Russia. There are similarities between their research, but an interesting point of difference is the attempts which Watson made to apply his conditioning experiments to humans as well as to animals. In one particular experiment, Watson conditioned a child to fear a white rat by frightening the child with a loud noise each time the child played with the animal. After a while, the child displayed fear of the rat even when the loud noise was omitted. This conditioned fear response was also extended by the child to other non-animal objects, like furry toys and fur coats. Obviously, it is not possible to conduct extensive experiments like this with humans, but from the work which has been done it seems clear that many emotional reactions like phobias, for example, are the result of conditioning which can be subsequently unconditioned.

EDWARD LEE THORNDIKE

At the beginning of the twentieth century another US psychologist named Thorndike was conducting studies which were concerned with problem solving in animals. As part of his experiments, Thorndike had designed a puzzle box in which he placed a cat, and later on other small animals. The problem for the cat was how to escape and reach the food which had been placed outside the box. A catch on the box could be released once the cat stepped on a lever which pulled a piece of string to which the lever was attached. After this the door of the box would open (see Fig. 6.2). Several trials later, the cat was able to manipulate the catch and escape fairly quickly. Thorndike noticed that the cat became more adept at the task as time went on, so that after about twenty trials it was able to escape almost immediately.

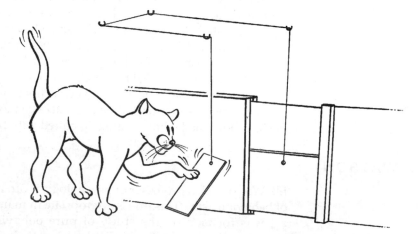

Fig. 6.2 *Thorndike's puzzle box.*

In view of these findings, Thorndike formulated what came to be known as the *law of effect*. The cat's learning was governed by this law, which states that if a response to a particular stimulus is followed by a reward, then that response will be repeated when the stimulus is met. Thorndike observed that the cat which he used in the experiment had made a great many random responses when it was first placed in the box, but eventually, and inadvertently, it stepped on the lever and thus released the catch of the door. This response of pulling the string was rewarded with pleasant consequences (i.e. escape), so the cat repeated the sequence over and over again. There is no evidence to suggest that the cat *understood* what it was doing, but it certainly did *learn* to escape from the box.

OPERANT CONDITIONING AND B. F. SKINNER

Another US psychologist named Burrhus Frederic Skinner (1904–90) extended and elaborated Thorndike's ideas many years after they were first published in the 1930s. Skinner based his work on Thorndike's law of effect and introduced the term *reinforcement* to describe the reward which makes the animal repeat the response. Reinforcement, in other words, increases the likelihood that the animal – or individual – will behave in a certain way. Skinner also used the term *operant conditioning* to describe the process of learning responses, because the responses are learned as a result of the animal or individual *operating* on the environment.

Skinner's operant conditioning differs significantly from the Pavlovian procedure in the sense that, in Skinner's experiments, it is the animal's own behaviour which determines whether the unconditioned stimulus is given. In other words, the animal is much more active than the animals used by Pavlov and Watson. Although operant conditioning has been used for hundreds of years by animal trainers, the process had not been clearly understood or analysed before Skinner conducted his experiments.

POSITIVE REINFORCEMENT – STRENGTHENS BEHAVIOUR

Skinner described two main types of reinforcers: positive and negative. *Positive reinforcers* are rewards which are given each time the animal gives the correct response to a stimulus. This positive reinforcer is usually in the form of food. Where people are concerned, money, comfort, affection and praise, as well as food, can act as positive reinforcers.

NEGATIVE REINFORCEMENT – STRENGTHENS BEHAVIOUR

Negative reinforcement involves the removal of an unpleasant stimulus once the correct response has been made. A person may learn, for example, that migraine headache is relieved through taking analgesic tablets. The successful relief of pain will increase the likelihood that the same response of taking analgesics will be repeated in the future. In a similar way, someone else might discover that boredom is relieved through socializing and activity, and if boredom is indeed banished in this way, then the same response to it will be made in the future. In these two examples, reinforcement occurs when something which the person (or, in the original experiments, the animal) does not want, is removed. Negative reinforcement is quite different from punishment, although it is sometimes confused with it.

Punishment is regarded by most learning theorists as a poor method of changing behaviour. Skinner considered it to be ineffective and even harmful. Punishment, which can be either verbal or physical, does tend to remove the likelihood that certain types of behaviour will be repeated, but it does not replace the undesirable response with a desirable one. The use of reinforcement to increase desirable behaviour is preferable to the use of punishment which has so many unfortunate side effects, including stress, anxiety and aggression. Punishment does, however, weaken undesirable behaviour and makes it less probable.

REINFORCEMENT SCHEDULES

It is not always the case that a reinforcer is given each time a particular response occurs. Skinner was concerned to study and experiment with various reinforcement schedules, and as a result five possible ways of reinforcing have been identified:

- *Continuous reinforcement schedule.* When a reinforcer is given, every time a response occurs it is called a 'continuous reinforcement schedule'. The response rate will progress at a slow, but steady pace.

- *Fixed-ratio schedule (FR).* Here the reinforcement is given after a certain number of responses. A cat might be given food, for example, after every sixth jump (FR6) or after every tenth (FR10). A car assembly worker might be paid an extra fifty pounds for every ten cars he helps to assemble.

- *Variable ratio schedule (VR).* Here the number of responses needed for reinforcement varies. The cat might be reinforced after ten jumps, then later on after twenty, and so on, with the number constantly changing. However, an average number of responses will be reinforced; on a VR40 the cat would be reinforced, on average, after every forty jumps.

- *Fixed-interval schedule (FI).* In this case, the reinforcement is given for the next response which occurs after a certain amount of time has elapsed since the last. On an FI20 schedule, the first response which occurs after twenty seconds have passed will be rewarded. This is like being paid weekly or monthly, for example.

- *Variable-interval schedule (VI).* In this last case, reinforcements are given at various intervals. The first response which is made, after perhaps thirty seconds, is reinforced, but the next reinforcement might be given after fifteen seconds, or sixty. Although reinforcement is given on average, perhaps every forty seconds, the intervals are essentially unpredictable. This is similar to the situation which obtains for many self-employed people who receive payment from customers on a fairly irregular basis.

PATTERNS OF RESPONSE

When reinforcement is given on a fixed-ratio schedule, a high rate of response will follow. This explains why production workers in industry are frequently paid on a piecework basis, according to the number of articles they produce. On a variable-ratio schedule, where reinforcement is random and unpredictable, a high rate of response is generated. Variable-ratio schedules are particularly resistant to extinction and the best example of human behaviour that operates on a variable-ratio schedule is gambling. On a variable-interval schedule, where the interval during which reinforcement is given changes from one occasion to another, a steady rate of response will follow, although the rate is not nearly so high as that produced on a variable-ratio schedule. However, a variable-interval schedule is also resistant to extinction.

EXTINCTION

The very high and steady response rate which is provided on a variable-ratio schedule is difficult to eliminate through extinction. The reason for this seems to be that the animal never quite knows when it is going to be reinforced again. In the case of human behaviour, the same principle applies, so that the gambler is kept in a permanent state of anticipation and hope, believing that he might just be lucky the next time round. It is possible to extinguish certain kinds of human behaviour, for example temper tantrums in children, by consistently ignoring it. After a certain period of non-reinforcement, the temper tantrums will eventually diminish and then disappear. What tends to happen in reality, however, is that the temper tantrum behaviour is reinforced by parents when they give the child attention, by trying to reason with him. If this is done occasionally, the child's behaviour will be even more difficult to control, since it will have been reinforced on a partial variable-ratio or variable-interval schedule. The general rule is that behaviour which has been learned under a partial reinforcement schedule is more difficult to extinguish than behaviour learned on a continuous reinforcement schedule. When reinforcement is unpredictable, extinction takes longer to occur.

SHAPING

Shaping describes the process whereby any response which is similar to the desired one is rewarded. Skinner and his colleagues taught pigeons to play table tennis by reinforcing their first attempts to move the ball across the table, and then by progressively reinforcing their attempts as they gradually improved. These experiments were surprisingly successful, in the sense that the pigeons learned quickly. Similar attempts were carried out with other animals with the same high degree of success. What is evident from the work that Skinner and his colleagues did, is that it is possible to shape behaviour in animals even when that kind of behaviour is not within the animal's usual repertoire of skills. Shaping is successfully used in human behaviour as well, and can be seen in the many areas of learning and teaching, including child rearing, school experience, sport and work. In all these activities, learning is guided through a gradual process of reinforcement for each attempt to reach the desired level of achievement.

SECONDARY REINFORCEMENT

Anything which is related to basic physiological needs is referred to as a *primary* reinforcer. Thus, water, food and sex are examples of primary reinforcers. Most of the reinforcers used in animal learning are primary reinforcers. Another category of reinforcers exists, however; these are referred to as *secondary* and are developed through association with primary reinforcers. Money is perhaps the best example of a secondary reinforcer for humans since it represents much more than coins and banknotes. It is the means whereby people acquire a whole range of primary reinforcers. Money and tokens have also been successfully conditioned as secondary reinforcers with monkeys and chimpanzees. Tokens are also used in behaviour modification to reinforce behaviour, and their value lies in the fact they can be used as currency to obtain concessions or privileges. Secondary reinforcers are essentially rewards which animals and people have learned to like. Even forms of social approval such as smiling are examples of secondary reinforcers for humans.

CONCLUSION

Some understanding of the principles of classical and operant conditioning is essential for students who are interested in working as behavioural counsellors. The work done by Pavlov, Thorndike and Skinner has given scientific validity to theories of learning which had never been tested before, and as a result of this we now know much more about the importance of reinforcement, for example. This has direct implications for the modification of objectionable behaviour, and for the establishment of more desirable forms of behaviour, both of which are important goals in behavioural counselling.

Social learning theory and observational learning

ALBERT BANDURA

In common with the behavioural psychologists, social learning theorists accept that children learn according to the principles of reinforcement and punishment. Social learning theorists differ significantly, however, from Pavlov, Watson and Skinner, in the sense that they do not regard the concepts of classical and operant conditioning as sufficient explanation for all learning. According to the social learning theorists, children also learn from the experiences of others, mainly through observation and imitation. A young child who observes that his playmates are rewarded when they behave in a certain way, is likely to imitate their behaviour. In the same way, a child who sees other children punished for misdemeanours, is unlikely to engage in similar behaviour. In both these examples, the children have learned associations, even though the events described have not happened to them personally. This kind of conditioning is described as 'vicarious'. In a number of experiments conducted in the 1960s, Albert Bandura, Professor of Psychology at Stanford University, California was able to show that when groups of children watched a film in which an adult attacked a Bobo doll, the children responded by imitating the behaviour which they saw rewarded. The film had three endings: in the first one, the adult was rewarded verbally by another adult and was also given sweets; in the second ending, the aggressive adult was punished by scolding and smacking; the final ending depicted a scene in which there was neither reward nor punishment. Bandura and his colleagues encouraged the children to play with the doll afterwards, and discovered that imitation of the aggressive behaviour was greatest among those children who had seen the adult being rewarded. As well as this, Bandura found that the children who were affected in this way by the film, were also disposed to be more aggressive generally as a result, and not just in relation to the doll.

The experiments which Bandura conducted, support the idea that learning can take place through *vicarious conditioning*. They also indicate that *observational learning*, i.e. learning new behaviours by watching the behaviour of others, is also likely to occur. A group of children who were shown the film version in which the aggressive adult was *not* rewarded, also acted aggressively when they were afterwards left alone with the doll. This was a group of children who were given no vicarious reward, in the form of either praise or sweets, so their behaviour seems to suggest that children will learn to imitate an adult (or others) even when there is no obvious reason for them to do so. On the other hand, those children who watched the film version in which the aggressive adult was punished, tended not to imitate what they had witnessed, though when bribed by sweets to do so, they were willing to perform the aggressive acts they had seen.

Although Bandura's experiments have been criticized – on the grounds that people are seldom rewarded for aggressive behaviour in real life – his work, overall, does seem to suggest that children are influenced by the behaviour of others, and that they are especially influenced by those people who are most important to them, and who show them affection and warmth. Obviously, those people who are closest to children are parents, relatives and teachers, and children will model their behaviour on them, even when no reinforcement is given. In many ways, learning by observation and imitation is more efficient than learning by trial and error, and many of the complex skills which children are required to learn, such as language, are partially accomplished through a process of observational learning and modelling. However, Bandura's theory of observational learning does not take into sufficient account the active part that children take in their own learning process. Children do not just copy what they see other people doing; whereas one child might imitate behaviour he has seen on television, another may choose to ignore it.

Bandura's original theories have been supplemented by his description of the four requirements which he regards as necessary if observational learning is to take place. These requirements are:

- *Attention,* without which no one can learn;

- *Retention,* which is essential if observed behaviour is to be remembered;

- *Ability to reproduce* the behaviour; and

- *Motivation* or a good reason to perform the act.

Bandura's work on observational learning is important in the context of behavioural counselling since he has highlighted the significance of modelling in the development, maintenance and modification of human behaviour.

JOSEPH WOLPE

In 1958, Joseph Wolpe, a South African psychiatrist, pioneered the development of procedures which could be used to relieve fears, stress and anxiety which had been created through classical conditioning. Wolpe's original work focused on the treatment of neuroses in animals; by producing fear reactions in them similar to phobias, he was able to show that a process of *systematic desensitization* could then be used to eliminate the fears. This form of treatment is now widely used in behavioural psychotherapy for the treatment of phobias and other irrational forms of anxiety, and will be described in more detail later in this chapter. In order to facilitate the process of systematic desensitization, Wolpe also used a technique called *progressive relaxation training,* which was designed to help clients overcome anxiety during treatment. In 1958, his book *Psychotherapy by Reciprocal Inhibition* was published, and served to highlight the contribution which his work was making to behavioural therapy generally.

HANS J. EYSENCK

Hans J. Eysenck is perhaps best known for his *Critique of the Psychoanalytic Approach in Therapy* (1952). Born in Germany, he later moved to France and finally settled in Britain where he became Senior Psychologist at the Maudsley Hospital in London. During the early 1950s he was appointed Professor of Psychology at the University of London. Eysenck disputed the effectiveness of psychotherapy and put forward the view that a large number of people who suffer from neurotic problems improve in the long term, regardless of whether or not they receive therapy. His criticism helped to focus attention on the work being done by clinical psychologists, work which had previously been almost ignored. These psychologists were making increasing contributions to the treatment of emotional problems, and during the 1960s their efforts were gradually recognized and further developments in behaviour therapy evolved, particularly at the Maudsley Hospital.

KEY WORDS

BEHAVIOURISM

This is the study of behaviour based on observable actions and reactions. Behaviourism focuses on analysing the relationship between behaviour and the environment and on the way that stimuli provoke responses. The benefit of this approach is that it is scientific, and does not rely on guesswork in order to arrive at a diagnosis or assessment.

BEHAVIOURAL PSYCHOLOGY

The aims of behaviour psychology are to study behaviour under scientific conditions, and to examine the influence of environmental factors in determining behaviour.

BEHAVIOUR THERAPY

Behaviour therapy is also sometimes referred to as 'behaviour modification'. Behaviour therapy uses treatments based on learning principles to help clients change from problem behaviour to more healthy ways of functioning. The approach involves teaching clients, through a variety of techniques, to act as well as to think differently. The term was first used by Skinner, but is also closely associated with Wolpe and Eysenck. Many of the behavioural techniques, especially those which have been developed during the past few years, emphasize cognitive processes and in doing so highlight the place of subjective experience (the person's thoughts and attitudes) in counselling and therapy.

The Model

The idea that behaviour is learned, can be unlearned and is not determined by instinctual drives, has separated the behaviourist and Freudian approaches in psychology, although there is some indication that this rigid division is now less marked. Procedures and techniques which have their origin in behaviourism are now being incorporated into various models of counselling and psychotherapy, and clients are increasingly encouraged to become more active in therapy, and to participate in the observation and measurement of their own behavioural change. Closer links have been established between behaviour therapy and the other models, including person-centered counselling, Gestalt, transactional analysis and rational-emotive counselling. This is not to say that these models have abandoned the theoretical principles upon which they were founded. However, many of their therapists and counsellors are now willing to use techniques which have proven effective in behavioural counselling and psychotherapy, as part of their repertoire of skills.

In the person-centered model of counselling, human behaviour is believed to be motivated by an innate drive towards growth and wholeness. Disturbed behaviour is seen as an indication that growth is blocked, either through lack of awareness, or distorted perceptions, or both. The aim of counselling is therefore to help clients to re-establish their natural growth processes, and the relationship between counsellor and client is based on equality. The counsellor is not seen as an expert, but rather as someone who is there to help create the right conditions for growth to take place. In the psychodynamic approach, behaviour is thought to be governed by repressed unconscious thought and by the ego's attempts to deal with psychic conflict which is caused by the pressure of living. Behaviour can be functional or dysfunctional, depending on the way the individual deals with this conflict. An important focus of psychodynamic counselling is to help the client achieve insight, and to recognize, understand and deal with the thoughts and emotions which cause his problems.

The behavioural approach to counselling emphasizes a very different kind of therapy. Behaviourism asserts that psychology should be much more scientific, should rely less on subjective experience and introspection, and should study people's *actual* behaviour instead of the supposed instinctual causes of it. Clients are encouraged to view their problems as learned behaviours which can be unlearned, without any recourse to prolonged analysis of motives and reasons.

The behavioural model is closely linked to the principles of learning examined earlier in this chapter. Although the original experiments were carried out on animals, later experiments focused on human behaviour. Perhaps the best known of these experiments was the one carried out by Watson and Rayner in 1920, on the child called Albert, who was conditioned to fear a white rat and later on various objects including furry toys. In other words, Albert had developed a phobia, and as a result of their work Watson and Rayner were able to show how emotional responses could be conditioned, then later unconditioned. Much later, in 1958, Wolpe published his book *Psychotherapy by Reciprocal Inhibition*, giving details of the work he was doing in his clinical practice on the subject of neurotic fear responses. It was largely during the 1950s and 1960s that the behavioural approach to therapy and counselling became firmly established.

VIEW OF THE PERSON

Behavioural counselling is based on a scientific approach to human behaviour. Disordered behaviour is seen as evidence of the dysfunctional thoughts and actions which clients have learned to use in different situations. These disordered thoughts and actions which have previously been learned, and which produce problems for people, can be clarified or solved through the provision of new learning experiences.

THE CLIENT–COUNSELLOR RELATIONSHIP

The emphasis on a strictly scientific approach can sometimes give the impression that behavioural counselling is soulless or non-caring, but this is certainly not the case. As in other forms of counselling, a good client-counsellor relationship is regarded as essential if progress is to take place. The health and wellbeing of the client is of paramount importance in the therapeutic endeavour, and behavioural counsellors are concerned to facilitate clients' growth, development, self-control and ability to cope effectively within their environment. When a good therapeutic relationship has been established, clients are more likely to feel confident, to explain their problems coherently, and to cooperate fully with therapeutic goals and procedures. The current trend in behavioural counselling seeks to give more control to clients in order to increase their freedom of choice as well as their ability to make effective choices. Past experience is regarded as relevant, only in so far as it influences present behaviour. For this reason, behavioural counsellors are not concerned to dwell on past or childhood events; instead, they are more interested in looking at current difficulties, especially those which are of great concern to the client.

There is no deliberate effort to establish an empathic relationship in the Rogerian sense, as this would be considered unnecessary in the behavioural counselling relationship. Warmth is not excluded, but clear communication is seen as more important, as is careful listing of the behaviours to be changed, and the treatment goals to be reached. Perhaps the most significant aspect of behavioural counselling, and the one which separates it from other models, is its strict adherence to measurement, recording and specification of problems and goals. Behavioural principles and procedures which have been scientifically tested, are openly stated and frequently revised, as and when revision is needed. Each client is seen as a unique individual with individual needs; techniques and procedures are adapted to meet those needs. There is a definite educational direction in behavioural counselling, and clients are taught skills which enable them to manage their lives more effectively. No psychodiagnosis is used, so that clients are not labelled as alcoholic or manic depressive, for example. Instead the counsellor seeks to uncover and help change the emotions, thoughts and behaviours which underpin these conditions. Research is an important feature of behavioural counselling, and is constantly taking place so that the whole approach is essentially dynamic and progressive.

By looking directly at observable responses, counsellors who use this approach believe there is less likelihood that they will make false assumptions about their clients' behaviour. Each 'symptom' which a client shows has been learned through a process of conditioning, and can, in turn, be dealt with or modified through the use of methods and techniques which are based on knowledge of learning theory. In other words, any learning which has developed through association and which produces problems for a client, can be removed through the application of the same principles.

CENTRAL AIMS

The client's ability to exercise control over his environment is the basic aim of the behavioural model of counselling. Control of the environment includes satisfactory adjustment to the norms of society, as well as satisfactory work and leisure experience, good relationships with other people and the ability to sustain intimate and sexual relationships. When a client's behaviour or activity is restrictive, the goal of behavioural counselling is to alter it, and to do so in a fairly short space of time. A range of methods and techniques is used to achieve this, and these are all designed to focus on the central problem and to deal with it in a straightforward and directive way. Once restrictive behaviour has been altered, other dimensions of the client's experience can be considered too. Even though there is no emphasis on an in-depth review of the client's past, there is certainly no prohibition of it either. Respect and consideration of the client's needs are fundamental prerequisites of the behavioural approach in counselling.

In order to achieve the central aims of the behavioural model, client and counsellor must always work together, and should reach agreement on specific goals. Any behaviour problems which are presented by the client should be clearly defined by him and related to the particular situations in which they occur. It is not enough, for example, for a client to say that he is 'highly anxious'. He needs to say clearly what situations specifically make him anxious. Motivation to work towards change is essential for clients to succeed, and a commitment to work, through homework and other assignments, is necessary as well. Although counselling is usually carried out on an individual basis, it can be used effectively in groups too. In many ways, behavioural group counselling is more effective than individual counselling, especially when clients' problems include difficulties in social relationships. The amount of feedback which is provided in a group is invaluable for clients who might not be able to get this experiential practice elsewhere.

THE INITIAL PHASE

The initial phase of the behavioural model of counselling involves gaining an overall picture of the client's problems so that an individual action plan can be formulated. This assessment of the client's problems will take place during the first interview with the counsellor. A good counsellor–client relationship based on respect and openness is also dependent on the initial rapport which is established at this time.

Behaviours which are problematic for the client need to be identified and related to the situations in which they occur, as well as to their physical, emotional and other effects on the client. The way the client reacts in particular situations is especially significant. If a client is frightened, for example, what does he do and what does he think? When did the client first experience the problem, and what happened in order to prompt it? What happened immediately following the experience and how long did it last? It is important to establish how frequently the problem behaviour occurs, and the factors which either exacerbate or relieve it. The effect that the problem has on the client's family and social relationship is an important consideration, so is the effect on his work and his lifestyle. The counselling skills of listening attentively, paraphrasing, summarizing, asking questions and focusing, are all essential in the behavioural model of counselling, as well as the ability to take rapid and unobtrusive notes in order to build up a detailed picture of the problems which the client describes.

GOALS

Once the initial assessment of the client's problems has been made, specific behavioural goals should be considered by both the client and the counsellor, and strategies developed to enable the client to deal with the problems. The client needs to understand the purpose of the goals, and also needs to be committed to them. For the client to be committed in this way, a contract should be made between him and the counsellor, and the changes which he wants to make should be clearly set out. Goals should be realistic and achievable, and should not be imposed by the counsellor. Negotiation between client and counsellor is important if the client is to feel that he has power to effect change for himself. When all the information about goals has been discussed, they should be clearly and correctly defined, and a plan of action to work towards them should be set up.

It is important to remember that clients who are suffering from severe psychological illness like depression are unlikely to be able to take part in the process of assessment and goal-setting. This is because their thought processes have been impaired as a result of the illness. The same is also true of those clients who are under the influence of alcohol or drugs. Behavioural counselling *can* be effective with clients who have a history of addiction, but it cannot usefully begin until withdrawal from addictive substances is, at least, in progress.

When goals are agreed upon by client and counsellor, a firm decision should be made by both either to continue working together or to consider alternative forms of therapy. It is necessary to do this because there are some people, especially those with severe depression or the kinds of addictive problems mentioned above, who do not benefit from behavioural counselling.

IMPLEMENTATION
OF GOALS

The methods and techniques used in behavioural counselling are always tailored to meet the needs of individual clients. Although behavioural counsellors are often described as active and directive, it is nevertheless also true that their main concern is to treat the client as a unique person whose welfare and cooperation are of paramount importance. The therapeutic techniques and procedures which are used, therefore, are not just randomly selected, but are carefully considered in the light of their proven effectiveness and their suitability for each client. Occasionally a procedure or technique may be used which proves to be ineffective for a particular client; when this happens the situation is reviewed, and a more appropriate direction is then taken. There is a wide range of therapeutic procedures and techniques available for behavioural counsellors to use, but it is possible for counsellors to be innovative in their approach, as long as they observe the principle that whatever is used must be appropriate for individual client needs.

RELAXATION METHODS

In the behavioural model of counselling, relaxation procedures are sometimes used along with other procedures, in particular with *systematic desensitization*, which will be described later. However, relaxation methods are also effective when used in isolation, especially for the treatment of anxiety and tension. Relaxation training also helps clients to cope with stress, but the ongoing practice of exercises is important if treatment is to be truly effective.

The progressive muscular and mental relaxation which is achieved through relaxation training is fairly easy to learn, though it does require both time and commitment on the part of the client. Initially, clients need to be seated in a comfortable position, preferably in a room where extraneous noise and interruption are excluded. The counsellor should explain the nature of the procedure to the client beforehand, and should also help the client to view it as a coping skill which can be used in a variety of anxiety- or stress-producing situations.

A starting point for most relaxation methods is a focus on the muscles of the body. The counsellor talks the client through the stages, asking him to alternatively contract and relax each muscle group. As well as this, the client is asked to breath deeply in a regular rhythm, and to focus on images which are pleasant and relaxing. If the procedure is carried out correctly, the client should experience a marked difference between the build-up of tension in his muscles and the subsequent pleasure of releasing it. Some clients find it more difficult than others to achieve deep relaxation, but

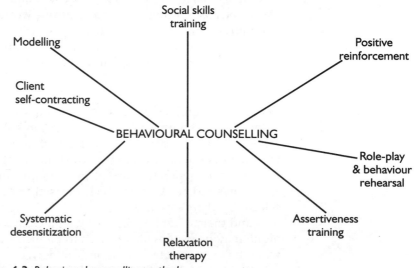

Fig. 6.3 *Behavioural counselling methods.*

with practice of, say, thirty minutes per day, it can become a learned response to various situations which have been problematic in the past. People who suffer from high blood pressure have found relaxation methods useful, and persistent headaches and insomnia have also been reduced when relaxation has been regularly practised.

SYSTEMATIC DESENSITIZATION

Systematic desensitization was based by Wolpe on classical conditioning techniques, and it is now widely used in behavioural counselling to enable clients to deal with irrational forms of anxiety and phobias. Wolpe believed that anxiety responses are learned or conditioned, and that they can be eliminated if the fearful person is kept calm and comfortable while being exposed gradually to whatever caused the anxiety in the first place. Pro-

Fig. 6.4 *Anxiety responses are learned or conditioned.*

gressive relaxation is used as an integral part of the treatment, so that clients learn a procedure which is incompatible with anxiety. After this, the fear-provoking object or situation is introduced, usually by asking the client to imagine it, and over a period of time the exposure becomes gradually more intense. Eventually, unpleasant experiences like fears and phobias become associated with the comfort of relaxation, until they are extinguished totally. Clients are not asked to endure too much anxiety at once, as a *desensitization hierarchy* is used where increasingly fear-provoking stimuli are presented over a period of time.

The following is an example of a desensitization hierarchy which was used with a client who had a phobia about birds. The client was asked to work through the hierarchy of fear-provoking situations, gradually imagining each scene. Moving from one scene to the next was done only when the client felt able to proceed without distress.

1. You are reading a magazine and you notice a picture of a bird.

2. You are watching the news on television when an item about birds appears.

3. You are walking down the street when you notice some birds flying overhead.

4. You are walking in the country when a flock of birds fly overhead.

5. You pass a pet shop where some birds are displayed in the window.

6. You visit a friend who has a pet bird in a cage in her sitting room.

7. You are standing beside the birdcage looking at the bird.

8. You visit the local zoo and watch all the birds in the aviary.

9. You stand close to the birdcages and listen to the noises the birds are making.

10. You watch the birds fly around in the cages.

11. You visit your friend with the pet bird and you touch its feathers.

12. You watch your friend opening the door of the birdcage.

13. You watch as the bird moves out of the birdcage.

14. You watch as the bird flies across the room.

When clients can stay calm and imagine themselves in fearful situations, they become more capable of dealing with them when they happen. Clients need to be involved with the design of the anxiety hierarchy, and it should be arranged that the least fear-provoking situation is presented first. It is important that the client gives a detailed history of his phobia beforehand, and special attention should be focused on those aspects of the phobia stimulus which influence the degree of anxiety it evokes. In the example of the bird phobia given above, it was the quick, unexpected movements of birds which disturbed the client most. During the first session it is a useful plan to find out just how rapidly and vividly the client is able to imagine each scene in the hierarchy and, more importantly, how he feels during the process. Deep relaxation should be maintained throughout subsequent sessions so that the desensitization itself does not acquire anxiety-producing properties. If a new item in the hierarchy repeatedly produces anxiety, items which were previously mastered should be re-presented. At the end of each session, the client should feel relaxed, and for this reason it is a good idea to end with an easy item. Certainly, no session should conclude while a client is feeling anxious, since in any learning series the last item is well retained, and any anxiety associated with it will take a long time to extinguish.

It is sometimes possible for people to treat their own phobias through the use of tape recordings or even self-help manuals. A person who is afraid of public speaking, for example, can undertake his own desensitization programme at home. Although it is often carried out in imagination alone, desensitization can also take place in reality, and this can prove particularly effective. However, this process is time-consuming, since the exposure to anxiety-evoking stimuli is very gradual; a client with agoraphobia, for example, will need to get used to walking down his own garden path before he ventures into a large shopping complex. People who do not respond to systematic desensitization in imagination, may respond to it in a real-life situation where practical retraining is used. There are, however, obvious difficulties in arranging graded stimuli in real-life. Certain phobias, such as thunder and lightening, are impossible to deal with in this way. When the phobia stimulus can be brought into the counselling session, successful desensitization to an imagined stimulus can be followed at once by presentation of the real stimulus. One client who had a fear of feathers was able to overcome his phobia in this way.

MODELLING

Modelling, or observational learning, can be used to help clients acquire new behaviour patterns. Through imitation of the desired qualities of someone else, clients can also deal more effectively with anxiety and develop social skills. Desensitization can be made more effective, for example, when the counsellor actually shows the client how to behave calmly in fearful situations. Modelling can take place either live or on videotape, and it is also sometimes combined with role-play. When clients see someone else behaving non-anxiously in a situation which provokes intolerable anxiety for them, the effect is to reduce the level of their fear and encourage them to imitate the model's behaviour.

Participant modelling refers to a process whereby live modelling is combined with gradual client practice. A counsellor can, for example, show a client how to behave calmly in a feared situation such as walking into a crowded room. The client can see quite clearly that the counsellor is relaxed and calm and that no harm has befallen her as a result of her action. Afterwards, the client can practise walking into a crowded room along with the counsellor, who acts as a guide. Gradually, the client should become more independent, and may then practise walking into the room while the counsellor simply observes him doing so. Eventually, the client's performance should become more self-directed and independent, so that he is finally able to walk into a crowded room on his own. Once clients have achieved this degree of independence, their confidence is heightened and their feeling of self-mastery helps to sustain the achievement. Modelling is based on the experimental findings of Bandura, and on the social or observational learning theory which he and his colleagues developed. Their work on conditioned emotional responses has shown that it is possible to help clients overcome phobias through a process of vicarious extinction. Clients who are afraid of cats, for example, can be helped to overcome this when they watch a model in a series of anxiety-producing situations, in which there is a gradual interaction with a cat. If clients are unable to master their fear through observation alone, however, they can be encouraged to participate slowly and gradually, in the model's interaction with the cat.

ASSERTIVENESS TRAINING

Assertiveness training aims to teach clients how to stand up for their rights and cope with life's challenges. The method reinforces positive attempts to deal with difficult situations (for example, dealing with angry or dissatisfied customers) while simultaneously reducing anxiety in those circumstances. Essentially, it is a procedure whereby clients are taught to interact more effectively and more comfortably with others, and in this respect it is a form of social-skills training. Assertiveness training can be done on an individual basis, or may be undertaken in groups. In many ways the group situation is an ideal forum for assertiveness training, since there are more people present and social interaction becomes more diverse. Modelling and role-play can be incorporated into both individual and group training. Clients who lack confidence in certain situations, such as work or social gatherings, can be taught to perfect the necessary skills through a process of repeated role-playing with a counsellor and/or other group members. Assertive responses are antagonistic to anxiety, so by practising these, clients not only become more effective communicators, they also reduce their own anxiety levels as a consequence. In recent years, assertiveness training has tended to become associated with women's groups only, but it is very effective for anyone who wishes to increase self-confidence, or for people who would like to become less passive or less aggressive. True assertiveness is not easy, especially for people who are habitually passive, so repeated practice in training is necessary if clients are to learn assertive responses.

POSITIVE REINFORCEMENT

Positive reinforcement is based on the application of Skinner's operant conditioning theory. Behavioural counsellors can use positive reinforcement to alter clients' dysfunctional behaviour. This is achieved through the systematic reinforcement of desired behaviour, while at the same time ignoring undesired behaviour which should eventually become extinct. Reinforcement procedures involve the strengthening of adaptive behaviour, and the elimination of non-adaptive behaviour. Reinforcers need to be identified for individual clients, and counsellors can do this by questioning clients and/or giving them questionnaires to complete. Various other aspects of the client's problem need to be clarified if counselling is to be really effective. These include:

- A precise definition of the behaviour which needs to be eliminated.

- A precise definition of each aspect of the behaviour to be increased.

- Identification of the factors which are reinforcing problem behaviour.

- Identification of the reinforcers which are applicable to individual clients.

When the behaviour which needs reinforcement is almost completely absent (for example in a client who is very passive), then each approximate response is reinforced by the counsellor. This method is based on Skinner's *behaviour shaping by successive approximations*, and it is used frequently in all aspects of everyday social interaction. Counsellors also use this approach in various models of counselling, since empathy, warmth, genuineness, praise, attention and listening, can all be viewed as methods of reinforcement for clients. In behavioural counselling, however, these methods may be used in an explicit way by the counsellor, when verbal comments like 'well done' are used with clients who have achieved some degree of success in specific areas.

In the behavioural model of counselling, clients can also be encouraged to identify and actively obtain their own reinforcers. This may involve increasing activities which are calming and pleasant, to replace behaviour which is maladaptive or dysfunctional. In fact, self-reinforcement, such as identifying and taking part in pleasant activities, should be an integral part of the counselling process, but clients sometimes need help in order to identify appropriate self-rewards. This is because people often lose sight of those aspects of living which give them true pleasure.

Self-contracting is another strategy which clients can use to help them follow through a successful plan of action. It involves consideration of all the variables which surround both adaptive and maladaptive behaviour, and a commitment to effective self-change. A behavioural diary is useful for those clients who want to monitor their own behaviour and increase self-awareness. When a particular behaviour (like smoking, for example) is recorded in terms of its occurrence and frequency, then a clearer picture of how to change should emerge.

TOKEN ECONOMY

This is a system for rewarding desired behaviour through the use of tokens which can be exchanged for privileges or gifts. The system has been used effectively with children in schools, with patients in hospitals and with prisoners. In order to develop a successful system of token economies, it may be necessary for counsellors to work with others outside the counselling situation, such as parents, teachers or nurses. However, when a group of people is involved in the process of therapy there is a danger that inconsistent information is given to clients, and there is the added danger that absolute confidentiality may become difficult to sustain. In any counselling situation, confidentiality is of paramount importance, and clients should always feel secure in the knowledge that this will be honoured.

FLOODING AND AVERSION THERAPY

Both flooding and aversion therapy are now seldom used with clients, except perhaps in a clinical or hospital setting. Aversion therapy is the use of punishment to remove an unwanted pattern of behaviour, such as drinking. One approach associates an emetic drug, or a mild electric shock with alcohol, over a period of time. Eventually, the drinker should develop an aversion to alcohol. Obviously, such a form of therapy raises certain ethical issues, along with theoretical and technical difficulties.

Flooding involves the client staying in the feared situation to experience all the anxiety which it evokes. Thus, a person with a fear of cats, for example, would be exposed to a situation where cats were actually present. Flooding requires maximum experience of anxiety on the client's part to cause it to be extinguished. There are certain situations in which flooding can be used successfully by clients themselves. One person who had a profound fear of snakes cured this himself by spending a whole day in the snake house at the local zoo.

Implosion therapy is a dramatic form of flooding in which the person is required to imagine the most terrifying situation he can think of. It has some resemblance to Wolpe's systematic desensitization, except that in implosion therapy there is no gradual exposure and no relaxation. In the first few sessions the client would be terrified, but later on his anxiety should diminish and then disappear.

CASE STUDY: JACKIE

Jackie was twenty years old when she came for counselling. She had suffered from a severe dog phobia since early childhood, and over the two years since she left home, her anxiety had become more marked. It had also become more socially inconvenient, since many of her new friends owned dogs – or their families did – and she found herself refusing to visit their homes because of this. Her GP, whom she had approached for advice, referred Jackie to a behavioural counsellor who agreed to see her at the local health centre the following week.

In common with many people who suffer from phobias, Jackie could remember the exact incident which triggered it off. At the age of three, she had been staying with her grandparents in the country when a large sheepdog jumped on her and knocked her over. As a result of this incident, she was kept overnight in hospital, and had to have stitches in her forehead. Over the years, her phobia had been reasonably well contained, because she simply avoided any situation which would bring her into close contact with a dog. She stayed well away from dogs in the street, and never visited people who owned them. Her father also disliked dogs, although his response to them was never phobic. However, he managed to convey to Jackie his antipathy towards them, and this served to confirm her deep fear which became exaggerated at times of stress. Since leaving home, her phobia had generalized to various animals, and even to pictures of dogs, and it was the incapacitating nature of these reactions which prompted her to seek help through counselling. When she thought about dogs she became anxious; her heart beat faster and she started to shake. She often became breathless and felt that she might lose control.

At the beginning of the first session with the counsellor, Jackie was nervous and apprehensive. The counsellor asked her to describe the problem she was experiencing and to say how often it occurred, how long it lasted, and whether it had changed in degree or intensity over the years. Jackie talked at length about her fear of dogs, and went on to assure the counsellor that she knew it was irrational since dogs did not objectively justify the anxiety she felt. The counsellor replied that she understood this, and after some further discussion about the subject, understanding and rapport were firmly established between client and counsellor. Jackie did not suffer from any other personal or health problems, and was not taking any drugs or medication which would have interfered with the effectiveness of the counselling process.

People often remember the incident which triggered the phobia.

In the behavioural model of counselling, the *initial assessment* of the client's problems is important since detailed and specific information needs to be obtained before planning and implementation of goals can be started. Assessment is also continuous throughout the sessions, so that procedures are carefully monitored and altered when necessary.

The counsellor listed the behaviours and thoughts which Jackie said she needed to change, and together they established the specific goals which she wished to achieve. These included:

- Being able to walk freely down the street without fear of meeting a dog.

- Being able to stay overnight with friends who own dogs.

- Being able to watch television programmes and read newspapers and magazines which feature dogs.

- Being able to think about dogs without anxiety or panic.

Since Jackie found herself increasingly handicapped by her phobia about dogs, she wanted to be free of it. In particular, she felt that her social relationships were suffering, and she was aware that this situation might worsen if she did not get treatment now. In the past, she had been shielded by her parents and her home life, but now that she was living and working away from home she felt that she could no longer tolerate her predicament. The counsellor could see that Jackie's commitment to treatment was strong, and that she was likely to work hard to achieve her goals. In view of this, the counsellor made a contract with Jackie to work together for eight sessions, and then to review the situation.

Jackie agreed to participate in a systematic desensitization procedure, and since the counsellor had explained this to her she knew exactly how it would work. At this stage, she was too anxious to undertake real life exposure, but agreed to try this later on once she had made some progress with imagined exposure. As part of her contract, Jackie had also agreed to carry out homework assignments which she would record in a diary and discuss with the counsellor at the beginning of each session. The first assignment involved going to the library each day to read books about dogs, and to spend time looking at pictures of them. Together, Jackie and the counsellor constructed a hierarchy of feared objects and situations in which the most frightening scene was placed at the top, and the least frightening at the bottom. In Jackie's case, the most frightening scene was one in which a large dog jumped up at her, and the least frightening involved looking at pictures of dogs.

Progressive relaxation was used by the counsellor to enable Jackie to become calm and comfortable. She also taught Jackie how to use the procedure herself so that she could practise at home with a prerecorded tape. Deep relaxation was maintained throughout the sessions so that Jackie was able to progress up the hierarchy towards the most frightening scene. Eventually, she was able to imagine a large dog approaching her, and at this stage she decided that she would like to expose herself to a real-life situation with a dog. Her best friend owned a dog, so it was arranged that she would spend two hours per day visiting her friend for the next week. Her friend was sympathetic and helpful, and since the dog was placid and old, it did not present any overwhelming threat to Jackie. She found that her anxiety level decreased towards the end of the week; she was able to touch the dog and did not even mind when he flopped down on the floor beside her chair. Some time later during a further session with the counsellor, she was able to imagine a playful dog jumping up at her, and to watch a video about Cruft's. At the end of eight weeks, Jackie was able to sit in a room with the counsellor who had brought along her own Labrador for the purpose of *modelling*. The counsellor petted the dog, and gradually Jackie was able to do the same.

Throughout her therapy programme, Jackie had conscientiously carried out and recorded her homework assignments. Through her reading activities at the library she had become something of an expert on different breeds of dogs, and was keen to discuss her newly acquired knowledge at counselling sessions. As a result of the visits to her friend's home, she found herself willing to socialize with other people too. The counsellor provided reinforcement through encouragement and praise. Jackie reported that she felt more confident generally, and that she no longer found herself thinking about dogs with fear and apprehension. At a review session with the counsellor she decided that she was sufficiently confident to finish counselling, but was keen to attend for a follow-up session three months later. When that time arrived, she had maintained her progress; her social life had improved enormously and although she said that she did not envisage owning one, dogs no longer exerted a negative influence in her life.

FURTHER READING

DRYDEN, W. (ed.), *Individual Therapy*, Open University Press, Milton Keynes, 1991.

FRITCHIE, R. and MELLING, M., *The Business of Assertiveness*, BBC Books, London, 1991.

NELSON-JONES, R., *The Theory and Practice of Counselling Psychology*, Cassell, London, 1990.

RICHARDS, D. and McDONALD, B., *Behavioural Psychotherapy*, Heinemann Nursing, Oxford, 1990.

SKINNER, B. F., *Science and Human Behaviour*, Collier Macmillan Publishers, London, 1953.

TROWER, P., CASEY, A. and DRYDEN, W., *Cognitive Behavioural Counselling in Action*, Sage Publications, London, 1990.

WALMSEY, C., *Assertiveness – The Right to Be*, BBC Books, London, 1991.

CHAPTER 7

Group counselling

The developmental background

Groupwork has been used as a method of training and therapy since the mid-to-late 1940s. Perhaps the most important of the early researchers into group formation and dynamics was the German psychologist Kurt Lewin who conducted laboratory experiments, and did extensive work with his students which involved experiental learning in the area of group theory and skills. His ideas led to the formation of the first training, or *T-groups*, in 1947. As a further result of Lewin's initiative, the National Training Laboratories was set up in Washington DC for the purpose of providing training suitable for people in management and industry. The principal focus of these groups was the development of effective human relationship skills which could be transferred to the job situation, and the personnel working within it. It was felt that in this way interpersonal communication would be enhanced and working conditions generally improved. Although the initial emphasis was on providing training which would be relevant to the work environment, it was later discovered that T-group interaction also exerted a positive influence on the individuals participating. Many of them reported that they had experienced beneficial personal change as a result of the training.

Carl Rogers, who pioneered the person-centered approach in counselling, was also involved in the development of group work in the 1940s. Just after World War II, he was working at Chicago University, where he set up a programme to train counsellors who would be available to help soldiers returning from the war. The participants in the group experience were primarily concerned to develop a deeper awareness of themselves in the belief that this would enable them to understand others more fully. The experiment was successful, not just in the area of growth and development, but also in the wider area of interpersonal and communication skills. As a result, groupwork, with its dual emphasis on personal growth and the development of communication skills, has become a recognized and powerful forum for counselling and psychotherapy generally.

In common with many other movements which have had their main impetus for growth in the USA, groupwork quickly became a focus for interest in Britain too. Indeed, while many of the key figures in the development of groupwork, including Kurt Lewin, had emigrated to America from Europe, others had settled in Britain where they played a prominent part in the evolution of new ideas and practice. Among those who moved to Britain, was the psychoanalyst Melanie Klein, whose work on the *theory of object relations* influenced many of the subsequent studies which took place in Britain on the subject of group dynamics. Bion, in particular, was influenced by the work of Melanie Klein. His work at the Tavistock Clinic, after World War II, was both original and innovative, and provided a framework for understanding the nature of group dynamics. Bion recorded his experiences and observations of group behaviour, and identified some of the common reactions which pertain to groups. His identification of group mentalities has provided a useful guide for group participants and leaders generally. Other important names associated with the group movement in Britain are Foulkes, Whittaker and Liberman, all of whom have contributed to a greater understanding of the unconscious processes which stimulate group dynamics.

Self-help groups

Although the work carried out by Lewin, Rogers and others has contributed significantly to the spread of interest in groupwork as a model for training and therapy, their initiatives were by no means the first in this area. Long before counselling and psychotherapy became popular, people with common illnesses or problems had come together to offer and receive mutual support and understanding. In 1905, a Boston doctor named Joseph Pratt set up weekly group meetings where patients who suffered from tuberculosis could support one another, discuss their illness, and receive information. In 1935, the first Alcoholics Anonymous group meeting was held in Ohio, and the organization which was formed as a result of this, has proved to be one of the most enduring and successful initiatives worldwide. In common with many other group movements, Alcoholics Anonymous started with people in crisis who came together because of mutual need, and because they could no longer cope alone with their condition. Exactly the same can be said about other self-help groups which have sprung up and continue to appear when a need is identified for them. There are now thousands of self-help groups all over the world and the fact that they proliferate serves to underline their effectiveness for the people who join them. Alcoholics Anonymous is perhaps the best example of the therapeutic effects of group support and community, but others, including support groups for drug users, Aids sufferers, problem eaters, schizophrenia, depression and diabetes, all appear to be beneficial for those who use them.

No two self-help groups ever function in exactly the same way, and there are vast disparities in terms of organization, structure, purpose and duration. There are obvious advantages in belonging to a group for someone who suffers, for example, from an addiction problem. In the first place, all the other people in the group will be fellow sufferers, and this fact alone seems to engender a sense of supportive community among the members. Destructive criticism is unlikely within such a setting, and coping abilities are enhanced through participation and cooperation in the group endeavour.

Many self-help groups are formed by people with the same health or social problems, but they can be set up for other purposes too, including activities as diverse as fund-raising and educative projects. What they all have in common, however, is a collective climate which usually facilitates personal growth, increases knowledge and improves self-image for members. Rules are an integral part of self-help group maintenance. Often these are stated explicitly or written down, but sometimes they are simply accepted as part of the ethos of the group. Members know that they are there to support one another, and the opportunity to provide this support – and to receive it – is a confidence booster for everyone. The ability to make progress without 'expert' help is further proof to members of a group that they, themselves, are capable of managing their own lives. Progress is not made, however, without a great deal of effort and commitment to change, and the importance of working towards goals is continually emphasized.

One significant aspect of self-help groups is the fact that *there are no experts within the ranks,* and very often there is no leadership either. This means, in effect, that everyone within the group feels equal, so it is unlikely that people will be sidetracked into seeking promotion or preferential treatment. Indeed, members of some self-help groups do not even meet as a body, but communicate instead by telephone, radio or newsletter. Although both the expression of emotion and the giving of emotional support are facilitated within self-help groups, there is greater emphasis on the sharing of information, and on practical ways of effecting change and achieving goals. The feeling of powerlessness which many people experience when they are ill, handicapped or in the throes of addiction or social ostracism, is often overcome as a result of the therapeutic effects of group membership. This is perhaps the main reason that self-help groups have increased so dramatically over the past twenty-five years.

Training groups

As mentioned earlier, training or T-groups originated with the work of Kurt Lewin in America. Their main focus was, and still is, on education and the development of life skills. A group of people who wish to improve the quality of their communication and other skills, meet together on a regular basis and follow a specific programme with clearly defined goals. The main emphasis is not on psychological growth, although this does often occur as a result of the interaction between group members. Participants are encouraged to explore group dynamics and processes, and to monitor their own contribution, and the contribution of others, to the communication which takes place during meetings. Many training groups are designed to encourage behaviour change, and assertiveness-training groups are an obvious example of this. Other examples include management-training groups, effective-parenting groups, retirement-training groups and job-search training groups. There is an increasing and varied range of training groups currently in existence, and their growing number appears to reflect the demanding and complex problems which people encounter in contemporary living. As well as this, it seems that people are developing a stronger sense of their own potential to manage and to overcome problems and challenges, without recourse to expert or professional assistance. In this respect, the growth in training groups runs parallel to the growth in self-help groups, and indeed, in many instances, the function of both frequently overlap or merge.

The educative nature of training groups is one of their most important features. Group leaders are often teachers in a specialized area of knowledge or skills, and their approach is usually instructive as well as facilitative. The setting is not formal as it would be in a class or lecture room, and experiential learning is an integral part of the exercise. Group members do not regard themselves as unhealthy or problematic, certainly not any more so than the rest of the population, and their main reason for participating is to improve the quality of their lives or work experience generally. Communication with, and encouragement from, other group members tends to give confidence to individual participants, so that personal growth takes place along with improvement in the specific skills area which the group is fostering.

Encounter groups

Encounter groups are also sometimes referred to as 'growth groups'. They were pioneered by Carl Rogers in 1946 and 1947, and differ from training groups in the sense that they emphasize personal growth as well as interpersonal and social skills. Through encounter group interaction, participants have the opportunity to see more clearly how they relate to others and how others relate to them, and in the process they learn to become more spontaneous and open in their communication.

The main focus of encounter-group activity is the improvement of interpersonal relationships *outside* the group, so that members will be able to lead more fulfilling lives once the experience is over. To this end, participants practise being open and expressive towards each other. The group leader or facilitator encourages the members to express their feelings in this way, in the hope that they will become less defensive and inhibited as a result.

People who take part in encounter-group work are usually concerned to develop a deeper awareness of 'self' which should, in turn, lead to a greater degree of self-actualization. Other reasons include a desire to be closer to other people, and to understand other people and their problems more clearly. Group members do not regard themselves as being ill or incapacitated in any way, but there is a shared recognition that the quality of most people's lives can be improved through enhanced communication with others.

Membership of encounter groups is entirely voluntary, and although the people who participate do have problems of everyday living, they are usually able to manage them without formal therapeutic intervention. Encounter-group leaders are usually non-directive in their approach, and this can have – initially at least – a disconcerting effect on the participants; it does not mean, however, that they are uninvolved in the group process. On the contrary, their function demands a great deal of commitment and skill, and involves such varied qualities as the ability to listen carefully, the ability to communicate empathy and understanding, as well as respect for group members. Along with all this, leaders or facilitators need to be confident about their work, and to have completed adequate theoretical and experiential training. Adequate training should ensure that group leaders are competent to help members relate what is happening to them in the group, to their own lives and relationships outside it. This requires sensitivity, tact, honesty and good communication skills, both verbal and non-verbal.

Theoretically, participants in group work should benefit from the feedback they receive from other members in the group, and from the acceptance which they feel they have achieved as a result of the group experience. This is not always automatically the case, however, and some studies of the effects of encounter-group participation suggest that the extent of positive behaviour change is often minimal or absent. In one study of more than two hundred US students who took part in group work with well-trained leaders, it was shown that only a small number experienced positive change as a result. Perhaps a more disconcerting aspect of this particular study is that it highlighted some negative changes which occurred in about one-third of the students taking part. These findings were based on self-reports as well as on ratings by close friends. (Lieberman, Yalom and Miles, 1973)

Task groups

Task groups are usually formed for a specific purpose, and in response to a particular problem, challenge or need. Goals are clearly defined and stated and, theoretically at least, all members of the group are committed to achieving these. Task groups may be set up for a wide variety of reasons, including planning for new initiatives or working on research projects. Many committees and community groups are task-oriented, and although their aims and objectives may differ, the basic structure and function of all of them are the same. A number of people meet to discuss, plan and decide on a course of action, and when the task is completed the group discontinues. There is no emphasis on personal growth and development since the task, and not the people addressing it, is the focus of attention. Nevertheless, participants in groupwork - regardless of the group's type or function – tend to learn something from the experience, and this in turn leads to increased self-confidence and improved social skills.

PSYCHOTHERAPY GROUPS

Psychotherapy groups are usually composed of people who could be defined as emotionally unwell, or at least unable to cope with the pressures of everyday living. Often group members are receiving medical care, either as patients in hospital or as out-patients who attend for treatment on a regular basis. Group members are also frequently seen for therapy individually by the group therapist.

Therapy groups are often psychoanalytic in orientation, and the group therapist may concentrate on a particular member of the group and highlight the ways in which he or she functions within this social setting. On the other hand, the group therapist may focus on the dynamics of the whole group, and in doing so examine, for example, the transference feelings and relationships between the participants, as well as transference to the therapist. In this way, thoughts, feelings and fantasies which were experienced in much earlier – usually childhood – relationships, are brought into the open and discussed. Group members are then encouraged to look at the similarities between past and present problems, especially those which apply to relationships.

The most important function of the group therapist is to sustain the role of transference figure, so that the group members are given the opportunity to work through their initial dependence on her, and then through their subsequent developing sense of autonomy and maturity. If this is to happen successfully, the therapist must be capable of staying as unobtrusive as possible, while at the same time monitoring and concentrating on everything which happens in the life of the group. The title 'group leader' is inappropriate for someone in this role, and the words facilitator, therapist or conductor seem better suited to describe her position.

The primary purpose of the psychotherapy group experience is to help members overcome their emotional and psychological problems. Since most of these problems are inseparable from family and social relationships, the group is an ideal medium for examining and working through them, and for looking at more healthy ways of relating to others. While encounter groups are more concerned to facilitate the development and growth of group members, psychotherapy group objectives go beyond this to a more radical and *remedial* approach which is curative as well as developmental. Group members may be severely incapacitated in their everyday lives, and may as a result be often defensive, even hostile, and lacking in basic self-esteem. This means that the therapist needs to be skilful and well trained if she is to be effective in encouraging change and growth where so little potential is discernible, on the surface at least. The psychotherapy group experience is concentrated, intense and generally extends over a longer period of time than either encounter or training groupwork. The therapist interprets what is happening within the group, but she does this sparingly and only offers interpretations when group participants are unable to see clearly themselves what is happening as a result of the group processes.

Insight is obviously much more valuable when group participants achieve it through their own efforts, and this is one of the guiding principles of psychotherapy groupwork. However, achieving insight can be a lengthy process, especially for those who are struggling with fairly severe emotional problems. Group participants may have difficulty in recognizing the benefits which arise as a result of group interaction, and for this reason – as well as for others – they often attend individual therapy sessions as well.

KEY WORDS

PSYCHODRAMA

The word 'psychodrama' refers to an approach which was first developed by J.L. Moreno in the 1930s. This method of group therapy uses role-play and creativity to help participants express themselves more fully. Moreno was a qualified doctor who moved from Vienna to the USA in 1925. He was particularly interested in the arts and theatre, and he adapted many ideas and techniques from these sources, which he then incorporated into his psychodrama workshops. A centre for psychodrama operates at the Holwell Centre in Devon. Workshops and courses are offered here for therapists who are interested in this medium.

FAMILY THERAPY

Family therapy is closely associated with marital therapy, and both are obviously concerned with the needs of more than one individual. The psychodynamic theory that most psychological problems are rooted in childhood and in family conflicts, has given impetus to an increasing use of family therapy as an approach to individual and relationship problems. The main goals of family therapy are to help individual members recognize the way they relate to each other, and to help them understand how their interactions contribute to the problems of the family as a whole. When each member of the family has a better understanding of family characteristics and dynamics, individual problems tend to be alleviated and deeper harmony is established in the group.

SYSTEMS THEORY

An idea central to all groupwork practice is that people need other people in order to give their lives meaning and purpose. The problems which occur in any individual's life are usually linked to interpersonal conflicts and relationship difficulties with close family members, friends or social acquaintances. Viewed in this way, it can be seen that dysfunctional relationships are rooted within a system, and that in order to improve the situation, the whole social network needs to be taken into consideration. Systems theory refers to the view, implicit in family therapy and in other models of groupwork, that the individual's needs can only be adequately addressed in the context of group interaction and communication.

The Model

The basic objectives of individual and group counselling are similar in that both approaches seek to help clients achieve greater self-awareness and autonomy, as well as control and direction in their own lives. Improved self-esteem is also an important outcome of group as well as individual counselling. Both approaches are often used to supplement each other, but group counselling has several important advantages over individual counselling, along with some disadvantages too.

ADVANTAGES

Perhaps the most obvious advantage of groupwork is that it is less time consuming for the counsellor since she can see a number of people all at once. Besides, groupwork tends to be less expensive for clients, as it meets the needs of a number of people together, many of whom might not be able to afford individual counselling.

Counselling groups enable clients to extend and develop their social skills. Experiences can be shared with other members of the group, and as a result, a deep sense of community and belonging is cultivated. Clients learn from both direct and indirect participation in the group process, and there are obvious advantages to be derived from groupwork when all the clients present share the same problem, (for example, addiction). Everyone else in the group is a fellow sufferer, and this fact alone seems to engender a sense of affinity which is both supportive and therapeutic. The sharing of experience is one of the most important dimensions of group counselling. It quite often leads to the setting-up of mutual support groups which are obviously less demanding on counsellors and likely to give an enormous boost to clients' self-esteem when they discover their own resources and ability to manage.

In group counselling, clients are afforded immediate opportunities to experiment with different ways of relating to others, and the physical proximity of people to one another can be emotionally reassuring as well as encouraging. Clients not only receive help themselves, but they also extend it to others in the group. In this way, helping skills are shared among a larger group of people, and this would certainly not be possible in individual counselling. Clients can also learn from one another through observation and modelling, and new ideas and attitudes can be explored through group interaction. The counsellor is also in a better position to observe the social and communicative dimensions of clients' behaviour, since the group represents a real-life social situation. Direct feedback can be given by the counsellor to the clients, as it can in individual counselling. In group counselling, however, feedback can also be shared among the clients themselves. In this way, group counselling allows the participants to act as both clients and therapists. Clients who have been defensive and guarded may be encouraged to share their feelings with others, and in doing so become more self-confident and self-accepting. Similarly, clients are encouraged to become more sensitive to the needs and feelings of others, and this tends to lead to the development of trust, respect and mutual understanding, both inside and outside the group. People who have experienced past difficulties in establishing or maintaining close personal relationships, are often encouraged to try new ways of relating to others as a result of their participation in groupwork.

In counselling groupwork, important and often traumatic issues like bereavement and loss are often discussed, and this may be a new and liberating experience for participants who may never have had the opportunity to address these concerns in a supportive environment before. Clients who take part in group counselling come from a variety of backgrounds, and bring to the experience a variety of problems, anxieties and personal difficulties. However, most clients tend to be interested in personal growth, self-knowledge and development, rather than radical or remedial change. Most clients function adequately in their everyday lives, and are not incapacitated in a way which requires either medical or psychiatric help. Strictly speaking, this is one of the ways in which counselling groups differ from psychotherapy groups, although the term psychotherapy group is now often used to describe a fairly wide spectrum of group practice.

Clients often learn to be more adventurous, and to become more socially involved as a result of their experiences within groups. Since the people who participate in group counselling frequently come from a variety of backgrounds, the encounter which they share is usually educative in the long term, not just socially but emotionally as well. Self-disclosure, which is painful for clients, can also have deep and beneficial effects when it leads to acceptance, not just by one person, but by a whole group. The cathartic effect of confiding to, and being accepted by, a group of people who have given a pledge of confidentiality, can be both curative and permanent, especially when feelings of shame and guilt are not disparaged, but understood by everyone present. Furthermore, through discussion and sharing of information, new perspective is gained and insight is achieved which can lead to therapeutic change for many or all of the group members.

DISADVANTAGES

Individual counselling has some advantages over group counselling. In the first place, individual counselling provides a safer environment for some people who may find it difficult to lower their defences. To participate in groupwork might seem very threatening to start with, and many clients benefit from a series of individual counselling sessions beforehand. With this approach, they can develop a trusting relationship with the counsellor prior to taking part in the more heightened atmosphere of group counselling.

The emphasis on free expression, which is embedded in the ethos of groupwork, may prove too confrontational or even harmful to people whose self-esteem is low, and they may be unable to withstand any criticism, however constructive, which is directed towards them. Many emotional problems involve the individual's difficulties in relating to others, and these tensions may be increased rather than decreased as a result of confrontation in the group. Although group counselling can give clients the opportunity to work on personal problems in the presence of others, as well as the chance to observe how others react to their behaviour, an essential starting point is that everyone should feel totally accepted by everyone else, even when criticisms are being voiced. This last point identifies a fundamental weakness in the groupwork approach to counselling, for it may be too much to expect that every person in a group will unreservedly value and accept everyone else. In addition, there is the important issue of confidentiality which, although easy to guarantee in a one-to-one counselling situation, may be more difficult to ensure when a number of people is involved.

Another practical disadvantage with groupwork is that participants may experience some degree of emotional catharsis, without adequate time or opportunity to work through the meaning of the experience in cognitive or intellectual terms. This deficit can be remedied, to some extent, when clients are also receiving individual counselling, but it is a problem, nevertheless, especially when a number of people in the group experience emotional upheaval.

Since the group counsellor is dealing with not just one person, but many, it is more difficult for her to monitor exactly what is taking place throughout the sessions. Whether or not this proves to be a significant problem depends on the degree of skill which the counsellor has acquired, and the adequacy of the training which she has undertaken. It goes without saying that the counsellor's training should include extensive experience of actually being in groups, as well as underpinning theoretical knowledge. Without this kind of experiential learning and background, it would be impossible for any counsellor to give the kind of individual attention to clients which is necessary in groupwork, while simultaneously paying attention to the processes which evolve within the group as a whole.

The possibility of scapegoating within the group is another potential disadvantage of the approach. However, scapegoating need not always be a disadvantage when the situation is dealt with skilfully by the group leader. What happens when it does occur, is that one individual is singled out by other group members and is subjected to hostility or ridicule. The reasons for this happening are complex, but usually involve the displacement of anger from its legitimate target on to a weak or vulnerable member of the group. It is often the case that the group leader is the real object of the negative feelings being expressed, but for different reasons, group members are unable to address their anger directly to her. The group leader can help the members to express themselves more appropriately by highlighting the situation, and by encouraging more honest and open discussion about what is happening.

We saw earlier that confidentiality becomes more complex in a group setting. There is an added consideration which is seldom mentioned in any of the literature on the subject: this concerns the rights of people outside the group to be respected. Since group members freely discuss personal and relationship issues, the confidentiality pertaining to others outside the group is indirectly violated. It is difficult to see what might be done to protect the rights of outsiders though, especially when the whole point of groupwork is that it affords opportunities for members to work through personal issues which nearly always involve other people. Perhaps there is a case for saying that all forms of groupwork have an intrinsic potential for exploitation which needs to be constantly measured against any benefits which are derived from their use.

LEADING THE GROUP

Anyone wishing to work with counselling groups needs to have received adequate practical training, including experience of groupwork participation. Along with this, a potential leader requires thorough working knowledge of group theory, as well as a commitment to all the qualities described by Rogers. These include the ability to communicate empathy and respect for clients, a willingness to be honest in relation to personal feelings and actions, and competence in making use of specific examples as opposed to intellectualizing and excessively relying on theory. The need for ongoing personal development, experience and supervision cannot be overstated, for when problems arise in group counselling – as they often do – everything hinges on the group leader's ability to conduct proceedings at a safe and therapeutic level. Also required are active listening, reflecting back and clarifying comments made by group members, as well as the skill of empathic challenging and the ability to connect and coordinate all the contributions made. Group participants need to be able to see some association between the group experience and their own lives outside it, and again, the leader must be able to point to any important links which are highlighted during the sessions.

CO-LEADERSHIP

Sometimes counselling groups have more than one leader, and there are certain advantages when counsellors work in pairs rather than singly. Quite often a situation arises in which one of the counsellors/leaders is more experienced than the other, and in this instance the less experienced leader has a chance to work and learn in an environment which is not too threatening. At the same time, clients are protected against possible ineptitude by the presence of a more seasoned leader. Other advantages of co-leadership include the supportive benefits which counsellors receive in this situation, as well as the benefits of sharing responsibility rather than carrying it alone. When two leaders are present in the group, each has more time and opportunities to observe the group process, and feedback can be given, between sessions, by co-leaders to each other. Nervous clients tend to feel more secure and supported when two leaders are present instead of one.

Co-leadership does have disadvantages, and these include the possibility of resentment or jealousy between leaders. Disagreement may arise about roles and responsibilities within the group, and even though these may be well disguised, they are often picked up by group members who may quickly exploit them. Sometimes group leaders agree with each other about everything because they sense that disagreement might lead to outright

Group counselling.

conflict which, in turn, might place their group plans in jeopardy. This latter situation is just as damaging as the former, because what is being avoided in both cases is free and honest discussion between co leaders about all aspects of the group experience. In order to ensure that the group is successful, counsellors need to be absolutely sure about their roles and responsibilities. They need to agree about certain fundamental issues, such as the purpose of the group and the ways in which they propose to deal with various situations likely to arise during sessions. It would be impossible to expect that all group leaders should be similar in style, but this is not important as long as differences are acknowledged, valued and accepted. Besides, any feelings of anger, uncertainty or frustration should be openly discussed by co-leaders, so that an atmosphere of trust and respect is fostered between them.

LEADERSHIP STYLE

Group leaders differ in terms of their personal characteristics. Some are authoritarian, directive and likely to retain most of the responsibility for the group in their own hands. An authoritarian leader is firm in her approach, and in many ways is similar to a benevolent but strict parent. She will have firm views about how things should be done, and although she will take the views of group members into consideration, she will be in charge of the overall structure and will probably stipulate the agenda from the outset. As far as group members are concerned, there are obvious advantages to be gained from having an authoritarian leader. In the first place, everyone understands the situation, and people are likely to feel safe when the rules are clear-cut and the leader is seen to be strong, even expert. If we accept that the group can be viewed as a metaphor for the family, then there is a distinct analogy between the leadership style and the parenting style. This means, in effect, that group members whose parents were strict, will want and expect the same guidance from a leader. But parents are human and capable of error, and in the end children grow up and become adults themselves. If there is not some degree of self-reliance and strength in adulthood, then everyday problems and more serious traumas become overwhelming and destructive. Individuation and maturity are impossible unless insight is gained about the way we all, to a greater or lesser degree, rely on the rules, strictures and prohibitions handed down to us by parents from early childhood onwards. The group setting is one way of achieving this knowledge and insight, but it can only be gained when an atmosphere conducive to free questioning exists, and when group members are allowed and encouraged to take responsibility for their own development.

There are other leaders who are more democratic in their approach to group counselling. A democratic leader is concerned to include everyone in decision making, and is also prepared to be flexible and adaptable according to the needs of group members. The democratic leader is aware that she is in possession of professional expertise, but also believes that group members have the potential to develop expertise if they are actually involved in the learning process. Group members often resent this style – initially at least – since many of them may interpret it as an abdication of responsibility. They frequently want to be told what to do by the leader, especially at the beginning when they feel vulnerable, insecure and nervous. The most positive aspect of allowing group members to determine their own rules, behaviour and strategy, is that it gives them real power and tends to lead to more energetic involvement in group tasks. It is not easy for the group leader to sustain a democratic style, especially in the face of opposition, and a temptation often exists to take the line of least resistance and become authoritarian. Moreover, the democratic style does not suit everyone and many group leaders are much happier, and therefore more effective, when they retain responsibility for the organization and overall functioning of the group.

A third leadership style is often referred to as *laissez-faire*, and implies an attitude which is essentially non-directive and permissive. A group leader who is *laissez-faire* will probably expect group members to work out their own rules and agenda. This is similar in some ways to the approach of the democratic leader, the main difference being that the *laissez-faire* leader places even more emphasis on exploration and experimentation by group members. Although there is always the risk that everyone will become frustrated and aimless as a result, such a stance often fosters creativity and imaginative thinking. An important point about the *laissez-faire* leader is that she adopts this attitude in order to encourage group members to accomplish their own goals with the minimum of interference from her. Like the democratic approach, though, it is difficult to sustain especially when group members see it – as they often do – as disorganized and inept.

In most counselling groups, the leader will evolve her own style to suit different situations and, more importantly, in response to the needs of the clients participating. The style of each leader will also depend, to some extent, on her own personality, but it is probably true to say that most group counsellors use a variety of styles which are flexible and interchangeable, as well as sensitive to individual needs.

PROBLEMS

Some of the problems which can arise in relation to the leader's role in the group include failure to be clear about group goals. Difficulties also arise when the leader tries to impose direction on a group whose members have a definite sense of purpose, and would prefer to proceed at their own pace. Sometimes group leaders are too quick to interpret what they think is happening in the group, a practice which can prove stultifying from the point of view of free expression. Other leaders are too constrained in their approach, and this can inhibit group spontaneity.

Although group leaders differ in their views about the degree of self-disclosure which they themselves should use, there can be no doubt that too much leader introspection draws attention away from participants, thereby sabotaging the whole purpose of the group endeavour. It is appropriate for group leaders to discuss their own reactions to group processes, but only in so far as this helps the clients within the group. The leader's principal task, regardless of her theoretical orientation, should be to facilitate and maximize the potential of all the group participants.

Group members need to feel that they are in an environment which is safe, and where they can express themselves in ways which might not be acceptable outside. These expressions often include emotional catharsis and other strong reactions, including anger and the verbalization of negative feelings. However, group participants should never feel compelled to react in these ways, nor should they be directed into deliberate conflict with each other. Some group leaders place a high premium on these displays of emotion and hostility, and problems can occur when they are deliberately engineered for the group leader's own benefit. Obviously, vulnerable members need to be protected within the group, and for this purpose the leader should be sensitive to everyone's needs, and capable of effective intervention as and when required. Such intervention is unlikely to be called for when clear guidelines have been established from the outset regarding unacceptable behaviour within the group. Participants should be aware that the group setting is not a free-for-all, nor is it a licence to abandon reasonable and civilized behaviour.

PLANNING

Before conducting a counselling group, there are several important issues which counsellors need to address. These include the following.

THE SIZE OF THE GROUP

Eight to ten is the usual number of group members. Some counsellors are willing to take more, but a large group is difficult to monitor and some

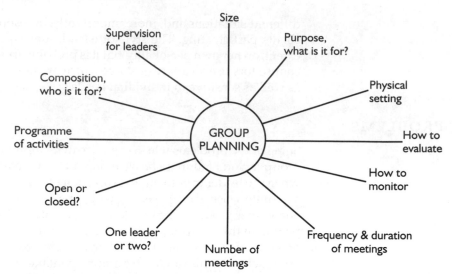

Fig. 7.1 *Group planning.*

members may avoid participation.) In a counselling group where self-disclosure is likely, membership is usually small. There are distinct disadvantages in large numbers, including loss of intimacy, as well as more reliance on the group leader and a greater need for rules and formality. If the group is too small, though, creativity is lessened and the range of personalities present is not enough to ensure varied interaction.

COMPOSITION OF THE GROUP

A counselling group can be made up of people of a similar age, or of people with similar problems. Groups may also be single-sex, or may be composed of people who come from similar backgrounds. Occasionally, decisions about group composition are already made for the counsellor, and depend on the context of the work being done and the reasons for doing it. One example of this is the group composed of clients who suffer from problems of addiction. A counsellor working in private practice will usually select group members from people within the community who suffer from stress, anxiety, loneliness or occupational dissatisfaction. One of the most important points about group structure is that it should include people who are likely to benefit from the experience, and who are capable of interacting effectively with others.

NUMBER, DURATION AND FREQUENCY OF MEETINGS

Obviously, the number and frequency of meetings will depend on the purpose of the group and the needs of participants. Weekly meetings are fairly usual, although some counsellors prefer to hold them twice a week. Meetings can last from about ninety minutes to three hours, and may continue for a period of ten weeks. If exploration is to be intense within the group, then more time will be needed to build up trust and to deal with issues which emerge. The advantage of weekly meetings is that interest, continuity and momentum are sustained. Group leaders can be flexible about the length of meetings once the group has been consulted and the needs of members have been established. It is important, though, to have an initial plan around which suggestions for change or alteration can be discussed.

THE SETTING

A closed group is one which runs for a predetermined number of sessions, and does not admit new members once it has started. An open group will admit new members at any time throughout the sessions, and members may leave when they wish to do so. There may be a fixed time span for the group, or it may run indefinitely to suit the needs of clients.

The main advantage of the closed group is that it is consistent and unified, with more chance of intimacy developing among members. It is also more likely that the different stages of group development will proceed unhindered without the disruption of people coming and going. The main advantage of the open group is that a wider array of thinking skills and resources is made available. This can mean more creativity, as well as providing learning opportunities relating to issues of change, separation and the beginning and ending of relationships.

There are several other important points which need to be considered before the group starts. These include:

- Whether to work alone or with a co leader.
- How to monitor the group and assess its benefits or deficiencies.
- Whether to use a programme of group activities.

Lastly, a great deal of care needs to be taken to ensure that the leader has a well-thought-out plan relating to the purpose of the group, and that decisions have been made regarding what to do if unforeseen problems occur. When the group experience is over, some post-group evaluation should take place, and the counsellor herself should have access to adequate support and supervision throughout.

STAGES OF DEVELOPMENT

All groups go through a series of developmental stages as they progress from the first meeting to the last. There is a substantial amount of literature available on the subject of group development, including studies by Tuckman (1965) who describes a sequential approach to group life. Carl Rogers (*Person-Centered Therapy*, 1991) has also illustrated the various characteristics of group dynamics, and Yalom (*The Theory and Practice of Group Psychotherapy*, 1970) has identified what he regards as the three main stages which are typical of early group life. Many of the stages of group life highlighted by these and other models, are fairly similar, and a predictable pattern of group development is illustrated in all of them. What all these studies have in common is some acknowledgement that groups, like individuals, are unique and will not therefore automatically follow identical patterns. In the process of group formation and development five *usual* stages can be described as follows.

ORIENTATION

When a group first begins, the members become acquainted and are concerned to identify the orientation and purpose of the group. Very often there is a preoccupation with rules and procedures, and members want to know fairly quickly what they are expected to do. There is heavy reliance on the leader for information and direction, and group members are wary of each other. At the same time, everyone is gathering information about everyone else, either directly through conversation, or indirectly through observation. Conversation at this stage lacks depth, and attempts are made to establish a sense of community based on social chitchat and well-mannered exchanges.

CONFLICT

When the group has formed, members start to compete with each other for roles and positions within it. This competition may be obvious or it may be well hidden, and people try to determine how much influence they will have in the group and the degree of commitment they will need to make to it. Considerable conflict may occur, although this too will tend to be masked. The organizational aspect of the group becomes a focus for attention, and often the leader is the subject of critical discussion. There is anxiety about how things should be done and what decisions should be taken. Alliances are formed and individual differences are brought out into the open. Sometimes group members will try to replace the leader by making 'Why don't we?' suggestions. Underlying most of this behaviour are issues relating to control, authority and status. The duration of this stage varies, but once it is completed, group members tend to be more deeply involved and firmly integrated into the group.

COMMUNITY

During this third stage, members develop a common perspective with regard to the group and how it will function. The conflict stage has been overcome, and a new closeness develops as a result. There is a sense of cooperation and bonding among group members which leads to the sharing of ideas and a willingness to participate fully in the group endeavour. Along with this, members feel more confident and are careful to respect one another and to avoid the risk of further hostility. There is a common belief that everyone is being more open, but unexpressed and unresolved tensions still exist, in spite of the laughter and banter which goes on at this stage.

ACHIEVEMENT

During this stage, group members concentrate on exploring personal issues, and there is substantial self-disclosure which encourages empathy, trust, acceptance and support within the group. People now concentrate on actively listening to each other, so that real work is accomplished and a high degree of psychic energy is consequently generated. There is a possibility that unexpressed conflict or tension will now emerge, but this is often constructive and can lead to more honesty and a new willingness to look at problems and issues previously ignored. A sense of freedom and openness exists which is conducive to sharing, so that group members act as counsellors for one another and become deeply aware of the interconnectedness of all their experiences.

ENDING   During the ending stage of the group life, members prepare to say good-
bye to one another. Before this, however, attention is focused on the achievements of the group and on the learning which has taken place throughout
the experience. Issues relating to separation and closure are discussed, and
this may be painful for group members, especially if strong emotional ties
have been formed between them. Sometimes there is regression to earlier
group behaviour, and this may include increased reliance on the leader.
Occasionally, attempts are made to reactivate old problems, while in other
instances group members may become less communicative and reduce their
overall involvement in the group. The longer the group has been together,
the more likely it is that expressions of loss and anxiety will surface in the
ending stage, although similar reactions may arise when a group has met
on fewer occasions. It is important for the counsellor to remember that the
ending of a group is like a bereavement for many of its members, which
means that extra support needs to be given to them if they are to deal effectively with the loss.

The group experience

The experience of group counselling will be different for individual participants and will depend, to some extent, on the issues, problems and expectations which prompted them to seek this form of help in the first place.
Another important factor in the outcome of group counselling for individual members, is the nature of the group, and whether, for example, it is
concerned with specific areas such as assertiveness, stress management or
addiction, or with the more generalized aims of personal growth and self-
awareness.

Regardless of the group's orientation, however, there are some areas of
experience which appear to be common to all participants. These include
initial worries concerning:

- Having to seek counselling in the first place.

- The possible effects of the experience.

- Whether or not it is the right course of action to take.

- Having to contribute to the group.

- Confidentiality.

- Ability to relate to a group of strangers.

- Whether it is really necessary.

- Whether it is the right approach.

Later on, once sessions are under way, clients may experience further anxieties, including:

- Embarrassment about speaking in the group.

- Fears about having to reveal too much to strangers.

- Fear of pressure.

- Fear of not having enough control in the group.

- Doubts about the leader's effectiveness, ability and training.

- Confusion about procedures and about the leader's response to questions.

- Conviction that the leader is not sufficiently forceful and positive.

When counselling sessions have become well established, group members often experience a mixture of bewildering emotions, preoccupations and worries. Among these are:

- Boredom and concern about what is happening.

- Worries about how other people view them in the group.

- Feelings of vulnerability and exposure, once they have spoken out.

- Inability to understand the purpose of group exercises and fears about wasting time.

- Mixed up feelings which appear to be heightened by the group experience, including feelings of rebelliousness.

- Awareness that other group members have had similar experiences.

- Fears about loss of control and about the new experience of introspection and self-disclosure.

- Awareness of new areas of self-discovery.

- Feelings of weakness and depression.

- Difficulty in expressing needs.

- Awareness of conflict within the group.

- A gradual sense of moving from reflections of the past towards consideration for the future.

- A new identification of personal and professional goals.

- The expression of personal needs.

Towards the end of the counselling group experience, client participants will usually have worked through to a more positive – though still somewhat confusing – array of feelings, expectations, goals and decisions. These may include:

- Acceptance of feedback from other group members.

- Increased self-knowledge as a result of the feedback.

- Exploration of personal goals.

- Trusting experience in the group.

- Experience of caring for others.

- Cohesiveness of the group.

- Insight as a result of supportive confrontation.

- Sadness when the group is about to disband.

And finally:

- Relief at the end, and a sense of freedom.

- Incorporation of gains into everyday living.

Counsellors can best help their clients to work through all the stages of the group experience by being organized and well prepared beforehand, and by being supportive and sensitive throughout. Good preparation depends, in the first place, on adequate training and experience, but also on thorough planning long before the first session begins. The group leader can also help to prepare clients by seeing them individually in advance, for a pre-group discussion. Some of the issues which might be discussed include:

- The length of sessions, when they start and the number of meetings overall.

- How many people will participate.

- Explanation of the leader's role in the group.

- What the group is about and what its objectives are.

- What activities will be used.

- The client's reasons for wishing to join the group.

- Problems or themes in the client's life which can be realistically addressed in the group.

- Negotiation of a contract with the client which includes clear statements about what he can expect from the group, and what he will be expected to give to it.

- Identification of the client's fears and anxieties.

Once the meetings have started, the counsellor needs to continue to be sensitive to the individual needs of clients. This means, among other things, showing respect by using their names when addressing them, and by using clear, informative language which avoids jargon and obscurity. It is important to make a contract with the group at the beginning which should include specific issues such as confidentiality, time-keeping and group objectives. Group members need some structure and some boundaries: the leader should respect this and show a willingness to take initial responsibility in these areas. Clients' need for direction is legitimate and should not be trivialized on the grounds that they ought to be responsible from the outset. Without some clear guidance from the leader, a group can quickly degenerate into a chaotic free-for-all without structure or logic.

Throughout subsequent sessions, the counsellor needs to maintain a climate which encourages group members to value and care for each other, especially during confrontation and periods of conflict. She also needs to have faith and trust in the group and in its ability to work through important issues without undue interference from her. Too much emphasis on directing the group can be life-destroying, as can too many inaccurate interpretations. When members believe themselves to be under constant scrutiny, they become inhibited and lacking in spontaneity. The counsellor does need to comment on what is happening in the group, but this should be done in a natural and unobtrusive way. Above all, the group counsellor should display attitudes of understanding and firmness, as well as the ability to give permission and protection when required. All this needs to be accomplished without infringing the participants' right to be self-directing and ultimately responsible for the life of the group. This is a lot to ask of any counsellor, but without these attributes, the effectiveness and safety of the group will be compromised.

FURTHER READING

AVELINE, M. and DRYDEN, W. (eds.), *Group Therapy in Britain*, Open University Press, Milton Keynes, 1988.

BENSON, J. F., *Working More Creatively with Groups*, Tavistock Publications, London, 1987.

CONYNE, R. K., *How Personal Growth and Task Groups Work*, Sage Human Services Guides, vol. 55, London, 1989

JOHNSON, D. W. and JOHNSON, F.P., *Joining Together – Group Theory and Group Skills*, Prentice-Hall International Inc., New Jersey, 1987.

NAPIER, R. W. and GERSHENFELD, M.K., *Groups – Theory and Experience*, Houghton Mifflin Company., Boston, 1985.

PECK, M. S., *The Different Drum*, Rider Press, London, 1987.

ROGERS, C., *Encounter Groups*, Allen Lane, The Penguin Press, London, 1971.

ROGERS, C., *Person-Centered Therapy*, Constable, London, 1991.

STOCK WHITAKER, D., *Using Groups to Help People*, Routledge & Kegan Paul Ltd, London, 1992.

YALOM, I. D., *The Theory and Practice of Group Psychotherapy*, Basic Books, New York, 1970.

CHAPTER 8

The eclectic or integrative approach

Introduction

Each client who comes for counselling is a unique individual whose needs are quite different from those of any other client. This means, in effect, that it is impossible to prescribe a formula approach which could be applied to all counselling situations. Eclecticism, which is the practice of selecting methods, techniques and concepts from a variety of approaches, does take account of client individuality and the diversity of needs, and for this reason, it is increasingly practised by therapists and counsellors generally. The term *integrative* is also sometimes used to describe the eclectic approach, and indeed many practitioners prefer it since it suggests a coherence and harmony which is not generally associated with the word eclectic.

A review of the seven approaches to counselling and therapy outlined in earlier chapters, will illustrate the point that although there are similarities among them, there are many striking differences as well. In particular, there are differences relating to theories of human nature, and in the practical application of these theories to the counselling situation itself. It is important to remember, however, that there are certain fundamental beliefs which are common to all of them. These include the following.

- Assurance of confidentiality is essential if clients are to feel safe in counselling.

- The relationship between client and counsellor is important and should be based on mutual respect and trust.

- Clients should achieve some understanding and insight as a result of the counselling they have received.

- Client growth and change should be facilitated within the therapeutic situation.

- Clients should experience themselves as active participants in counselling.

THE COUNSELLOR'S PERSONALITY

The counsellor's own personality, along with the skill and qualities which she possesses, will obviously have an influence on the process and outcome of therapy. Even within a given school, different counsellors may use the same approach with varying degrees of success. Indeed, it is probably true to say that in counselling, everything hinges on the personality and behaviour of the counsellor, and on the unique relationship which she has with the client. There is always the danger that overemphasis on methods and techniques will diminish the importance of the client/counsellor personality interaction and undermine the effectiveness of the therapy. This is why experiential learning, self-development and growth are regarded as essential elements in the training of student counsellors. It is only through this kind of experience that students truly appreciate the significance of client/counsellor personality interaction, and the way that it influences the work between them. For this reason also, student counsellors need to be committed to self-development and learning, as an ongoing process which should be continued even when other work commitments loom large.

READING

Reading is a key element in the education and training of student counsellors. This should not be confined to the fairly restricted area of counselling theory, and ideally should include works of literary merit, which offer a much wider view of human nature, and all its attendant difficulties. Reading within a narrow framework does nothing to help students understand the vast spectrum of ordinary human behaviour, and tends to encourage

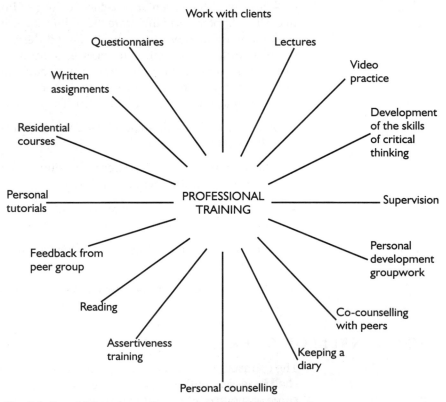

Fig. 8.1 *A model for trainee self-assessment and self-development.*

instead an emphasis on that which is pathological or problematic.

Students should also try to read as many relevant newspaper articles as possible, especially those which deal with the subject of therapy and the general reactions of the public to it. There is increasing public interest in the use of counselling and therapy, and in recent times some criticism has been directed against it. This criticism can only prove to be beneficial in the long term, since it serves to focus attention on the possibility of exploitation and abuse by practitioners, and it also helps to identify the areas in which opportunism is most likely to take place. Students need to be aware that the potential for abuse is always present in counselling, and though this is an area which should be adequately considered throughout basic training, it needs to be addressed at frequent intervals thereafter too.

THE COUNSELLOR'S EXPERIENCE OF TECHNIQUES

The discipline of reading a wide range of books, including literary works and media coverage relating to therapy, will obviously provide students with the intellectual stimulation and the theoretical information which is necessary for the practice of eclectic or integrative counselling. Reading on its own is not enough, however, and students need to have some personal experience of the techniques which are central to the various models of counselling. This includes experience of a wide range of methods and procedures, including role play, script analysis, Gestalt work, cognitive homework and disputing irrational beliefs, as well as practice in early recollection and dreamwork. It is only through experience like this that students can begin to understand how well they themselves are suited to using particular techniques, and how comfortable they feel with them.

Some understanding of the feelings which clients might experience, is also gained through the use and practice of a range of procedures which are integral to a variety of approaches. Because each client is a unique individual, and each client/counsellor relationship is unlike any other, it is impossible to generalize on set procedures. This means that the counsellor needs to respond to each counselling session as it evolves, for although she might have some idea of what might happen, she cannot possibly know for sure. It is this very lack of certainty which necessitates good preparation on the counsellor's part, in terms of both practical training in a wide range of approaches, and in-depth knowledge of all the relevant theory.

THE CLIENT'S CHOICE

It is sometimes the case that clients who are well informed about therapy, choose the model that they themselves prefer, and which they believe will suit their own individual needs. Thus, a client who suffers from phobic reactions, for example, may decide to seek out a behavioural counsellor who will use the technique of systematic desensitization. Such a client may be only minimally interested in his past life experience, although there is always the possibility that he may develop an interest during the course of therapy. There are many clients, however, who have no idea what to expect from a counsellor, and certainly most ordinary people are unacquainted with the spectrum of therapies now available to the public.

To make matters even more confusing for them, some clients live in areas where counselling and psychotherapy are provided free of charge, while others are less well served and need to be prepared to make enquiries further afield. Clients who can afford to do so, may opt for private counselling, while others who are less well off may be lucky enough to find a therapy group in their own area. It is comparatively easy for articulate and financially secure clients to shop around for the model of counselling which they want, but it is obviously much more difficult for those who are inarticulate, lacking in confidence, or poor. Regardless of levels of confidence and financial status, however, most clients are understandably apprehensive about venturing into the unknown area of counselling, and this apprehension tends to make it even more difficult for them to make clear and well-informed choices. One client who spent some considerable time locating the kind of counselling which she wanted, recounted the following concerns:

> The areas which gave me most concern were those related to counsellor qualifications and the various approaches used. I was also worried about training, and how many years they needed to practise in order to become proficient. I didn't know how long the whole process would take, and I didn't know how the sessions would be organized or how long they would last. Someone had mentioned to me that counsellors should belong to a professional organization and that they should also receive supervision – although I had no idea at the time what this meant.
>
> What did I want at that time? Well, I wanted to be listened to, and I had a vague feeling that I might get some useful advice or information. Apart from all this, I needed understanding and support, and although I knew what my main problems were, nothing was specific or clearly defined. I was confused, upset and a bit demoralized, and it took me some time to actually pluck up the courage to go for counselling eventually. I suppose if I had to sum it all up, I would say that my main fears were about qualifications, training, the cost and the amount of time it would all take. And, of course, the main question was – would it really help me?
>
> (Hayley, a client, 1993)

The above passage indicates some of the worries that clients experience before they embark on counselling. The issue of different therapeutic approaches is probably one of the most perplexing for them, and one which they sometimes find too intricate to tackle. There is no easy way for clients to overcome this problem – short of carrying out extensive research – so the onus is on counsellors and therapists to clarify, in unequivocal and jargon-free language, what it is that they do. Since there is no foolproof way for prospective clients to find a counsellor whose orientation will suit their individual needs, counsellors and therapists generally should be happy to discuss the methods which they use, the training and experience which they have had, as well as the professional organizations to which they subscribe.

Why therapy?

There is an increasing demand for counselling and psychotherapy; arguably, this is related to changing public attitudes to fitness and health generally. Within medicine itself there is a new stress on individual accountability for health, and this is reflected in many areas, including advertisements for wholefoods, campaigns against smoking, excessive drinking and irresponsible sex. The emphasis has shifted away from illness towards a positive awareness of the benefits of full health. Members of the public no longer want or expect to be given drugs for every ailment, and they are more aware of the emotional and psychological causes of many physical conditions. In addition to this, the stigma which once attached to psychological problems is now fading, so people feel less embarrassment about asking for therapy.

General practitioners no longer have the time – or the resources – necessary to help patients cope with a myriad of contemporary problems ranging from broken family relationships, isolation, alienation, and unemployment. Psychiatry, which was once regarded as the only treatment for emotional disturbance, is still firmly aligned with the world of medicine, and still continues to use drugs as a routine part of many treatments. As well as this, patients in psychiatric treatment are quite often very ill, passive, and seldom encouraged to take a full and active part in their own recovery. This kind of approach is clearly not appropriate for the vast majority of people who are not ill in the strict sense, but who, nevertheless, feel that their emotional problems hamper their everyday living.

Changes in public perception about health have prompted many people who once consulted doctors for advice and medication, to search for alternative forms of help. Churches, from which many people in the past obtained spiritual and emotional support, are now less influential in this respect. In view of all this, it is understandable that counselling and therapy are increasingly regarded as desirable and instrumental, not just by members of the public, but by many doctors too. The number of general practitioners who now employ counsellors is increasing all the time, and many more routinely recommend this approach for their patients. This is not to say that everyone is now unreservedly and enthusiastically in favour of counselling and therapy; on the contrary, there are many critics, some of whom are concerned with what they see as a lack of spiritual dimension in this new trend. Other critics see it as a fashion which will eventually disappear, while still others are rightly concerned with the possibility of abuse, an issue we have already referred to. Undeniably, the increasing interest in counselling and therapy does create an ideal opportunity for unscrupulous people to step in and exploit the situation. This makes it imperative that everyone involved in both training and practice should be vigilant in safeguarding and maintaining standards.

Let us now look at the way counselling has evolved historically and consider the relative merits of the three main approaches and the counselling models which have stemmed from them.

The three main approaches to counselling and therapy

Historically, the three principal orientations in counselling and therapy are grouped under the headings of:

- Psychoanalytic
- Behavioural
- Humanistic

These headings are, in turn, subdivided to include a wide variety of theoretical schools or models which have evolved from them. These subdivisions can be outlined as follows.

PSYCHOANALYTIC

All psychodynamic approaches which have their origins in Freudian ideas, including Jung's Analytical Psychology, Adler's Individual Psychology, as well as the therapies of the Neo-Freudian school and the Object Relations theorists.

BEHAVIOURAL

This group includes those models of counselling and therapy which are directly linked to the learning theories of Behavioural Psychology. However, there has been a progressive movement away from the more rigid ideas of pure behaviourism, towards a wider view of personality which encompasses cognition and human interaction. This has led to the evolution of cognitive therapies, one of the most enduring of which is Albert Ellis's rational-emotive therapy.

HUMANISTIC

The humanistic group of therapies includes Rogers's Person-Centered Counselling, Fritz Perl's Gestalt Therapy, and Eric Berne's Transactional Analysis. Existential approaches to therapy are also grouped under this heading, although in many respects this is an area which is quite independent of any of the others.

This tripartite grouping of therapeutic approaches can be misleading, however, since transactional analysis is sometimes also referred to as a cognitive model, and Gestalt Therapy is occasionally called an 'affective' approach. As well as this, rational-emotive therapy is often listed along with other cognitive approaches, as if it had somehow evolved quite separately from behavioural influences. These anomalies and inconsistencies can be confusing for students who are trying to make sense of the ways in which different schools have evolved historically. In addition, group counselling can be linked to a variety of models and new approaches to therapy generally are appearing at a very fast rate.

What matters most is that students should understand the theoretical bases of the main individual models, along with the goals of each approach, the techniques used in them, the nature of the client/counsellor relationship emphasized by them, and the applications and limitations of all of them.

THE PSYCHOANALYTIC APPROACH AND PSYCHODYNAMIC COUNSELLING

Freud's psychoanalytic approach developed partly as a result of his medical practice during the late 1880s. His curiosity about hysterical conditions led him to use hypnosis as a method of curing patients who suffered from these. However, this approach was only partly successful and Freud later went on to use free association or the 'talking cure' in order to help his patients uncover childhood memories.

Freud was surprised by the number of patients whose symptoms seemed to be linked to experiences of sexual abuse by a close relative during childhood. This suggested to him that sexual abuse was either very widespread in Vienna, or that his patients were mistaken in the accounts which they gave him. Later on, he suggested that his patients' hysterical symptoms could be based on unconscious fantasies and wishes, and that these memories of sexual abuse might reflect an early wish for such an experience. These views led to the theory of the Oedipus complex, and to an emphasis on the exploration of unconscious conflicts and wishes.

Psychoanalysis evolved, therefore, as a treatment which would enable clients to achieve insight through recognition and understanding of emotions and unconscious thoughts which lie at the roots of their problems. There is a further emphasis on the connection between unconscious thoughts and the way these influence relationships with other people and behaviour in general. People are seen as determined by early experience and irrational forces, as well as sexual and aggressive impulses which are always present and striving for recognition. Conflict between the id and super-ego produces anxiety which the rational ego seeks to reduce through a variety of defence mechanisms. This process uses up a great deal of psychic energy, and psychoanalytic treatment is aimed at uncovering the original source of the conflict. The methods used to do this include:

- *Free association* or the 'talking cure', which encourages clients to recall incidents and information from the past and from childhood.

- *Interpretation*, which is meant to lead to insight and to the assimilation of new information by the ego.

- *Dream analysis*. The idea that our deepest wishes and fantasies are experienced in dreams is the basis of dream analysis.

- *Analysis of resistance and analysis of transference*. Both are meant to help clients gain access to unconscious conflicts and feelings.

The psychodynamic approaches which have evolved from Freudian theory, however, tend to place less emphasis on sexual and aggressive impulses, while social interaction is increasingly regarded as an important element in the individual's development. There are many varieties of psychodynamic therapy but, overall, the length of therapy has been considerably decreased in recent times and fewer sessions are likely to take place. Today, the psychodynamic counsellor, while obviously influenced by Freudian theory and its emphasis on past events, is equally interested in the client's ability to cope with everyday needs, events and problems. Although free association is still used in psychodynamic counselling, just as differing forms of it are used in many therapeutic approaches, open discussion between client and counsellor is regarded as an important component of therapy and one which helps to equalize the balance of power between them. While the concept of transference is central to the psychodynamic approach, the counsellor is concerned to limit the intensity of the client's feelings in this regard, although unconscious problems which are highlighted in the therapeutic relationship are certainly used as a means to address relationship problems outside it.

One of the problems associated with the psychodynamic approach is that the emphasis which has traditionally been placed on the importance of childhood events, may obscure or mask some of the client's current problems and difficulties. These include financial and other material forms of deprivation, issues which need to be addressed if the client is to make any real progress in dealing with emotional distress. Many clients who come for counselling are simply not interested in an introspective approach to

Fig. 8.2 *Clients may be preoccupied with issues relating to childhood experience.*

their problems, but prefer immediate and more direct means of tackling issues which cause them concern. Others just want to speak freely in the presence of someone who is willing to give them individual attention, and help them clarify and make sense of their difficulties. Psychodynamic counselling can be geared to short-term objectives, and listening attentively to the client is a fundamental principle of its use. Supportive interventions, including paraphrasing, summarizing, asking questions and addressing practical issues, are not inconsistent with the approach.

While some clients are not interested in unconscious motivation and past events, many others are keen to look at these areas, and deliberately seek out psychodynamic counsellors who will help them to do so. Occasionally, clients come for counselling with no idea of the counsellor's theoretical orientation. They may be seeking help in a vague and uninformed way, but once counselling has started it may become clear fairly quickly which method is best suited to their needs.

Clients who are keen to gain intellectual as well as emotional understanding, may welcome the counsellor's interpretations as a means of helping them achieve those ends. Interpretation can only be done correctly, however, when the counsellor knows the client well and is familiar with his past history and the ways in which this history might be affecting his current problems. Clarifying and translating the client's past experiences obviously takes time and effort, and they will only make sense to him when they are appropriately made and he is ready to consider them. Many clients are unwilling to contemplate this kind of approach, and again, may prefer more immediate or directive ways of tackling their problems.

BEHAVIOURAL COUNSELLING

Behavioural counselling, which has traditionally been regarded as a directive approach, is in many respects concerned with client self-management and client self-directed behaviour. It is true that there is less emphasis on subjective experience than there would be in a person-centered approach, for example, and less stress is put on introspection, which is valued highly in the psychodynamic model. However, clients are encouraged to view their problems as learned behaviours which they *themselves* can unlearn in a reasonably straightforward way.

Overt behaviour is identified, goals of therapy are specified, therapy plans are developed and their outcomes are evaluated objectively at the end. This approach suits a great many clients, especially those who are interested in a direct and specific plan which will address the needs of their own immediate problems. Since the nature of the client/counsellor relationship is not usually highlighted in any of the literature which describes behaviour therapy, there is a common and mistaken belief that the approach lacks warmth and is therefore not appropriate in a true counselling situation. However, it is usually counsellors who are genuinely concerned to meet the many and diverse needs of clients who use behavioural techniques when they feel that the client will benefit from such an approach. This sensitivity to client needs is at the very heart of good counselling practice, so the charge that behavioural practice lacks warmth is certainly open to argument.

The educational dimension of behaviour therapy can be used effectively in the counselling context when clients express a desire to be taught certain skills. Assertiveness training is one example of an area which clients increasingly value. Relaxation techniques can also be taught in a wide spectrum of counselling situations, and such teaching is an effective way of helping clients to manage their own problems (especially those related to anxiety and stress) and to become more self-reliant generally.

Both role-play and modelling can also be used effectively within counselling, regardless of the theoretical orientation of the counsellor. Clients can practise role-play in order to help them develop confidence in the use of communication skills, especially when they need these for particular situations like job interviews. Although behaviour therapy deals with what many psychodynamic therapists would regard as the symptoms only of a client's problems, the techniques used within it are often very helpful in enabling clients to deal with immediate and perhaps incapacitating difficulties. It could be argued that a behavioural procedure like modelling is unlikely to encourage clients to become independent and autonomous, since what they are being asked to do is to rehearse and act out behaviour which really belongs to someone else. However, the truth of the matter is that for many clients, confidence and independence are unlikely to develop until pressing problems are eased or solved. Modelling, as well as role-play, can be used within counselling to help clients overcome certain blocks or impediments which would hamper their chances of moving forward and becoming self-sufficient. In this respect, behavioural procedures can be said to help clients grow towards self-actualization, a concept which is central to the person-centered model of counselling.

In addition to this, behaviour therapy – through its strict adherence to explicitly stated goals, procedures and outcomes – is unlikely to confuse clients. On the contrary, the clarity and sense of purpose which is integral to the model, can have the effect of providing the impetus necessary for perseverance and full commitment.

Behaviour therapy encompasses a wide range of techniques and procedures which can be used to meet the diverse and changing needs of clients. For this reason, it can be said to contribute a great deal to the comprehensive and holistic view of clients which is increasingly valued by counsellors generally. Encouraging clients to read books so that they become better informed, or teaching them various skills, for example, will address needs which might be overlooked by counsellors who stick rigidly to one model. In order to make them work effectively, these procedures need to be used with clients who welcome such measures. The practice of using behavioural techniques like positive imagery or time projection is also consistent with a broad view of human requirements, and therefore valuable in any counselling situation which identifies clients' needs. All this does not mean that behavioural procedures should be used in a haphazard or unplanned way in counselling; their use needs to be indicated as appropriate and suitable, and clients need to be fully involved at every stage in order to make them work.

THE ECLECTIC OR INTEGRATIVE APPROACH   173

PERSON-CENTERED COUNSELLING

The core conditions of the person-centered approach to counselling are central to many other models as well. Counsellors generally believe in the importance of respect for clients and in the need to be genuine or congruent with them. Most approaches accept that the client/counsellor relationship is the most significant element in counselling. However, some approaches, like rational emotive therapy for example, place less emphasis on the need for empathy in counselling. Indeed, staying detached from the client's frame of reference is regarded as essential, since this is seen as the only sure way of remaining uncontaminated by the client's irrational thinking. A similar situation obtains in behavioural counselling where understanding and rational thinking are highly valued, and empathy is underplayed. In both these approaches (rational-emotive therapy and behavioural counselling) there is a strong educational bias which, in the long term, is incompatible with the kind of relationship which Rogers advocates.

Is it ever possible, therefore, to integrate techniques and procedures from other models of counselling with the person-centered approach? It seems that a sizeable number of counsellors who are person-centered in their basic orientation, do in fact select and use ideas from other models, when and if clients request or need them. Clients can be given unconditional positive regard, empathy and congruence, and be helped in other ways too. It is true that a directive or teaching approach cannot be used consistently with person-centered counselling if the distinct features of the latter are to be retained. It is still possible – and frequently desirable – to use elements of rational-emotive, behavioural, Gestalt or psychodynamic counselling within the framework of the person-centered approach. Relaxation techniques, positive imagery or rational-thinking exercises are all useful adjuncts to short-term and crisis counselling in particular.

Perhaps one of the most useful contributions of the person-centered approach is its applicability to groupwork. In this respect, it is much safer than many other models since a basic tenet of the approach is that each individual must be valued, accepted and appreciated, regardless of any other considerations. People who feel vulnerable, socially insecure, or unable to cope with an openly directive or confrontative groupwork ethos, may well benefit from the therapeutic conditions of respect, genuineness and empathic understanding which are central to the person-centered approach. If these conditions are really present in the groupwork situation, it is unlikely that any participant will be harmed by the experience, and it is quite likely that individuals will be encouraged to become more self-sufficient and confident generally. The tendency to become more responsible for self is very much part of the person-centered groupwork involvement; so too is the corresponding tendency for group members to become therapists for one another. These two related developments effectively locate power within clients themselves, which in turn leads to personal growth and deeper awareness of individual potential.

Short-term and crisis counselling were referred to above in order to highlight the usefulness of various procedures like relaxation methods, and rational-thinking exercises in these contexts. It should be added, however, that the core conditions of unconditional positive regard, empathy and congruence are essential elements of crisis counselling in particular, regardless of the theoretical orientation of the counsellor. Clients whose lives have been suddenly thrown into chaos by events such as bereavement, divorce or illness, need to know that they will be listened to, accepted and understood when they come for counselling. This listening, acceptance and understanding is very often *all* clients want from counselling, since many of them are aware that only they can deal, ultimately, with the difficulties they describe.

Relatives and friends are often unable to provide the support which clients need in a crisis situation, either because they themselves are emotionally involved and in need of help, or because they are afraid of saying or doing the wrong thing. The following is an account given by a client who found herself in a crisis situation with no one to turn to within her own family.

> I've been feeling terrible since yesterday. When I got home from work, Mark, my youngest, had broken the television, and the dog had been gone from early morning. My mother is staying with us for two weeks until my father gets out of hospital, and she's not very well herself. Well, my husband isn't very happy with this situation and he's been drinking more than usual. It's the deceit that I can't stand. That and the way he and my mother bicker all the time. Everything is just left for me to do when I come home – the cleaning, the cooking, everything. I have been feeling so tired, and when I discovered this lump in my breast – well that was it! I don't know how I'll ever get the time to go for all those tests. I know my husband is worried about it too, but somehow we never get the chance to really talk to each other. He finds it difficult to discuss emotional things like that, anyway, and sometimes I wonder if it is really worth trying to communicate with him anymore.   (Jo, a client, 1992)

In this particular situation the client did not expect or need direction, teaching or interpretation. What she wanted was an opportunity to think out loud, to clarify her thoughts, to be heard, and above all to be accepted and valued so that she could gather sufficient courage to deal effectively with her immediate problems. Crisis situations are not always as dramatic as this, however, and very often events or circumstances which might seem insignificant or trivial on the surface, are in fact deeply critical for the clients who experience them. The following is another account given by a client in crisis, this time precipitated by the break-up of a relationship.

> Most of my friends seem to have no difficulty with girlfriends. My best friend has been going out with a girl for two years now, and they will probably get engaged. I thought Lynda was the one for me, but she was just like all the others. As soon as she met a better-looking bloke with more money, she was off. I've always had a bit of a hang-up about my looks – the doctor says that my acne will disappear in a couple of years, but that's not much good to me now. I suppose if I had a proper job, things would be better. I don't have much money to spend going out in the evenings. Funny thing, I never thought money mattered all that much to Lynda, and she always said it didn't matter. But this other bloke

definitely has money. So what am I to think when she goes off with him? She says she got fed up with my self-pity and moaning, but I think she's using that as an excuse to get back at me.'   (Ken, a client, 1992)

As far as Ken was concerned, he too wanted to talk about his problem, to be heard and to be understood. Initially, the person-centered approach to counselling was effective in helping him to clarify the various aspects of his problems, but later on the counsellor encouraged him to look more closely at some of the beliefs expressed by him during the counselling sessions. In this way, he was helped to gain insight into his problems and to adopt more rational views about himself generally.

RATIONAL-EMOTIVE COUNSELLING

Rational-emotive counselling is effective in helping clients to look more closely at the beliefs which they hold so that irrational thinking can be identified and changed. The ABC model which Ellis designed to explain the relationship between thinking and emotion, can be used in some counselling situations to enable clients to see the connections for themselves. In Ken's case (described above), rational-emotive counselling was used successfully to help him identify his irrational belief that other people were exempt from problems in relationships. Later on, when he became more confident, several other irrational beliefs which he tenaciously held, were analysed, debated and challenged. As well as this, Ken was encouraged to look at the ways in which his negative thinking was causing him emotional upset, including self-pity and depression. The kind of behaviour which accompanied his negative thinking was also discussed; since the break-up with his girlfriend, Ken had become reclusive and solitary, which served to increase his loneliness and sense of failure.

When Ken first came for counselling he felt that his life was in crisis. His immediate need was to talk through his experiences in order to clarify and make sense of them. The counsellor was aware that the core conditions of empathy, unconditional positive regard and congruence were necessary at this first stage to help him deal with the emotional turmoil and loss of confidence which he was experiencing. It was only when he became stronger and more confident, that rational-emotive procedures like debate and use of the ABC model were introduced. These procedures appealed to Ken, and he enthusiastically applied himself to a fuller understanding of his problems.

The contract between client and counsellor, which is an integral part of both rational-emotive therapy and transactional analysis, can also be used in a variety of counselling situations, especially when specific goals have to be outlined. Rational-emotive techniques are tailored to accommodate individual client needs, and for this reason they are diverse and wide-ranging. A great many clients benefit from keeping a *diary*, for example, so that they can record their thinking and behaviour over a period of time. *Homework* arrangements can encourage clients to practise new skills or to modify dysfunctional behaviour, and reading – or *bibliotherapy*, as it has come to be called – also encourages the development of self-help skills, as well as fostering habits of critical thinking and enhancing creativity. Through the use of *imagery* techniques, clients can be helped to imagine different situations, and the ways they might respond to these. In rational-emotive counselling, this procedure is often used so that clients can, for instance, imagine a feared situation in the future in order to test the validity of their apprehensions. As mentioned earlier in Chapter 5, imagery can also be used to help clients who want to practise coping strategies. These strategies can be imagined or visualised by the client at frequent intervals, so that self-confidence is gradually increased.

Rational-emotive counselling is by its very nature eclectic since it uses a variety of procedures, some of which are borrowed from other theoretical models. These include assertiveness-training techniques, role-play and a wide range of behavioural techniques. A danger of using rational-emotive procedures too early in counselling, however, is that they are often too confrontational for vulnerable clients, and do not address their affective needs

Fig. 8.3 *Bibliotherapy and homework.*

in the way that some other approaches do. Counsellors can be tempted to push their own belief systems in the hope that clients will change quickly and alter their irrational thinking. This is something that counsellors need to be aware of when using rational-emotive techniques, even in situations where clients appear to be enthusiastic about participation. However, many clients value the teaching and direction which they get in rational-emotive counselling, and the idea – central to the approach – that everyone is capable of learning and of changing, is very encouraging and empowering for them too. Perhaps the most important point to remember about the rational-emotive approach, is that real understanding of the client's experience is essential before any of his beliefs are labelled as irrational by the counsellor. The counsellor's task is to judge whether clients are capable of dealing with rational-emotive concepts and procedures without becoming intimidated by them. This kind of judgement can only be made when a good client/counsellor relationship based on knowledge, trust and respect has been established.

TRANSACTIONAL ANALYSIS COUNSELLING

A thirty-five-year-old mature student recently came for counselling, and she recounted the following experiences.

> Right from the start I've had problems with this particular teacher. I don't think she likes me. She's about my age, but she acts like she's my mother or my boss. Without even consulting me she decided that I shouldn't do this shorthand exam. When I saw her in class this morning she told me – in front of the others – that I probably wouldn't pass it anyway, and that therefore she didn't intend to put me in for it. I'm really worried about the way she treats me, and I don't think I shall get my diploma at the end of the year because she'll do something else to undermine me. When I tried to talk to her about everything that's happening at home, she didn't want to know. She got upset and said that we all have problems and we just have to get on with them. It's all right for the other students in the group because most of them are young anyway, and they don't seem to mind her talking down to them. They've all come straight from school and that's what they're used to. But she really upsets me, and I feel myself acting like a child with her because that's how she makes me feel. I was always taught to look up to teachers, and my mother would never allow me to cheek them, or anyone else in authority for that matter.   (Debra, a client, 1992)

Debra was crying and visibly very upset when she talked to the counsellor about the problems she was having. In common with many mature students in education, she lacked confidence, not just in terms of her abilities, but also in her communication skills with lecturers and staff generally. Mature students often come to counselling because the stress of dealing with home commitments, financial hardships and the burden of assignment work and exams, becomes overwhelming. It seems surprising that at a time when increasing numbers of people are returning to education later in life, so little attention is focused on the special problems facing them There is a dearth of any serious research on the subject of adult experience in education, and this partly explains why there is often a lack of real understanding and communication between mature students and the people who teach them. Most mature students come back into education after an absence of perhaps ten years, or even more. Very often their memories of school are unpleasant or traumatic. Teachers were figures to be revered and feared, people whose opinions were accepted without question. Worse still, teachers were people who punished you if you got it wrong. Learning was essentially passive. Above all, education contained no element of fun. Sarcasm and ridicule were often the order of the day. Given such a background, it is little wonder that students like Debra are often anxious and defensive when they find themselves in a classroom once again. This attitude then serves to alienate a teacher or lecturer who is perhaps riddled with self-doubt anyway. Many university and college lecturers are still reluctant to admit that they are fallible, and that mature students return to education with valuable experience which should be acknowledged and appreciated.

In Debra's case, transactional analysis (TA) was used very effectively in later counselling sessions to help her understand what was happening in her relationships with staff, and in particular, in her communication with the teacher who caused her most concern. One of the major strengths of TA is that it can be clearly and quickly understood by clients, and in this respect it is one of the most useful models which eclectic counsellors have at their disposal. The structure of personality and the principles of TA are easy to explain, and although recent developments seem to have made TA more complex, the basic model remains the same.

Transactional Analysis is ideal for use by counsellors who find themselves in situations where a teaching approach is needed, and where clients wish to develop better communication skills. The basic structural diagram is instantly accessible, and everyone can understand the ego states which Berne described. Through its use, Debra was able to recognize her Child ego state with all its recorded messages from the past. She was further able to see how she reacted in her Child to situations in which she currently found herself. Her Parent and her Adult ego states were also identified and discussed, so that Debra eventually developed the ability to think and act in a planned and realistic way. When she did this, she was able to respond in her Adult to the member of staff who had intimidated her in the past, and this invited an Adult response which ensured that complementary transactions and real communication took place.

Transactional analysis is very effective in showing clients how the early decisions which they have made continue to influence their lives and their behaviour. The cognitive dimension of the model also encourages clients to analyse their beliefs and assumptions, and in this respect it has some similarity with rational-emotive therapy. The contract which client and counsellor develop between them, means that clients experience personal power and responsibility in therapy, and sometimes this is the first time they experience equality and control over what is happening to them. *Script analysis* is also helpful in showing clients the life patterns which they have chosen, and in this way, new decisions can be made and new choices identified. Clients can also be made more aware of the *games* which people, including themselves, play, and through this identification of game-playing, new and more open behaviour can be adopted. *Script analysis* and *game-playing* take some time to recognize and discuss, which means that it is not always possible to incorporate these procedures into a short-term eclectic approach.

As far as Debra was concerned, a person-centered approach was necessary in the initial counselling session, because what had happened in her life was a crisis to her, and she needed this kind of help to work through her own emotional distress. Later on, in subsequent counselling sessions, she was keen to look at structural and transactional analysis to enable her to understand what was happening in her communication with other people. However, she was happy to leave it at that, and was not concerned with a detailed appraisal of her past life and decisions, nor was she particularly interested in looking at game-playing in depth.

It is important when using TA with clients – particularly in crisis situations – not to overplay its distinct terminology. The language of TA can be intimidating for clients, and this is something that Berne never intended to happen. His concern was always to facilitate better understanding, but even though TA is readily understood by most clients, counsellors can get carried away by their own enthusiasm for the technical language. When this happens, the whole purpose of the approach is negated. As well as this, clients in crisis often need to have their affective or emotional needs addressed, before they can become intellectually engaged in counselling. Concepts like script analysis, crossed transactions and game playing, can all appear confusing and meaningless to clients who are in the throes of emotional turmoil.

Transactional analysis is ideally suited to group work, where communication is highlighted and participants can easily see how people interact with one another, and general awareness is raised. It is suitable also for use with all age groups and for a wide variety of problems, especially those involving interpersonal difficulties, and those relating to issues of authority and power.

GESTALT COUNSELLING

Gillian came for counselling because she was confused and emotionally upset over a number of issues in her life. She was nineteen years of age and engaged to be married in the near future to a boyfriend she had known for just over a year. Shortly before she came for counselling, she had suffered a miscarriage and this had left her depressed and in two minds whether or not she should proceed with the wedding. The marriage plans had been prompted by her pregnancy, and now that this was over she felt that there was no good reason to go ahead. Her boyfriend, who was six years older than Gillian, was keen to get married and her parents, who had been very supportive during her pregnancy, were also enthusiastic about wedding plans. Both sets of parents lived in the same village and knew each other well. Gillian's mother and her boyfriend's mother had been lifelong friends and everyone seemed anxious for the two families to stay close. Gillian had had a previous boyfriend who had died of cancer, and she found it difficult to stop thinking about him, especially after the miscarriage. She would burst into tears at work, or at home, but people, although sympathetic, did not really ever listen to her, or help her to sort out the turmoil in her mind. Her mother and her boyfriend's mother were preoccupied with making dresses for the wedding, and arranging the reception, and when Gillian mentioned her fears they put it all down to pre-wedding nerves.

Gillian found it difficult to articulate and make sense of her problems when she first came for counselling. She had talked to so many people who had given her conflicting advice, that she became more and more muddled and distressed. The counsellor taught her some simple relaxation exercises which helped Gillian to calm down and to think more clearly. She wanted to tell the counsellor how she felt, but said that she could not describe this in words. The counsellor asked her if she could draw what she felt instead, to which Gillian answered with alacrity that she could. She then proceeded to draw what looked like a ball of tangled wool, and said that she felt she was right in the middle of this and could not get out. Together, Gillian and the counsellor looked at the drawing and discussed it.

COUNSELLOR: Tell me something about the picture.
GILLIAN: I feel I'm in the middle of all that jumbled stuff.
COUNSELLOR: What does that jumbled up stuff look like to you?
GILLIAN: Well, like unravelled wool.
COUNSELLOR: So what might be the best way to get out of there?
GILLIAN: By knitting up the wool again.
COUNSELLOR: So that would smooth out the wool and make it into a garment again?
GILLIAN: Yes, but it would take time to do that.
COUNSELLOR: So when things are very jumbled, it takes time to smooth them out and make things whole again?
GILLIAN: Yes.

Although Gillian and the counsellor were speaking metaphorically throughout this exchange, both understood exactly what Gillian was trying to describe. Gillian decided to come for further counselling, and to take time to sort out her problems relating to her boyfriend, both sets of parents and the wedding plans. A wide range of techniques can be used in Gestalt counselling, and ideas borrowed from this approach can be employed in many situations, especially those situations where clients find it difficult to become aware of 'self'.

The counsellor encouraged Gillian to recognize and accept the mixed-up feelings which she was experiencing, and to get in touch with her own innate ability to solve her problems. Because so many other people had been telling her what to do, Gillian was convinced, at first, that she was hopeless and incapable of understanding and dealing with her own conflicts. Gestalt counselling demands an innovative and creative approach, but this should be geared to the needs of individual clients. In Gillian's case, the idea for drawing her problem came from the counsellor, but it was right for Gillian and she understood it perfectly. More importantly, it enabled her to start looking at her problems in a clear way, and to focus on her own needs, instead of on the needs of other people.

Focusing on what clients experience in the 'here and now' also helps them to become aware of 'self', and to express feelings which have been suppressed or denied in the past. In Gillian's case, it helped her to acknowledge the sorrow which she felt when her first boyfriend died, and the subsequent reawakening of that feeling when she had the miscarriage. Since there are no prescribed techniques in Gestalt counselling, it is possible to use ideas which present themselves, and which seem right for the client at the time.

During a later session, Gillian asked the counsellor to look at a short story she had written as a way of helping herself to disentangle her mixed-up feelings. This was the starting point of some useful discussion, again some of it metaphorical to begin with, but later becoming deeply personal for Gillian as she talked in great detail about the recent events in her life, and re-experienced the emotions connected with these. Since some of Gillian's difficulties lay in the lack of real communication between herself, her boyfriend and her parents, the counsellor helped her to look more closely at this, and to identify the ways she was responding to all of them, so that she could change her reactions and gain more control.

Gestalt counselling can lead to the expression of intense emotion which will not in itself produce understanding unless it is followed up by discussion and cognitive appraisal of what has taken place. Integration of all aspects of the client's experience should be addressed, including integration of feelings, thinking and behaviour. Gestalt procedures are powerful in the sense that they overcome difficulties related to verbal expression of feelings. People who cannot clearly say how they feel, can be shown how to express themselves in other, often more potent, ways. However, people who are naturally inhibited or reserved will not benefit from this approach, nor will those who have been culturally conditioned not to express their feelings too openly. This means that the counsellor needs to be accurate in her assessment of the client's problems and clear about his willingness – or lack of it – to participate in Gestalt methods or procedures.

Much of the unfinished business which Gillian brought into counselling related to her unexpressed feelings about her miscarriage and her bereavement. There were unexpressed feelings connected with the lack of real communication with the significant people in her life as well. Though drawing and writing had acted as catalysts for a fuller exploration of emotional experience, they had also, paradoxically, enabled her to avoid the uncomfortable task of dealing more directly with her feelings. Over a period of time, the counsellor helped her to look at this avoidance and to overcome it through a process of confronting and experiencing the sadness, grief and anger which had never been fully expressed. In addition to this, she was helped to develop new communication skills, and to become more responsible for herself, especially as far as future plans for the wedding were concerned.

Procedures which are used in an eclectic way like this, must always be correctly timed to suit the needs of individual clients, and if they are to be beneficial they must feel right for clients and their purpose must be understood as well. Because of the effectiveness and potency of Gestalt techniques, in particular, a high level of training in both theory and practice is necessary for counsellors who intend to use them. Anyone who is inexperienced or inept will do more harm than good through the use of powerful procedures which elicit strong feelings kept in abeyance for many years.

Group counselling

A common feature of the six main models of counselling described above, is that all of them can be used in a groupwork context. The chief benefit of using a groupwork setting – regardless of the theoretical orientation underlying it – is that clients have greater opportunities to practise social and communication skills, and to gain help and support from other participants. Group counselling has other advantages too, including the fact that it meets the needs of a number of people at once, and tends to be less expensive for clients.

Adlerian individual psychology, which was outlined in Chapter 1 can also be applied to groupwork, and in many ways the group approach is more appropriate for this model. This is because one of the main goals of individual psychology is to encourage clients to develop social interest and to contribute more to society generally. Encouragement, which is an important feature of Adlerian therapy, can be given by group members to one another, while self-defeating attitudes and behaviour can be identified and challenged in a supportive way. Participants in Adlerian groupwork can come to see that many of the problems which they experience are interpersonal or social in origin, and they are also given the opportunity to experience a sense of belonging in the group, and a chance to contribute something to it. Cooperation is the key word in both individual and group Adlerian therapy.

Rational-emotive therapy can also be used successfully in groupwork. In fact, in many ways the group is an ideal forum for this approach since the teaching dimension – which is so much a part of it – is enhanced when so many different views and ideas are generated. As in all forms of group counselling, participants can act as therapists for one another, and individuals in the group are encouraged to contribute, to discuss their problems, or to remain silent if they wish to do so. However, rational-emotive therapy is essentially challenging, and for this reason group members who appear passive and disinterested will be asked to contribute at some stage. There is no emphasis on catharsis, although group members often do experience strong emotional reactions when they are encouraged by others to express themselves more freely. Homework assignments may be given by group members to one another, and this can prove to be very effective. When an individual is asked by a group of people to fulfil a certain task, there is often a greater incentive to comply than there is when just one person makes the request. In individual counselling, clients often give what they believe to be accurate accounts of their social and inter-personal skills, but frequently their views are mistaken or distorted. In group counselling, each client's social skills can be observed in his interaction with the others. Thus the feedback which clients receive in groups is much more reliable and based on observable facts. Irrational beliefs can be iden-tified and challenged, and socializing problems can be brought into clearer focus when rational-emotive groupwork is used.

Transactional analysis is also ideally suited to groupwork since one of its main objectives is to help clients achieve social control. Again, the way in which members interact within the group, will help clients become aware of their own individual transactions. Communication between group par-ticipants can be analysed in order to focus on the part of personality – Parent, Adult or Child – which is speaking at any given time, and the intent of the message is analysed as well. Ulterior transactions or games are identified and discussed, and new, more open forms of communication are encouraged among members. There is an emphasis on the cognitive and behavioural dimension in TA groupwork, and an underlying assump-tion is that people are capable of change once they have identified the changes which need to be made. There is perhaps some danger that the affective or emotional dimension of people's experiences might be over-looked in transactional analysis groupwork, and for this reason it might not be suitable for those clients whose problems are directly related to unexpressed feelings, certain crisis situations, and trauma. Person-centered group counselling, with its emphasis on respect and empathy, probably provides a safer environment for those clients who are vulnerable, or emo-tionally upset. One of the main objectives of this latter approach is to help clients work towards personal growth and change, so that they may become more self-actualized, more open to different experiences, and more willing to trust themselves and their own judgement. Everything is viewed from the client's own subjective experience, and it is the clients themselves who determine what will happen in counselling, and what goals they want to achieve. There is no emphasis on specific skills, but there is a great deal of potential for individual growth.

In the Gestalt model of counselling, groupwork is an intrinsic part of the therapy and, in fact, it is often regarded as preferable to individual work. Frequently, the Gestalt counsellor will work with one individual in the group who has volunteered to be the client. Participants are not requested or told to be clients during therapy; they always volunteer to do so, and the rest of the group remains silent while the session is in progress. Fritz Perls be-lieved that it was important for group members to be aware of the rules beforehand, and that no group member should be put under pressure to contribute if they do not wish to do so. To a large extent, this provides safety for those clients who are not ready to participate for whatever their own individual reasons. The intensity of feeling which can be generated in a Gestalt group setting, is not to everyone's taste, and one criticism which could be levelled against it, is that insufficient attention is given to the cog-nitive and intellectual aspects of participants' experiences.

Behavioural counselling has a wide range of methods and techniques which are ideally suited to the groupwork medium. These include assertiveness training, relaxation training, modelling, social-skills training, and behaviour rehearsal. There is a clear-cut set of procedures which is attractive to many clients, and the counsellor functions as teacher, model and reinforcer. In the group context, clients observe, communicate with, and learn from one another, so they tend to make progress much more readily than they would in individual counselling. The educational bias of the approach, along with its insistence on the learning of practical skills, means that there is a definite focus which clients can see and work towards. Ongoing assessment and monitoring of progress throughout ensures that this sense of direction is never lost.

For those clients who are more interested in looking at past causes of their present behaviour, the psychodynamic approach in groupwork is more appropriate. Whereas the behavioural model has been criticized on the grounds that too much attention is paid to overt behaviour – and not enough to the client's history – the psychodynamic model has been criticized for placing too much emphasis on the past, and not enough on the present. The model is certainly much more suited to those clients who are interested in looking at unconscious motivation, and the events in the past which might have been responsible for current problems. All the techniques of the psychodynamic model of counselling – including free association, dream interpretation and the study of transference – can be applied to group, as well as individual counselling.

Conclusion

In every individual counselling situation, one person is there to help another person who has experienced, or is experiencing, emotional or psychological problems. This is true, regardless of the theoretical orientation of the counsellor, and regardless of the procedures which she uses or the goals of her particular model.

There are several important factors which have a bearing on the methods which might be used in counselling, and these include:

- The client's problems.
- The client's preferences.
- The client's financial circumstances.
- The amount of time available for counselling.
- The counsellor's theoretical orientation.
- The counsellor's experience and ability to use certain techniques.
- The relationship which is established between counsellor and client.

Most trained and experienced counsellors do not stick rigidly to one particular method or set of techniques. As the most important aspect of counselling is the relationship between client and counsellor, many counsellors will select the procedures which they believe to be right for individual clients at any given time. This flexibility of approach is essential to meet the wide-ranging needs of so many people; however, flexibility is probably also one of the reasons why it has been so difficult in the past to gather reliable information regarding the effectiveness of different therapeutic approaches.

FURTHER READING

CORRY, G., *Theory and Practice of Counselling and Psychotherapy*, (4th edn) Brooks/Cole Publishing Co., CA, 1991.

DRYDEN, W. (ed.), *Integrative and Eclectic Therapy – A Handbook*, Open University Press, Milton Keynes, 1992.

KOVEL, J., *A Complete Guide to Therapy*, Penguin Books, London, 1991.

Bibliography

ADLER, A. *What Life Could Mean To You*, One World Publications Ltd, Oxford, 1992.

ADLER, A., *Understanding Human Nature*, One World Publications Ltd, Oxford, 1992.

ATKINSON R. L., R. C. ATKINSON, E. E. SMITH & E. R. HILGARD, *Introduction to Psychology*, Harcourt Brace Jovanovich, Florida, 1981.

AVELINE, M. & W. DRYDEN (eds), *Group Therapy in Britain*, Open University Press, Milton Keynes, 1988.

BANDURA, A., *Principles of Behaviour Modification*, Holt, Reinhart & Wilson, London, 1969.

BENSON, J. F., *Working More Creatively with Groups*, Tavistock Publications, London, 1987.

BERNE, E., *Games People Play*, Penguin Books, London, 1968.

BERNE, E., *Transactional Analysis in Psychotherapy*, Souvenir Press, London, 1991.

BERNE, E., *What Do You Say After You Say Hello?*, Corgi Books, London, 1992.

BERNSTEIN, D. A., E. J. ROY, T. K. SRULL & C. D. WICKENS, *Psychology*, Houghton Mifflin Company, Boston, 1988.

BROME, V., *Jung – Man and Myth*, Paladin, London, 1985.

BROOKFIELD, S. D., *Developing Critical Thinkers*, Open University Press, Milton Keynes, 1987.

BROWN, D. & J. PEDDER, *Introduction to Pychotherapy*, Tavistock/Routledge, London, 1991.

BURKE, J. F., *Contemporary Approaches to Psychotherapy & Counselling*, Brooks/Cole, California, 1989.

BURNS, R. B., *Essential Psychology* (2nd edn), Kluwer Academic Publishers, Lancaster, 1991.

CHAPMAN, A. J. & A. GALE, *Psychology & People – A Tutorial Test*, The British Psychological Society/The Macmillan Press Ltd, London, 1982.

CLARKSON, P, *Gestalt Counselling in Action*, Ed. W. Dryden, Sage Publications, London, 1990.

CONYNE, R. K., *How Personal Growth and Task Groups Work*, Sage, London, 1989.

COOPER, J. (ed.), *Lexicon of Psychology, Psychiatry and Psychoanalysis*, Routledge, London, 1988.

COREY, G., *Theory & Practice of Counselling & Psychotherapy*, Brooks/Cole, California, 1991.

CULLEY, S., *Integrative Counselling Skills in Action*, Sage, London, 1991.

DAVENPORT, G. C., *Essential Psychology*, Collins Educational, London, 1992.

DRYDEN, W., *Current Issues in Rational Emotive Therapy*, Croom Helm, London, 1987.

DRYDEN, W. (ed.), *Individual Therapy in Britain*, Harper & Row, 1994.

DRYDEN, W. (ed.), *Psychotherapy Handbooks – Individual Therapy*, Open University Press, Milton Keynes, 1990.

DRYDEN, W., *Rational Emotive Counselling in Action*, Sage Publications, London, 1990.

DRYDEN, W. & C. FELTHAM (eds.), *Psychotherapy and its Discontents*, Open University Press, Milton Keynes, 1992.

EGAN, G., *The Skilled Helper*, Brooks/Cole, Monterey, 1986.

ELLIS, A., *Reason & Emotion in Psychotherapy*, Citadel Press, New York, 1990.

FAGAN, J. & I. L. SHEPHERD (eds), *Gestalt Therapy Now*, Penguin Books, London, 1972.

FORDHAM, F., *An Introduction to Jung's Psychology*, Penguin Books, London, 1991.

FREED, A. M., *TA for Teens – and Other Important People*, Jalmar Press, CA, 1988.

FRITCHIE, R. & M. MELLING, *The Business of Assertiveness*, BBC Books, London, 1991.

GOBLE, F.G., *The Third Force*, Pocket Books, New York, 1975.

GROSS, R. D., *Psychology – The Science of Mind & Behaviour*, Edward Arnold, London, 1987.

HARRIS, A., *I'm OK – You're OK*, Pan Books, London, 1970.

HOUSTON, G., *The Red Book of Gestalt*, The Rochester Foundation, London, 1990.

JACOBS, M., *Psychodynamic Counselling in Action*, Sage Publications, London, 1990.

JACOBS, M., *Key Figures in Counselling & Psychotherapy – Sigmund Freud*, Sage Publications, London, 1992.

JOHNSON, D W. & F. P. JOHNSON, *Joining Together – Group Theory & Group Skills* (3rd edn), Prentice Hall International, New Jersey, 1987.

KOVEL, J., *A Complete Guide to Therapy*, Penguin Books, London, 1991.

LAKE, T. & F. ACHESON, *Room to Listen, Room to Talk – A Beginner's Guide to Analysis*, Bedford Square Press, in association with BBC Radio 4, London, 1988.

LIEBERMAN, M. A., I.D. YALOM & M. B. MILES, *Encounter Groups – First Facts*, Basic Books, New York, 1973.

Longman's Dictionary of Psychology & Psychiatry, Longman, New York & London, 1984.

MARTIN, K., *Psychology (Made Simple Books)*, William Heinemann Ltd, London, 1992.

MASLOW, A., *Towards a Psychology of Being* (2nd edn), Van Nostrand, Toronto, 1968.

MASLOW, A., *Motivation & Personality* (2nd edn), Harper & Row, New York, 1970.

MASSON, J., *Against Therapy*, Fontana/Collins, London, 1990.

McGUIRE, W. & R. F. C. HULL (eds) *C. G. Jung Speaking – Interviews & Encounters*, Picador/Pan Books, London, 1980.

MEARNS, D. & B. THORNE, *Person-Centered Counselling in Action*, Sage Publications, London, 1988.

MEDCOFF, J & J. ROTH (eds), *Approaches to Psychology*, Open University Press, Milton Keynes, 1991.

MEYER, V. & E. S. CHESSER, *Behaviour Therapy in Clinical Psychiatry*, Penguin Books, London, 1970.

MILLER, A., *Breaking down the Wall of Silence*, Virago, London, 1992.

MURGATROYD, S. *Counselling & Helping*, The British Psychological Society & Methuen, London, 1988.

NAPIER, R. W. & M. K. GERSHENFELD, *Groups – Theory & Experience* (3rd edn.), Houghton Mifflin Company, Boston, 1985.

NELSON-JONES, R., *The Theory & Practice of Counselling Psychology*, Cassell, London, 1990.

PECK, M. S., *The Different Drum*, Rider Press, London, 1987.

POPKIN, R. H. & A. STROLL, *Philosophy (Made Simple Books)*, Butterworth–Heinemann Ltd, London, 1991.

RICHARDS, D. & B. McDONALD, *Behavioural Psychotherapy*, Heinemann Nursing, Oxford, 1990.

ROGERS, C. R., *Encounter Groups*, Alan Lane, The Penguin Press, London, 1971.

ROGERS, C. R., *Client-Centered Therapy*, Constable, London, 1991.

SCHIFFMAN, H. R., *Sensation & Perception – An Integrated Approach*, John Wiley & Sons, New York, 1982.

SKYNNER, R. & J. CLEESE, *Families & How to Survive Them*, Mandarin, London, 1990

STAFFORD-CLARK, D., *What Freud Really Said*, Penguin Books, London, 1992.

STEWART, I., *Transactional Analysis Counselling in Action*, Sage Publications, London, 1989.

STEWART, I., *Eric Berne (Key Figures in Counselling & Psychotherapy)*, Sage Publications, London, 1992.

STEWART, I. & V. JOINES, *TA Today – A New Introduction to Transactional Analysis*, Lifespace Publishing, Nottingham, 1987.

STREET, E. & W. DRYDEN, *Family Therapy in Britain*, Open University Press, Milton Keynes, 1988.

TUCKMAN, B. W., 'Developmental Sequence in Small Groups', Psychological Bulletin 63, 6: 384 99.

WADE, C. & C. TRAVIS, *Psychology* (2nd edn), Harper Collins, New York, 1990.

WALMSLEY, C., *Assertiveness – The Right to Be*, BBC Books, London, 1991.

WHITAKER, D. S., *Using Groups to Help People*, Routledge & Kegan Paul Ltd, London, 1992.

WILLIAM, R., *Gestalt Therapy*, Pennsylvania State University, taken from *A Lexicon of Psychology, Psychiatry and Psychoanalysis* (ed. Kuper, J.).

YALOM, I. D., *Theory and Practice of Group Psychotherapy*, Basic Books, New York, 1970.

Index